The Gods Within

AN INTERACTIVE GUIDE TO ARCHETYPAL THERAPY

Peter Lemesurier

Winchester, UK
Washington, USA)

First published by O Books, 2007
O Books is an imprint of John Hunt Publishing Ltd., The Bothy, Deershot Lodge, Park Lane,
Ropley, Hants, SO24 0BE, UK
office1@o-books.net
www.o-books.net

Distribution in:

UK and Europe
Orca Book Services
orders@orcabookservices.co.uk
Tel: 01202 665432 Fax: 01202 666219 Int. code (44)

USA and Canada
NBN
custserv@nbnbooks.com
Tel: 1 800 462 6420 Fax: 1 800 338 4550

Australia and New Zealand
Brumby Books
sales@brumbybooks.com
Tel: 61 3 9761 5535 Fax: 61 3 9761 7095

Far East (offices in Singapore, Thailand, Hong Kong, Taiwan)
Pansing Distribution Pte Ltd
kemal@pansing.com
Tel: 65 6319 9939 Fax: 65 6462 5761

South Africa
Alternative Books
altbook@peterhyde.co.za
Tel: 021 447 5300 Fax: 021 447 1430

The Gods Within

AN INTERACTIVE GUIDE
TO ARCHETYPAL THERAPY

Peter Lemesurier

BOOKS

Winchester, UK
Washington, USA

The details in the various gods' 'sub-personality' sections are reprinted from the author's *The Healing of the Gods* by permission of Thoth Publications.

Cover photo: The temple of Hera at Agrigento in southern Sicily

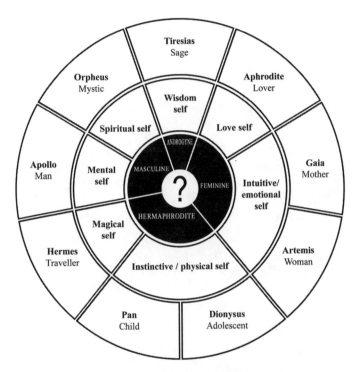

THE CIRCLE OF KNOWING

CONTENTS

AUTHOR'S FOREWORD

THE ANCIENT GREEK GODS ARE NOT DEAD. They are still running around inside us. Today we call them our complexes and neuroses, our compulsions and quirks, our instincts, emotions and everyday personal characteristics. Jungian psychologists usually refer to them as the 'Archetypes'. Either way, they are what make us 'tick'.

All the while we ignore them, they exert a dark power over us that is not always to our benefit. It is not just that they become our masters and we their tools. Rejected, they can wreak inner and outer havoc on our lives. But if we can first make ourselves aware of them and then learn to co-operate with them, they can turn into invaluable friends and guides in our quest for self-knowledge, self-fulfilment and ultimate wholeness.

And it is that knowledge that can eventually set us free.

In the following pages, then, each of the main gods and other mythical entities that are prone to haunt us is revealed in turn in his or her true colours, as are some of their common 'sub-personalities'. Their individual characteristics as we experience them are spelt out in detail, as are some of the vital actions that we consequently need to take if we are to learn to know and befriend them. Not all of those characteristics are pretty. Some of them, in fact, are quite shocking. So, consequently, are some of the therapies that they demand. Neither the Greek myths themselves, after all, nor the therapies that they enshrine, could ever be accused of pussyfooting. Yet all of them have to be faced, and sufficient of the resultant therapies applied (insofar as current social rules allow, that is), if we are truly to come to terms with them.

Be prepared, then, to be shocked. It may well be what your system needs.

To assist in the initial task of self-analysis, you will find at the end of the Introduction (below) a personal diagnostic test to help you discover just which of your inner gods is in most urgent need of attention and therapy at this moment. You may well care to consult it before you read anything else.

The very word 'therapy' comes from the Greek *therapeia*. It originally meant not merely 'healing', but 'service' and 'worship', too. The Greeks, evidently, knew what they were about. Add to the word 'therapy' the word for 'god', of course, and you have the invented word *theotherapy*. This single word neatly sums up the principle involved. It is by learning to serve and even worship our inner gods that we ourselves can be both healed and made whole.

For, ultimately, we and the gods are one.

You shall know the truth,
and the truth shall set you free.

Jesus of Nazareth (Jn.8.32)

INTRODUCTION
A WORLD IN THRALL TO
THE SOLAR GOD

Man is the measure of all things.
Protagoras (quoted by Plato)

Our current Western tradition of knowledge and thought has a long pedigree. True, in its most recent form it goes back only as far as the European Renaissance. But the Renaissance in turn based its own attitudes and procedures firmly on classical precedent. This fact has important consequences. It means that, far from being inborn or inevitable, our established outlook – including the very basis of our science, our philosophy and our way of coming to terms with the world – was effectively invented by the ancient Greeks, and thence passed on to us by the great philosophers such as Socrates, Plato and Aristotle.

This suggestion may at first sight seem far-fetched, if not actually contrary to common sense. It is, after all, natural to assume that our own traditional way of looking at the world is the only possible one – or, at least, the only reasonable one. Time, causality, reductionism, idealism, morality and the dualism of 'good' and 'evil', in other words, are facts of nature, givens of life. So, indeed, they were assumed to be for many centuries. It was only after those great emissaries of eighteenth-century Europe's Age of Reason, the explorers Bougainville and Cook, had encountered highly successful native civilisations in the South Seas who believed in few, if any, of these 'givens' that Westerners in general started to realise that such things were neither as factual nor as given as they might once have seemed.

The only *reasonable* way of looking at the world they might well be, but then even reason itself is not a given. What we call 'reason' is only one among many possible approaches to reality – and specifically one of those originally devised and bequeathed to us by the ancient Greeks.

Thus, to attribute our current way of looking at things to the great Greek philosophers of the fifth and fourth centuries BC is by no means as far-fetched as it may seem. Our philosophy, outlook and attitude to the world are far from natural or inevitable. Their pedigree is clearly traceable through the centuries for anybody who cares to trace it. Their paternity, in consequence, is not in doubt, even in the most respected academic circles.

And it has to be assigned above all to Socrates, to his pupil Plato and to *his* pupil Aristotle.

The servants of the Sun

As portrayed in Plato's *Phaedo*, Socrates claims to be the sanctified prophet and servant *of Apollo*. And certainly he is known to have had close dealings with the god's oracle at Delphi. As for Plato himself, venerable tradition has it that he, too, was a 'son of Apollo' and a priest of his cult. Both claims, if true, are highly significant.

True, such claims cannot now be proved definitively either way. Yet there is nothing particularly improbable about either. In classical Greece the priesthood (unusually for the ancient world) was rarely a full-time job, still less a kind of numinous alternative to worldly power. Religion had, as it were, become democratised and laicised – or possibly it was everyday life that had instead become sacralised. At all events, worship of the gods being a direct part of everyday life, the role of priest was generally vested simply in local worthies whose families had in many cases fulfilled the office for centuries – rather like a hereditary version of the British magistrature. Except at the major cult-centres, it involved little more than officiating at the annual (or quadrennial) festival of the god at the local temple.

Thus, it would have been nothing unusual or out-of-the-way had either Socrates or the aristocratic Plato fulfilled the role of priest. Indeed, Aristotle was likewise quite distinguished and high-born enough to qualify for priestly office. And if in his case too the cult in question was that of Apollo, the fact would explain a great deal.

For it has to be said that the basic approach of all three philosophers, with its belief in God-given reason and its emphasis on the supremacy of the intellect and the transcendence of the human spirit, is suffused with typical Apollonian thinking and teaching; and even their conclusions, when closely examined, turn out in practice to be little more than re-expressions and elaborations of the Apollonian myth.

Which might account for the fact that our own age, too, is (as we shall see) patently in thrall to the self-same myth, and consequently runs the whole gamut of mortal dangers which wholehearted self-dedication to any one of the gods *in isolation* has always been known to pose for those foolish enough to undertake it.

Apollo at large

Apollo was – and is – the sun. Not the sun *god* – for the truly ancient Greeks knew no difference. Like radiant Helios before him, Apollo was simply the sun, and the sun was the god.

In that simple statement his whole myth is enshrined and comprehended. By taking as a symbol the solar orb itself, the Greeks contrived to sum up a whole human archetype, a whole, complex outlook, a particular, characteristic way of approaching the world.

As Above, so Below.

In Chapter 1 we shall first lay bare in detail the characteristics of that myth on the personal level, then assess its results and lessons for each of us. Consequently I shall not anticipate them in any detail here. However, even the broadest outline of them must prompt us to enquire into the effects of our communal adoption of his 'knowing', or *scientia*, on the world at large. In what ways, in other words, does our inheritance of rampant Apollonianism modify our natural cognition, condition the preconceptions that we bring to bear on the world about us and so, to a very large extent, mould that world itself?

Suffice it to note for the moment that Apollo is concerned less with subjective knowledge than with what purports to be 'objective' knowledge – with knowledge, moreover, of a particularly intellectual kind. Being the sun, he needs to throw light on anything and everything. He needs to research, to describe, to explain. He is appalled at ignorance, affronted by the inexplicable, positively *angst*-ridden in the face of undefined mystery of any kind.

In the service of this quest, Apollo naturally needs some kind of order and discipline in the world about him – indeed, where he cannot find it he is perfectly prepared to impose it. Where previously nature simply *natured*, now it must be subjected to laws – to regularities, that is, whether observed or assumed, that Apollo himself lays down for it. In the process, the wilderness must be destroyed, the forests cut down, its indigenous peoples tamed and/or decimated, its wild animals reduced by Apollonian hunting to near extinction. On the theoretical level, similarly, the universe as a whole must be reduced to a kind of all-embracing piece of clockwork, a cosmic machine which functions according to known and immutable principles. But laws and principles have no existence in themselves. They are purely abstract in character. It follows, therefore, that Plato's world of abstract principles is as much the province of Apollo as is Aristotle's world of mechanical fact. Even spirituality itself can be intellectualised. Indeed, where Apollo is concerned, it almost invariably is.

And so the god reigns as securely in the kingdoms of philosophy and theology as in those of science and technology. Order is all. Predictability is a *sine qua non*. And acquiring knowledge is thus essentially a matter of routine, of methodology, of procedure. As, indeed, the ancient Greek philosophers were themselves at such pains to demonstrate.

Apollo's approach might thus be described as essentially classical, never as romantic.

This approach is duly reflected in modern science and technology of every kind. Nothing can be accepted which cannot be explained. Not that this rules out intuitive leaps of the imagination – for these, too, are second nature to Apollo. But each insight must be examined and tested repeatedly, to the point where it can be confidently expressed in *predictive* form. Not merely 'Whenever this... then that' in the context of *the past*, but in that of the future too.

Prediction, after all, is (as we shall be seeing) likewise the province of Apollo.

But such testing and research involves detailed observation, and detailed observation means dissecting what is observed into its minutest constituent parts. Not merely the argument, not merely the claim under consideration, but frequently the very object of all the observation, too.

That is no doubt why, as a healer, Apollo tends to be much more interested in individual symptoms than in the whole patient who is displaying them, and much keener to resort to cutting the patient apart – i.e. to invasive surgery – than to simple preventive medicine or holistic therapies. Indeed, as a natural technician, he is keener still on all the gadgetry that this involves.

And meanwhile the world, too, must be taken apart, divided into its constituent parts. In order to be understood, the very universe itself must be reduced to atoms, the atom analysed into its various particles (notwithstanding the fact that the Greek word *atomos* originally meant 'indivisible'!), the particle itself split into such constituent sub-particles as neutrinos and quarks, and so on *ad infinitum* – or rather *ad destructum*. And this despite the fact that the unwitting devotee of Apollo can never bring himself to believe in that *infinitum,* since infinity, by definition, cannot be grasped or comprehended. Nevertheless, it is that basic refusal to believe which actually fires his passion to unearth the ultimate *finitum*, the supposed 'basic particle' the search for which ultimately fires the whole enterprise in the first place.

And if in the process the atom is blasted into smithereens, *bio*logy turned into *necro*logy, living frogs into small, dead corpses, what price the universe itself? There is more than a suspicion, in other words, even in the scientific camp, that what we finish up by observing is not a living universe but a dead one, or rather one that never existed in the first place – not nature itself but merely our own way of observing it. Just as measuring a tyre's air-pressure, or

The story of the solar divinity

The sun has been venerated as divine since time immemorial - especially by highly ordered societies. In ancient Japan, in Egypt (first as Ra, then as the Aten, or sun-disc), in Persia (as the Zoroastrian Ahura Mazda), in Greece (first as Helios, then as Apollo) and in Rome (particularly in connection with the adopted Persian cult of Mithras), it was always regarded as the model and guarantee of creative, live-giving reliability and regularity. Surprisingly, perhaps, the Hebrew Essenes of around the time of Christ seem to have prayed to it as it rose each morning, while it has been suggested that even the disc-shaped holy wafer that the Christian priest elevates before the altar at Mass is far from being the mere loaf of bread that it is supposed to be, but is in fact a carry-over from the ancient Mithraic rite at which the solar disc was regularly venerated and sanctified. Modern holidaymakers may be unaware of all this - but most of them still remain extraordinarily keen on what they are quite happy to call 'sun-worshipping'.

inserting a thermometer into a refrigerator to measure its temperature, changes what is being observed and so actually *prevent*s its observation, so at the level of subatomic particles the very light (or other projected particles) that we use to observe them changes what we are trying to observe. What we finish up observing is in fact what we ourselves have created. Or, in Heisenberg's sobering words, 'What we observe is not nature itself, but nature exposed to our methods of questioning.'

And endlessly dissecting a living world, it seems, must in the end inevitably produce a dead planet.

Pursued to its logical conclusion, in other words, unmitigated Apollonianism always finishes up by invalidating and destroying itself. But then, so does *any* '-ism' pursued to its logical conclusion – not least because logical conclusions are in any case by definition the copyright of Apollo. As the ancient Greeks were perfectly well aware, no single god has a monopoly of the truth. And Apollonian reductionist logic in particular merely finishes up by taking *itself* apart, only to disappear in a puff of metaphorical smoke.

Yet such is the path to which Western civilisation has committed itself – and, with true Apollonian arrogance, most of the rest of the world, too – ever since the time of the Renaissance. Officially, at any rate. And so it, too, has its terminal puff of smoke to look forward to.

*Un*officially, however, the victory of Apollo is far from complete. Politicians and businessman trying to arrive at logical decisions still use nothing more scientific than hunch and intuition to decide when they have examined sufficient of the evidence to base those decisions on, or to determine at which point the initial assumptions stop and the actual logic begins. Scientists who have proved paragons of logic and academic rigour all week will still cheerfully attend church on a Sunday. Technologists used to solving all their problems by a process of careful, measured deduction and ordered investigation will not hesitate to row with their marriage-partners or lose their tempers with their children. Brilliant, middle-aged executives who take inordinate pride in the extent to which they have maximised their opportunities by organising their lives in the minutest detail suddenly find their emotions in turmoil and their plans in tatters on encountering some seductive adolescent of whichever sex. And Einstein, the 'ultimate scientist', duly goes on to demonstrate the inherent relativity of the whole scientific exercise.

In all this there is actually some measure of hope. For Apollo, as we shall see, is not by nature a god of permanence. He has his days and seasons, and must be allowed to depart in due time if major *dis-asters* (literally 'derangements of the stars') are not to ensue. All work and no play, as the saying has it, makes Jack a dull boy. And so Dionysus in particular (whose way of knowing we shall likewise be considering later) must also be allowed his fling.

Apollo within

As on the collective level, so on the personal level, too, our Apollonian inheritance has its inevitable consequences. The majority of Western men, especially in the so-called White Anglo-Saxon Protestant nations, attach extraordinary significance to logic and the world of the head, and have the greatest difficulty in dealing either with their emotions or with women. Many of them, indeed, would deny that they have any emotions at all, and so are embarrassed should they ever surface (even though, curiously enough, embarrassment is an emotional reaction in itself). By the same token, they are quick to ridicule or decry the expression of emotions in others. Even women find themselves drawn into this particular trap. Even children are taught not to cry. The media report as a matter of curiosity and even astonishment that such-and-such a couple were 'seen holding hands in public', or that shattered victims of personal or collective tragedies 'cried openly', almost as if it were possible to cry in some other way, or as if such things were in some way scandalous or taboo.

Curiously enough, this anti-emotional stance (ably supported by post-Apollonian Christian morality – for early Christianity was itself strongly influenced by the teachings of the Apollonian Plato) then goes on to bedevil men's sexuality. Not only does sex all too easily become for them divorced from love, a purely physical rather than an emotional act, but their natural, Apollonian affection for other men has to be denied too. Thus, except in such permitted contexts as football or gay bars and clubs, touching other men is 'out', holding hands with them strictly taboo, publicly kissing them a cause for public outrage. Attitudes which, it needs to be pointed out, are by no means a matter of course, as cultures as diverse as the Arab, the Hindu or the Burmese persist in demonstrating.

In the process, of course, Apollo's incipient homosexuality is denied its proper outlet, and this inevitably tends to intensify his other characteristics – and particularly his more 'negative' aspects. For it seems to be a fixed rule of the gods that the repression of any of their aspects always evokes some kind of negative revenge. A god or goddess who is ignored always makes his or her presence felt in uncomfortable and unpleasant ways.

A fact which, of course, at least has the positive benefit that we can then always use our 'troubles' and 'symptoms' as keys to understanding what is really *a-miss*, what god or goddess is currently 'feeling offended'.

Which, as it happens, constitutes the core principle of this book.

So it is, at all events, that male sexuality becomes warped in a variety of extraordinary ways. Sadism, masochism, rape and child-abuse flourish. Sex, even of the heterosexual kind, becomes an obsession, even an illness. And meanwhile the other pole of the argument becomes commensurately intensified, too. The intellect arrogates to itself even further powers. Reductionism becomes rampant. Nothing – not even music – can be experienced until it has first been 'explained' and dissected. Other people, similarly, have to be pigeon-holed, analysed, criticised, reformed, 'treated' and generally homogenised. There arises a 'tyranny of the normal' from which nobody can be allowed to escape. Apollo's gift for self-restraint becomes warped into a mania for repressing others.

And so the path lies open for social, psychological and genetic engineering, for autocratic regulation, for state control, for totalitarianism of every kind – whether political, religious, moral, medical or scientific. Moreover, once in place, it becomes regularised and fossilised in true Apollonian fashion. *Rigor mortis* sets in. And so the resultant regimes, of whatever kind, become inflexible, set in concrete. The young Apollo turns into the ageing Cronus, who cannot and will not let go and insists on imposing his will on everybody and everything. Only a bloody revolution can then disempower and overthrow the reigning order, and chaos and destruction are bound to follow in its wake.

All of which, it has to be said, is the very reverse of the true nature of the ever-young Apollo. Merely denying even one of his aspects, it seems, is liable to lead to a whole string of *disasters*. Refusing to accept him in his totality leads to a whole chain-reaction of self-contradiction, self-denial and eventually self-destruction.

And yet, at the same time, whatever aspect of the god is rejected still continues to force itself into expression – but now in essentially negative ways. Thus, in the more youthful areas of society, Apollo's fresh, boyish outlook now starts to be transformed into sheer neophilia (obsessive love of the new). And so nothing can be left alone for two minutes together. Everything must constantly be re-examined, changed, replaced. Perpetual revolution becomes the order of the day.

By the same token, newness and youth are all. Enormous resources are devoted to staying young, feeling young, looking young. Apollo's characteristic healing skills are obsessively invoked to improve health, to delay the onset of old age, to prolong life. (The old, by contrast, are scorned, ignored, shut away out of sight.) Death is not merely devalued, resisted, tabooed and swept under the carpet: an absolute war starts to be waged against its very existence.

At which point Apollo's nature as an ever-*dying* god is *itself* denied. And so self-contradiction and self-destruction enter the picture all over again.

The process goes on. The negative, self-defeating chain-reaction spreads further. Apollo's awareness of solar time merely produces a world ruled obsessively by the clock. His consciousness of causality leads to a form of awareness which insists on living constantly in the past, incapable of experiencing the present on its own terms. His moral sense turns into guilt and self-disgust on the one hand, and into intolerance and bigotry on the other. His sense of the duality of good and evil divides both his own psyche and the world about him into opposing camps, for ever at war with each other. His obsession with order, predictability, science and the claims of the intellect causes him to undervalue entirely the apparent chaos and irrationality that are inherent within the natural world, as also within his own inner world, so that ecological *dis-aster*, both outer and inner, in due course results. His mania for purity and cleanliness render him vulnerable to all kinds of ailments, both physical and psychological, to which he has never had the chance to develop any immunity. And his devaluing of the feminine results not merely in a failure to understand either women or the feminine side of his own nature, but in a compulsion to repress and do violence to both. This in turn must sooner or later result in a violent backlash which – as ever – can only result in his own eventual downfall.

Apollo none the less

Apollo's way of knowing thus has its own clear characteristics and its own equally clear results for us all. Be it noted, moreover, that they are by no means *all* negative. The life of the head has a perfectly valid *raison d'être*. A chicken without a head may run around frantically, but for all practical purposes it is no longer a chicken at all.

It is perfectly in order, in other words, to divide up the world, to name it, to understand it and even to manipulate it. Time, causality, morality and duality have proved valuable tools in the past (even though, like many a tool, they also have their dangerous, sharp edges) and will undoubtedly prove just as valuable in the future.

Science, technology and mathematics likewise have their honoured place in our midst. Idealism has its clear uses as a tool for human manifestation and achievement. Combined, they are capable of producing technological miracles such as the American space-programme (crowned as it was by the triumphant series of lunar space-missions to which NASA, with remarkable insight, gave the name 'Apollo'). Philosophical tunnel-vision and practical single-mindedness are not so very far removed from each other. Discipline and routine are the very wheels of our social machine, and have helped enormously to get us where we are. Health and hygiene are not things to be ignored.

The sphere of purely masculine endeavour, too, has undoubted benefits for society at large. It secures our borders, guarantees our safety, protects our interests, boosts our self-confidence. Even homosexuality, in man as in the rest of the animal kingdom, has its natural place. And a wariness of women has helped to preserve many an over-protected and ill-prepared young man from untimely emotional disturbance and intellectual confusion at some critical stage of life.

Yet all these are only one side of human nature – one side, indeed, of masculine human nature in particular. And while the female sex, too, has its Athenas, its Amazons and its Caeneises – i.e. its masculine, politically-minded pillars of society and its militant, confrontational man-women – the true voice of woman also needs to be heard in our midst.

Indeed, all the while the two are not in balance, society itself is in danger of toppling and collapse. And not only these particular two, but all the other archetypes within us that constantly demand *ac-knowledge-ment*, respect and due expression.

There are, admittedly, enough of us – all of us different in various ways – to ensure that all these archetypes do indeed find expression. But too often that expression is not acknowledged or respected by society at large. Too often, for that matter, it is actually *repressed* in favour of the accepted, reigning view.

For some centuries now this view has been that of the solar Apollo. Our reigning form of knowing has been exclusively that of the light, of the day, of reason and intellectual awareness. Our world, consequently, has not only reflected that light, that particular form of knowing, but has also lived under the dark, threatening shadow which it inevitably casts at one and the same time across both our outer and our inner lives.

But now the time is upon us when the light of reason is starting to pale and grow thin. The touching belief that 'reason

The American space-programme

Early American space-launches were based on the Titan rocket. Later, the launch-vehicle became the Saturn - the Roman name for the Greeks' Cronus (king of the gods before Zeus). Appropriately, the space-vehicles that arose on their shoulders were named after Mercury (i.e. Hermes), Gemini (i.e. the Greek Dioscuri) and finally, for the moon-landings, Apollo. Thus, the increasing sophistication of the technology was mirrored more or less exactly in the evolution that led, in ancient myth, from the primitive Titans to the summit of godly brilliance in Apollo.

will prevail', it is increasingly clear, is a statement of Apollonian dogma, not of actual fact. Deep shadows of irrationality and chaos, of environmental pollution and ecological *dis-aster*, of self-engineered famine and pestilence are spreading ever more widely across not only our outer world, but across our inner landscape too.

And before they finally destroy us, we need at long last to *let* the sun go down, and to allow other divinities entirely to mount into their rightful place aloft the starry firmament.

As ever, then, the process needs to start with *me*...

PERSONAL DIAGNOSTIC

T HE FOLLOWING DIAGNOSTIC TEST will help you determine which of your inner gods or other inner entities most urgently needs attention. It is perfectly simple to operate.

All you need to do is allow your eye to run down the following list of characteristics and symptoms in a perfectly relaxed and playful way. Almost at once, you will find that some of them jump out at you as being your own. Opposite these, you will find one or more gods' names. Make a rough mental note of them. There is no need, though, to write anything down.

WARNING: DO NOT JUMP TO IMMEDIATE CONCLUSIONS ON THE BASIS OF ANY ONE CASE ALONE.

Now continue with the exercise. As you come to the next familiar characteristic, mentally note the relevant gods' names again. The name following a slash-mark refers to a 'sub-personality' of the particular god in question. Carry on until you either reach the end of the list or you notice that one particular god keeps jumping out at you. In this case, that god is the one on whom you need to concentrate first.

It may well be, though, that *several* gods' names demand your attention. In that case *all* of them need your attention.

Once you have determined who they are, you need merely turn to the Table of Contents at the beginning of this book to discover which sections you particularly need to study and apply. You should return to this list from time to time. As *you* change, so will your gods. And so, consequently, will the *therapy* that you owe them.

able to change: Aphrodite/Adonis

absentee from work: Gaia/Demeter, Pan

absent-minded: Gaia/Demeter

abused as child: Apollo/Hippolytus, Hermes/Odysseus

accepts challenges: Artemis/Cyrene, Hermes/Heracles/Perseus

accepts death: Artemis/Persephone

accepts too heavy responsibilities: Zeus/Atlas

accident-prone: Apollo/Actaeon/Hippolytus

acquainted with death, life and birth: Gaia

acquisitive: Gaia, Zeus/Poseidon

active: Aphrodite/Adonis,Dionysus

activist: Zeus

actor: Apollo/Muses/Narcissus, Dionysus

acts first, talks afterwards: Zeus

adaptable: Apollo, Dionysus, Hermes, Zeus

addicted to change: Dionysus, Hermes

addicted to moonlight: Artemis

administrator: Hermes, Zeus

admired anonymously: Apollo/Narcissus

admirer of father: Hermes/Heracles

admires spirited women: Zeus

adolescent: Dionysus

adolescent beauty: Aphrodite/Adonis

adventurous: Hermes

advocate of genocide: Zeus

aerial joy-rider: Apollo/Ganymedes

afraid of opposite sex: Apollo/Actaeon, Artemis/Daphne, Orpheus

afraid of the dark: Pan

afraid of sex: Artemis/Daphne

afraid of snakes: Artemis/Persephone

afraid of women: Apollo/Actaeon

ageing: Zeus/Cronus

aggressive: Artemis, Dionysus, Hermes/Heracles, Zeus

agile: Hermes

alchemist: Hermes

alcoholic: Artemis/Selene, Dionysus

alive to own instincts: Artemis

alleycat: Dionysus

all-rounder: Hermes/Heracles

always changing: Artemis, Dionysus, Hermes

always on the go: Artemis,

Aphrodite, Dionysus, Pan

always right: Orpheus

always shouting: Pan

Amazon: Artemis

ambiguous: Hermes

ambitious for children: Artemis/Medea

anaemic: Artemis

analytical: Apollo

angry: Hermes/Odysseus

angst-ridden: Zeus/Prometheus

animal: Pan, Dionysus

animal lover: Orpheus

animal tamer: Apollo

anorexic: Apollo/Narcissus, Artemis,
    Aphrodite, Gaia/Demeter

antagonises women: Hermes/Heracles

anti-domestic: Artemis/Amazons/Cyrene

antiintellectual: Gaia

antimale dominance: Gaia

anti-men: Artemis

anti-monogamy: Artemis/Amazons

antiphysical: Orpheus

antipromiscuous: Orpheus

antispiritual: Gaia, Zeus/Typhon

antitaboo: Dionysus

anxious to please: Artemis/Persephone

'anything for a quiet time': Gaia/Hestia

'anywhere but here': Dionysus

apparent cruelty: Hermes

archer: Apollo, Artemis

architect: Apollo

ardent lover: Aphrodite/Eros

arrogant: Apollo, Zeus

arthritis: Zeus/Prometheus

arthritis in legs: Dionysus/Centaurs

artistic: Apollo, Gaia

ascetic: Apollo, Orpheus

asthmatic: Hermes/Odysseus, Pan

astronomer: Apollo

athletic: Apollo, Artemis, Hermes

attentionseeker: Artemis

attracted by light: Artemis

attracted to childbirth: Artemis

attracted to magic and occult: Apollo,
    Artemis/Hecate

attracted to opposite sex: Aphrodite,
    Eros, Apollo/Actaeon

attractive: Aphrodite/Eros,
    Apollo/Narcissus,
Artemis/Hecate

attractive voice: Artemis/Sirens

authoritarian: Zeus

autoerotic: Aphrodite, Dionysus, Pan

autocrat: Zeus

aware of coincidences: Hermes

aware of dreams: Apollo/Asclepius,
    Hermes

aware of own emotions: Dionysus

bachelor: Apollo, Orpheus

back problems: Zeus / Atlas / Poseidon /
Prometheus / Typhon

back-to-the-womb: Apollo/Narcissus

bad dreams: Hermes/Heracles,
Zeus/Typhon

balanced: Gaia/Hestia, Hermes/Theseus

balletomane: Apollo, Orpheus

ballistics expert: Apollo

bandit: Hermes

banished as youth: Hermes/Perseus

bearded: Dionysus

'bears world on shoulders': Zeus/Atlas

beautiful: Aphrodite,
Apollo/Ganymedes/Narcissus,
Artemis/Selene

befriends adolescent girls: Artemis

believer in progress: Zeus/Prometheus

belligerent: Zeus/Ares

bellylaugher: Dionysus

bereaved: Orpheus

beside oneself: Dionysus

beside oneself with ecstasy: Orpheus

bestial: Pan, Dionysus

bigot: Apollo, Orpheus

bipolar: Zeus

bisexual: Apollo, Aphrodite/Eros,
Dionysus, Hermes, Pan, Zeus,
Orpheus

bitchy: Artemis

bites off more than can chew: Zeus

bitter: Hermes/Heracles

black mischief: Dionysus

blazing eyes: Zeus/Typhon

blind: Zeus/Hades

blind folly: Dionysus

bloodyminded: Aphrodite,
Hermes/Heracles

bloodthirsty: Artemis/Medea

blows hot and cold: Gaia

blusterer: Zeus

boaster: Hermes/Odysseus

bodyorgan fetishist: Dionysus

bold: Pan, Zeus

boxer: Hermes

boy racer: Apollo/Hippolytus

brave sufferer: Orpheus

breast-cancer: Artemis/Amazons

breathing problems: Pan

broad: Gaia

broadcasts own problems:
Artemis/Sirens

broadminded: Gaia

broods on own problems: Artemis

brutal: Zeus

bubbly: Aphrodite

by turns spiritual and demonic: Gaia

calming: Gaia

can't cope with women: Apollo

can't get up in the morning: Pan

candid: Aphrodite

can't cope with teenagers: Gaia/Hestia

can't hold drink: Dionysus/Centaurs

can't understand own children: Zeus

cantankerous: Pan, Zeus

capricious: Pan

careless parent: Gaia/Demeter

carer: Gaia, Orpheus

caring: Aphrodite

cattlerustler: Hermes

catty to other women: Artemis

causes female jealousy:
    Apollo/Ganymedes

cautious: Hermes/Odysseus

caver: Gaia

celibate: Artemis/Daphne, Gaia/Hestia,
    Orpheus

centred: Gaia/Hestia

centre of male rivalries: Aphrodite

chameleon: Dionysus, Zeus

champion of just causes: Zeus

changeable: Artemis, Dionysus

characterless: Gaia/Hestia

charlatan: Hermes

charmer: Aphrodite,
    Artemis/Selene/Sirens

charming when she wants to be:
    Artemis/Hecate

chaste: Apollo/Hippolytus, Artemis

chauvinist: Apollo,
    Hermes/Heracles/Theseus, Zeus

cheat: Aphrodite/Eros

childcarer: Artemis, Aphrodite

childless: Artemis/Persephone

child-maltreater: Artemis/Amazons,
    Gaia/Demeter, Zeus/Cronus

child of nature: Artemis, Zeus

child prodigy: Hermes

childish: Apollo

childlike: Hermes

chip on the shoulder: Zeus/Prometheus

city planner: Apollo

civicminded: Zeus

clairvoyant: Apollo, Gaia

classically minded: Apollo

cleanliving: Apollo

clearheaded: Apollo

cleptomaniac: Hermes

clinging: Dionysus

clumsy: Dionysus, Zeus/Cronus

clutcher at straws: Zeus/Epimetheus

coarse: Dionysus, Gaia

cold attitude: Zeus/Cronus

coldheaded: Artemis

combative: Hermes/Heracles, Zeus/Ares

comic: Dionysus

compassionate: Zeus

competitive: Zeus/Ares

comradely: Dionysus/Dioscuri

concerned with own appearance:
Aphrodite

conciliator: Orpheus

confident: Zeus

confrontational: Apollo,
Hermes/Heracles/Perseus, Zeus

confused: Dionysus

conservative: Gaia/Hestia, Zeus

consistent: Zeus/Hades

constant: Artemis/Medea

constrictive: Zeus/Cronus

construction engineer: Apollo

contemptuous of law: Zeus/Ares

control freak: Apollo, Zeus/Ares

convivial: Pan

convulsive: Dionysus

cool skin: Artemis/Selene

counsellor: Orpheus

courageous: Artemis, Dionysus/Dioscuri,
Hermes/Perseus/Theseus, Orpheus,
Zeus,

courier: Hermes

courteous: Hermes/Heracles

coward: Zeus

coy: Artemis

craftsman: Hermes, Zeus/Prometheus

craftswoman: Gaia

crafty: Hermes/Odysseus,
Zeus/Prometheus

crazed: Dionysus

creative: Aphrodite/Eros

crude: Gaia

crude sense of fun: Hermes

crudely sexual: Artemis, Dionysus, Pan

cruel: Aphrodite, Artemis/Medea/Sirens,
Zeus

'cruel to be kind': Apollo/Asclepius

cult figure: Orpheus

cult freak: Dionysus

cunning: Aphrodite/Eros, Hermes, Zeus,

dancer: Artemis, Dionysus/Silenus,
Orpheus

dancing mad: Dionysus

daring: Artemis, Hermes/Theseus

dark instincts: Dionysus

dead from head downwards: Orpheus

dealer in abstracts: Apollo

death-denier: Zeus/Hades

death-wish: Apollo/Narcissus

debauched: Dionysus/Silenus

deceitful: Hermes, Pan

deep negative moods: Aphrodite

deluded: Orpheus

delusions: Zeus/Typhon

demanding mistress: Aphrodite

demands blood: Artemis

demonic: Pan

demure: Artemis

depressed: Artemis, Orpheus,
    Zeus/Cronus

depressed: Aphrodite, Hermes/Heracles

depressed by loss of children:
    Gaia/Demeter

deprived in youth: Zeus

deserted by mother: Pan

destroyed by own success:
    Hermes/Odysseus

destroys own children: Gaia

destructive: Aphrodite, Dionysus, Pan,
    Hermes/Perseus

destructive of men: Artemis

detached: Hermes

determined: Apollo, Artemis/Medea,
    Gaia/Hestia, Zeus

determinedly virginal: Artemis

devastating: Zeus

devilish: Pan, Dionysus

devious: Apollo/Hippolytus, Hermes,
    Zeus/Prometheus

devoted: Aphrodite

devoted to illusion: Orpheus

devourer of loveobject: Dionysus

dictator: Zeus

different: Dionysus

digestive problems: Zeus/Prometheus

diplomat: Hermes

dirty: Pan

disapproved of by older women:
    Aphrodite

disapproving of others' sexuality:
    Artemis

disciplined: Apollo

discus-thrower: Apollo

disguised: Gaia/Demeter

dishonest: Aphrodite/Eros

dislikes bright light: Pan

disreputable: Hermes

dissector: Apollo

dissembler: Zeus

dissimulating: Artemis/Medea,
    Dionysus/Dioscuri, Hermes, Pan,
    Zeus

dissolute: Dionysus

diviner: Apollo, Zeus

doctor: Apollo, Athene, Hermes

dogged: Hermes/Perseus

dogmatic: Orpheus, Zeus

domestic servant: Hermes

domineering: Gaia, Zeus

doorkeeper: Hermes

down to earth: Dionysus, Gaia

dozer: Hermes, Pan

dragon: Gaia

dragon-slayer: Hermes/Perseus

drama fan: Apollo

drawn to esoteric and occult: Gaia

dream interpreter: Apollo, Hermes

dreamer: Dionysus

dresses in rags: Hermes/Odysseus

drinker: Dionysus, Hermes

dropout: Dionysus

drugged: Dionysus

drunk: Apollo/Aristaeus, Dionysus,
    Zeus/Ares

durable: Zeus

dry: Zeus/Hades

dying: Zeus/Cronus/Hades

dynamic leader: Apollo/Aristaeus

early riser: Apollo

earth-worshipper: Artemis/Daphne

earthy: Dionysus, Gaia,
    Zeus/Prometheus

easily influenced: Dionysus

easily wounded emotionally: Aphrodite

easy-going: Apollo/Ganymedes,
    Dionysus/Silenus

ecstatic: Dionysus, Orpheus

effective: Zeus

effeminate: Dionysus

egocentric: Apollo/Narcissus,
    Hermes/Theseus

eloquent: Hermes

elusive: Pan, Dionysus, Hermes

emotional: Artemis

emotionally selfsufficient: Artemis

emotionally vulnerable:
    Aphrodite/Adonis, Hermes/Odysseus

enchanter: Artemis/Selene

energetic: Aphrodite/Eros, Dionysus

enjoys sex within stable relationship:
    Gaia

enjoys uncertainty: Hermes

enraged: Zeus/Ares/Prometheus

enthusiastic: Artemis, Dionysus, Pan

entranced: Dionysus

ephemeral: Dionysus, Aphrodite, Hermes

epileptic: Pan, Orpheus

erotic: Dionysus, Aphrodite

escapist: Orpheus

escort: Hermes

evanescent: Aphrodite

evangelical: Orpheus

everchanging: Dionysus, Zeus

everwelcoming: Gaia

exaggerated maleness: Dionysus

experienced: Dionysus/Silenus, Hermes,
    Zeus/Hades

exploiter of own sexuality: Aphrodite

explosive: Dionysus, Zeus/Typhon

failed lover: Apollo, Zeus

fair-dealer: Artemis/Amazons

fairminded: Apollo

faithful: Artemis/Persephone, Orpheus

false prophet: Orpheus

fanatic: Pan

farmer: Apollo

fascist: Zeus

fashion mad: Aphrodite, Dionysus

fat: Dionysus/Silenus, Gaia

father: Zeus

fears change: Zeus/Cronus

fears rejection: Apollo/Narcissus

fears sexual failure: Dionysus

feigns madness: Hermes/Odysseus

feminine: Gaia/Demeter

feminist: Artemis

ferocious looking: Zeus

fertile: Aphrodite, Artemis/Selene, Gaia,
  Zeus/Ares

festivalgoer: Dionysus

feverish: Artemis/Sirens, Zeus/Typhon

fiery speaker: Zeus/Typhon

finds men hard to cope with: Artemis

firebrand: Aphrodite/Eros

firemaker: Gaia

firewalker: Hermes

flatterer: Hermes

fleet of foot: Hermes/Perseus, Zeus/Ares

flexible: Hermes

flirter: Aphrodite

floosie: Aphrodite

fluid: Dionysus

fluteplayer: Pan, Dionysus

focused: Gaia/Hestia

follower of herd: Dionysus/Centaurs

fond of animals: Dionysus

fond of loud music: Dionysus

fond of sound of own voice: Orpheus

foolish: Hermes

football fan: Dionysus

forecaster: Hermes

foresight: Hermes/Odysseus

forgiving: Dionysus/Dioscuri

formal dancer: Apollo

foultempered: Aphrodite, Zeus

fraud: Hermes

frenzied: Pan, Dionysus

friendly: Artemis/Amazons, Dionysus,
  Hermes

frigid: Artemis

frustrated: Zeus/Epimetheus/Prometheus

full of nervous energy: Pan

gambler: Hermes

gangster: Dionysus/Dioscuri

gardener: Aphrodite

gauche: Dionysus

generous: Aphrodite, Gaia, Zeus

gentle: Aphrodite, Apollo/Asclepius,
Gaia/Demeter, Hermes

genuine: Gaia

gets things done: Zeus

giddy goat: Dionysus

gift of gab: Hermes

girlish whisperer: Aphrodite

gloomy: Zeus/Hades

gnostic: Orpheus

goalorientated: Artemis

going through hell for sake of truth:
Orpheus

goodhumoured: Dionysus, Zeus

good appetite: Artemis/Sirens

good learner: Apollo/Muses

good memory: Apollo/Muses

good sense of taste: Dionysus

good with children: Aphrodite,
Gaia/Demeter

gourmet: Artemis/Sirens

gracious: Artemis/Persephone

grand: Zeus

grateful: Gaia/Demeter

great: Zeus

gregarious: Dionysus, Pan

grounded: Pan

group aggression:Dionysus/Centaurs

group hysteria: Artemis/Sirens, Dionysus

group murderer: Dionysus

groupie: Artemis/Sirens, Dionysus

growing: Dionysus

growing spirituality: Zeus/Prometheus

guide: Hermes

guiltobsessed: Apollo

guiltridden: Zeus/Epimetheus, Orpheus

guitarmad: Dionysus

gullible: Artemis/Persephone/Selene,
Zeus

guru: Hermes

guruhunter: Dionysus

gymnast: Hermes

hander-on of culture: Gaia/Hestia

happy memories: Zeus/Cronus

has casual affairs: Aphrodite, Artemis

has nightmares: Pan

hates household tasks: Artemis/Cyrene

hates snakes: Apollo, Zeus

hates washing: Pan

headorientated: Apollo, Orpheus,
Zeus/Prometheus

headstrong: Zeus/Prometheus

healer: Apollo, Artemis, Gaia, Hermes,
Orpheus

healing presence: Gaia/Demeter, Hermes

heartless: Artemis/Sirens

heart-problems: Zeus/Atlas/Prometheus

heavy: Gaia

heedless: Zeus/Epimetheus

henpecked: Hermes/Heracles

hepatitis: Zeus/Prometheus

herbalist: Hermes

hermaphrodite: Hermes/Theseus, Pan

hermit: Orpheus

hermit tendency: Apollo

hero: Hermes/Heracles

hernia: Zeus/Atlas

herpes: Hermes/Heracles

hidden powers: Artemis/Hecate

highly active: Artemis

historian: Apollo/Muses

hoarder: Zeus/Hades

hoaxer: Aphrodite

holistic: Apollo/Asclepius

holy idiot: Hermes

Holy Joe: Orpheus

home-loving: Gaia/Hestia

homemaker: Gaia

homosexual: Apollo, Artemis,
    Dionysus/Dioscuri, Orpheus

homosexual escapades: Hermes/Heracles

honest: Aphrodite

hooligan: Dionysus

horny: Pan

horrors: Zeus/Typhon

horseman: Zeus

hospitable: Gaia/Hestia

hotheaded: Apollo

hot tempered: Zeus

humble: Gaia

humorist: Pan

humorous: Pan, Dionysus,
    Gaia/Demeter, Hermes

hunched shoulders: Zeus/Atlas

hunted: Dionysus

hunter: Apollo, Artemis

hunter of men in pack: Artemis/Sirens,
    Dionysus

hyperactive: Aphrodite

hypersensitive: Hermes/Heracles

hypertension:
    Zeus/Atlas/Prometheus/Typhon

hypnotist: Hermes

hypocrite: Orpheus

hysterical: Dionysus

idealistic: Aphrodite/Eros, Apollo,
    Dionysus, Orpheus

ignores world outside: Gaia/Hestia

immature: Dionysus,
    Aphrodite/Adonis/Eros

impetuous: Zeus/Ares

implacable fury: Zeus/Atlas

impotent: Zeus/Cronus/Hades

inaccessible: Zeus

incestuous: Aphrodite/Eros, Zeus

incompetent: Zeus/Epimetheus

incomprehensible: Zeus/Typhon

inconsistent: Artemis, Pan, Hermes

inconspicuous: Hermes/Odysseus

inconstant: Artemis, Dionysus

independent: Apollo, Artemis, Pan

indestructible: Zeus

individualist: Pan

ineffectual: Zeus/Epimetheus

infant hardship: Hermes/Perseus

infantile: Pan, Hermes

inferiority complex: Zeus

inflexible: Apollo, Zeus/Hades

information clerk: Hermes

inhospitable: Zeus/Atlas

initiative: Hermes/Odysseus

initiator: Apollo, Artemis, Hermes

inner pilgrim: Orpheus

inner rage: Zeus/Ares

innocent: Dionysus

inquisitive: Hermes/Odysseus

insecure: Apollo, Pan, Gaia/Hestia,
Hermes

insensitive: Zeus/Ares

insightful: Hermes/Theseus

insistent on rights: Gaia,

Hermes/Odysseus, Zeus/Prometheus

insolent: Hermes

insomniac: Zeus/Cronus

insulter: Dionysus/Dioscuri

instinctive: Artemis, Pan, Gaia

instinctive healer: Dionysus/Centaurs

instructor: Dionysus/Centaurs

integrated: Dionysus/Silenus

intellectual: Apollo, Zeus/Cronus

intelligent: Pan, Hermes

interested in military: Apollo, Zeus/Ares

interpreter: Hermes

intimate: Dionysus

intoxicated: Dionysus

introverted: Apollo. Zeus/Cronus

intrusive: Artemis/Selene

intuitive: Artemis, Hermes/Theseus,
Zeus

involuntary nocturnal emissions: Zeus

irascible: Hermes/Odysseus

irrational: Aphrodite, Dionysus, Pan,
Zeus/Ares/Typhon

irrational fears: Apollo/Actaeon

irregular: Pan

irrepressible: Dionysus

irresponsible: Aphrodite/Eros,
Artemis/Cyrene

jealous: Apollo, Aphrodite,

Artemis/Medea, Zeus/Ares

jealous of rights: Zeus

joker: Dionysus, Hermes

jovial: Zeus

jumps to conclusions: Artemis

junior gangster: Dionysus

junkie: Dionysus

keen on alternative religion: Dionysus

keen on new ideas: Dionysus

keensighted: Pan, Hermes

keeps problems to herself: Artemis

killjoy: Orpheus

kind: Gaia, Hermes

knowall: Apollo

knowing: Hermes

knowledgeable: Zeus

knows the sea: Zeus/Atlas

lacks foresight: Zeus/Epimetheus

lame: Hermes/Odysseus

larger than life: Zeus

latent paedophile: Apollo

lateral thinker: Artemis, Hermes, Zeus

laughs: Aphrodite

lawyer: Apollo, Zeus

lazy: Dionysus/Silenus

leader: Hermes/Odysseus, Zeus

left-handed: Zeus/Cronus

lesbian: Artemis

lethargic: Apollo/Narcissus,
   Gaia/Demeter

lets hair down: Dionysus, Pan

lets herself go: Gaia/Demeter

lets it all hang out: Dionysus

lewd: Dionysus/Silenus

liable to be kidnapped:
   Apollo/Ganymedes

liar: Apollo/Muses, Hermes

lifegiver: Gaia

lightfingered: Hermes

lightning decisions: Zeus

likes citylife: Artemis

likes flowers: Aphrodite

likes long clothes: Dionysus

likes seabathing: Aphrodite

likes seafood: Aphrodite

likes slim women: Apollo

likes strife: Aphrodite

linguist: Apollo/Muses, Hermes

links music with sex: Pan

lives on knife edge: Hermes

lives through own children: Gaia

logical: Apollo, Zeus/Prometheus

loner: Apollo, Artemis, Orpheus

long hair: Apollo, Dionysus

looter: Dionysus

lopsided: Dionysus

lost innocence: Artemis/Persephone

loud: Dionysus

loud voice: Aphrodite/Eros, Pan

lout: Dionysus

lovable: Aphrodite

loveshy: Artemis, Ganymedes

love-filled: Apollo/Aristaeus, Orpheus

lover of the new: Aphrodite

lover of the wild: Artemis

lover of wilderness: Gaia

loves animals: Artemis

loves baths: Artemis

loves challenges: Hermes/Theseus

loves company of own kind: Dionysus

loves dancing: Artemis

loves dark: Aphrodite,
Artemis/Persephone/Selene

loves dogs: Artemis

loves female company: Artemis/Daphne

loves flying: Apollo/Ganymedes

loves gadgets: Apollo

loves high life: Artemis/Cyrene

loves in excess: Orpheus

loves insecurity: Hermes/Odysseus

loves jewellery: Aphrodite

loves mountains: Artemis

loves nature: Apollo, Artemis

loves own children obsessively: Artemis

loves pets: Aphrodite

loves showers: Artemis

loves solitude: Artemis

loves sound of own voice:
Apollo/Narcissus

loves strenuous activity: Artemis/Cyrene

loves summer and sea: Aphrodite

loves symmetry: Apollo

loves the unattainable: Apollo/Narcissus

loves water: Apollo/Narcissus, Artemis

loves wilderness: Apollo/Actaeon

loves wind instruments: Pan

loves young wild animals: Artemis

loving: Aphrodite

lucky: Artemis/Hecate, Hermes

lustful: Aphrodite/Eros, Zeus

machismo: Hermes/Heracles

mad: Artemis, Hermes/Heracles, Pan,
Zeus/Epimetheus

mad on music: Pan, Dionysus

magician: Artemis/Hecate/Medea,
Dionysus, Hermes

magnanimous: Zeus

male chauvinist: Zeus

maltreater of aged partner: Aphrodite

manhunter: Artemis

manager: Zeus

mania for order: Zeus/Cronus

manic: Dionysus

manic depressive: Aphrodite/Adonis,
  Artemis/Persephone/Selene, Gaia

manipulative: Gaia

manipulator: Apollo, Artemis

manly: Hermes/Theseus

manually agile: Hermes

many-faced: Artemis/Hecate

marriage problems: Zeus/Epimetheus

marriage-resister: Gaia/Demeter

married late: Apollo/Hippolytus

married to older partner: Aphrodite

masculine: Zeus/Ares

masochistic: Hermes/Odysseus

mass hysteria: Dionysus/Centaurs

mass militant: Dionysus/Centaurs

masturbator: Aphrodite/Adonis,
  Apollo/Narcissus, Pan

materialist: Pan, Gaia

mathematician: Apollo

matriarchal: Artemis/Amazons

mediator: Gaia, Orpheus

medic: Apollo

medical knowledge: Apollo/Asclepius

medical specialist: Apollo

meditation junkie: Dionysus

meditator: Apollo

medium: Artemis

melancholic: Aphrodite, Zeus/Cronus

menstrual problems: Artemis/Selene

mentally disturbed: Pan

mentally disturbed at times: Artemis

methodical: Apollo

midwife: Artemis

migraine sufferer: Dionysus, Pan

militant: Zeus

militarily effective:
  Dionysus/Centaurs/Dioscuri

mineralogist: Zeus/Hades

miser: Zeus/Hades

misfit: Zeus

missionary: Orpheus

mistress: Aphrodite

mistrusts women: Zeus

moderate: Apollo

modest: Artemis

monk: Orpheus

monopoliser of truth: Orpheus

monotheist: Orpheus

moody: Artemis, Zeus

moral: Orpheus

morally upright: Gaia/Hestia

morbid: Zeus/Epimetheus

moralistic: Apollo, Orpheus

mother: Artemis, Aphrodite, Gaia

mother-abuser: Zeus/Ares

motherer: Artemis

mountaineer: Gaia

mournful: Hermes/Heracles,

Zeus/Epimetheus/Hades

muddled: Zeus/Typhon

murderer: Dionysus/Dioscuri, Zeus

murderous: Zeus/Typhon

murky motives: Dionysus

musical: Apollo, Artemis/Sirens,
Dionysus, Hermes, Pan

musician: Apollo, Artemis, Hermes,
Orpheus

music mad: Dionysus

music therapist: Apollo

naive: Apollo, Artemis

narcissistic: Apollo, Aphrodite

narrowminded: Orpheus

natural: Pan

naturist: Apollo, Aphrodite, Hermes

needs to learn hard way: Apollo

negative: Aphrodite, Dionysus,
Zeus/Hades

negative effects on women:
Apollo/Aristaeus

neglects wife: Hermes/Odysseus

neophile: Aphrodite

nightbird: Pan

nightmares: Apollo/Actaeon

nocturnal wanderer: Hermes

noisy: Dionysus, Pan

nomad: Hermes

noncommonsense: Hermes

nonsmoker: Orpheus

nostalgic: Hades,
Zeus/Cronus/Epimetheus

not made for marriage: Orpheus, Zeus

nudist: Pan, Aphrodite, Hermes

nymphomaniac: Aphrodite,
Gaia/Demeter

obdurate: Zeus/Cronus

obese: Gaia

observant: Pan

obsessed with death: Artemis/Persephone

obsessive counter: Zeus/Cronus

obsessive nomad: Hermes/Odysseus

obsessive washer: Artemis/Daphne

obstinate: Pan, Zeus/Hades

occasional pederast: Zeus

occultist: Artemis

omnivorous: Pan

only child: Artemis/Hecate

openminded: Hermes

open to the spiritual: Artemis/Persephone

opportunist: Hermes

opposed to grandfather: Hermes/Perseus

optimist: Dionysus

orator: Apollo/Muses

orderly: Apollo

organiser: Zeus

orgiastic: Dionysus/Centaurs,
  Apollo/Muses, Pan

original: Aphrodite, Hermes

orphan: Zeus

otherworldly: Orpheus

out of control: Dionysus

out of touch with real world: Orpheus

out of mind: Dionysus

outwardly devilmaycare: Dionysus

overachiever: Apollo

overactive: Apollo, Dionysus

overconfidence: Dionysus

overeater: Gaia

overerotic: Aphrodite

overexcitable: Dionysus

overreacts: Apollo

oversensitive to women's needs:
  Orpheus

oversexed: Aphrodite, Dionysus, Zeus

overflowing with life: Gaia

overweight: Gaia

overwhelms women initially: Pan

pacifier: Orpheus

paradoxical: Artemis, Hermes

paralysed by deeper self: Zeus

paralysis of right side: Zeus/Cronus

paralytic: Dionysus, Zeus

paranoid: Apollo/Actaeon, Zeus

passionate: Pan, Aphrodite

passive: Apollo/Ganymedes

paternal: Zeus

patient: Dionysus/Dioscuri

patriarch: Zeus

patricide: Zeus

pedlar of illusion: Orpheus

pensive: Zeus

periodic depression: Apollo/Asclepius,
  Artemis/Selene

periodic insanity: Artemis/Persephone

perjurer: Hermes, Zeus/Cronus

permanent: Zeus

persecuted child: Dionysus

persistent: Apollo, Hermes/Heracles

perspicacious: Gaia/Hestia, Hermes

persuasive: Hermes/Perseus, Orpheus

Peter Pan: Aphrodite/Adonis,
  Apollo/Ganymedes/Narcissus

petrifying: Zeus

petulant: Zeus

philanthropist: Zeus/Hades/Pormetheus

philosopher: Apollo, Hermes

philosophical paralysis:
  Apollo/Asclepius

physical: Pan, Aphrodite

physically orientated: Pan

Pied Piper: Orpheus

pioneer: Hermes/Heracles

pilgrim: Dionysus, Orpheus

pillar of society: Zeus

pitying: Zeus

planner: Hermes, Orpheus, Zeus

playful: Hermes

pleasure-loving: Dionysus/Silenus

plotter: Dionysus/Dioscuri,
	Hermes/Odysseus

poetic: Apollo/Muses, Orpheus

poisoned legs: Dionysus/Centaurs

poisonous: Artemis/Medea

pokerplayer: Zeus

political: Apollo, Zeus

polygamous: Zeus

poor eyesight: Zeus/Hades

poor health: Zeus/Epimetheus

pop music fan: Dionysus

popular: Hermes/Perseus

possessed: Dionysus

possessive: Aphrodite,
	Artemis/Persephone, Gaia/Demeter,
	Zeus/Ares/Hades

possessive of mother: Hermes/Perseus

possessive of own children: Gaia

potential murderer: Dionysus

potential rapist: Zeus/Typhon

powermad: Zeus

power-freak: Apollo/Asclepius

powerful darker side: Gaia

powerful personality: Zeus

practical joker: Aphrodite

pragmatic: Hermes/Perseus

prankster: Dionysus

preacher: Orpheus

precocious in youth: Zeus/Cronus

precognitive: Gaia

predictable: Zeus/Hades

prefers animals to people: Artemis

prefers female company:
	Artemis/Persephone

prefers male company: Apollo

prepared to be persecuted: Orpheus

priest: Hermes

primal: Pan, Gaia

profligate: Aphrodite/Eros,
	Zeus/Epimetheus

promiscuous: Aphrodite, Apollo/Muses,
	Artemis/Amazons, Hermes/Heracles,
	Zeus

promoter of civilised values: Zeus

prone to change character: Zeus

prone to despair: Artemis

prone to infections: Apollo, Artemis

prone to overkill: Hermes/Perseus

prone to VD: Aphrodite

prophet: Apollo/Aristaeus, Gaia,
	Orpheus

prophetic abilities: Apollo,

Artemis/Sirens, Dionysus/Silenus, Zeus/Cronus

prosperous: Hermes/Perseus

prostitute: Aphrodite

protective of oppressed: Apollo

protector of own children: Gaia

proud: Hermes/Odysseus, Zeus

prudish: Artemis

psychic: Artemis, Gaia

psychological balance: Artemis/Amazons, Dionysus/Centaurs

psychological problems: Dionysus

psychological disintegration: Apollo/Actaeon

psychosomatic illness: Zeus/Epimetheus

psychotherapist: Hermes

pure: Apollo/Hippolytus

purist: Apollo

puritanical: Hermes/Odysseus, Orpheus, Zeus/Hades

pursued by men: Artemis/Daphne

pyromaniac: Aphrodite/Eros, Zeus/Typhon

quarrels with extravert brothers: Apollo

quarrelsome: Zeus

quick decider: Zeus

quick learner: Apollo, Hermes

quicktempered: Gaia

raconteur: Dionysus/Silenus

rages: Zeus

randy: Pan, Dionysus

rapes own daughter: Zeus

rapid moodswings: Artemis

rapist: Pan, Dionysus, Zeus

raucous: Pan, Dionysus

raver: Dionysus

realist: Artemis

reasonable: Apollo

reassuring: Zeus

rebellious: Apollo, Zeus

reclusive: Apollo, Artemis/Sirens, Zeus/Hades

reclusive at times: Aphrodite

recuperates quickly: Zeus/Prometheus

red clothes: Aphrodite

red hair: Hermes/Odysseus

reductionist: Apollo

reformer: Apollo/Aristaeus, Orpheus, Zeus

refuses to eat, drink, wash: Gaia/Demeter

regenerator: Orpheus

regretful: Orpheus, Zeus/Cronus/Epimetheus

regrets loss of virginity: Aphrodite

regular: Apollo, Zeus

rejects dogmas: Aphrodite/Adonis

rejects love: Apollo/Narcissus

rejects the new: Zeus/Cronus

relates well to grandparents: Dionysus

reliable: Apollo/Aristaeus, Gaia, Zeus

religious: Apollo/Hippolytus, Orpheus,
    Zeus,

religious ecstatic: Dionysus

religious idealist: Orpheus

religious maniac: Orpheus

religious propagandist: Orpheus

religious revolutionary: Orpheus

remote: Apollo, Zeus

repressed unconscious urges:
    Zeus/Typhon

represses sexuality: Orpheus

repressive: Zeus/Cronus

resentful: Zeus/Epimetheus

resentful of parents: Zeus/Cronus

resents control by others: Gaia

resilient: Dionysus

resists dominant women:
    Hermes/Perseus

resists sex: Artemis/Selene

resolute: Zeus

resourceful: Hermes/Odysseus, Zeus

respecter of received wisdom:
    Hermes/Odysseus

responds to challenges: Dionysus

responsible: Dionysus, Gaia

responsibly creative: Gaia

responsive to dreams: Dionysus

responsive to gut instincts: Pan

responsive to intuitions: Dionysus

restless: Apollo, Hermes, Pan, Zeus

restorer of others:
    Artemis/Hecate/Persephone,
    Orpheus

retiring: Artemis

retrospective: Zeus/Epimetheus/Hades,
    Orpheus

reveller: Pan

revolutionary: Zeus/Prometheus

rich: Artemis/Hecate, Zeus/Hades

rightbrained: Artemis

rigid: Zeus/Cronus

rigid sense of values: Gaia/Hestia

riotous: Pan, Dionysus

risk-taker:
    Hermes/Odysseus/Perseus/Theseus

rogue: Hermes/Odysseus

romancer: Dionysus

rounded: Gaia

routinebound: Apollo, Zeus/Hades

runner: Hermes

rustler: Dionysus/Dioscuri

ruthless: Aphrodite, Artemis/Medea,

Hermes/Odysseus/Perseus, Zeus

ruthless with own children: Gaia

sacraliser: Artemis/Hecate

sadistic: Apollo

sadomasochist: Dionysus

savage: Dionysus, Gaia

saviour and protector: Zeus

schemer: Hermes/Odysseus

scientist: Apollo

scolder: Gaia/Demeter

scorns clothes: Hermes

scorns sleep: Zeus

scorns the unconscious:

   Zeus/Prometheus

screamer: Dionysus

screams when hurt: Zeus/Ares

seasonally depressed: Gaia

secretive: Artemis, Hermes

secret worrier: Hermes/Odysseus

seditious: Zeus/Atlas/Prometheus

seduced: Aphrodite/Eros

seduced in youth: Apollo/Hippolytus

seducer: Aphrodite, Hermes

seeker: Orpheus

seeker of higher consciousness: Gaia

seer: Gaia

sees things in black and white: Apollo

selfabandoner: Aphrodite

self-admirer: Apollo/Narcissus

selfaware: Hermes

selfbeautifier: Aphrodite

selfcentred: Apollo

self-confident: Apollo/Narcissus,

   Hermes/Perseus

self-destructive:

   Apollo/Actaeon/Narcissus,

   Zeus/Cronus

selfdisgusted: Apollo, Orpheus

selfdoubting: Dionysus

self-destructive if scorned:

   Artemis/Sirens

self-effacing: Gaia/Hestia

selfexpressive: Dionysus

selfish: Hermes/Theseus

selfgiver: Aphrodite

selfhealer: Dionysus, Zeus/Cronus

self-justifier: Zeus/Cronus

selfmutilator: Artemis/Amazons,

   Dionysus

selfobsessed: Apollo

selfrecollected: Hermes

selfsacrificial: Aphrodite/Eros, Dionysus,

   Gaia, Orpheus

selfseeker: Apollo

self-sufficient: Apollo/Narcissus

sense of fun: Aphrodite, Dionysus

sense of honour:

   Hermes/Odysseus/Perseus

sense of justice: Apollo/Aristaeus

sense of mystical: Dionysus

sense of order: Gaia/Hestia

sense of place and belonging:

Gaia/Hestia

sense of propriety: Zeus

sensitive: Pan, Dionysus

sensitive to nature: Artemis/Daphne

sensitive to omens: Hermes/Heracles

sensitive to own unconscious needs:

Artemis, Gaia

sensual: Dionysus

serendipitous: Hermes

serene: Zeus/Cronus

serial lover: Aphrodite

setting affairs in order: Zeus/Hades

severe on self: Apollo/Hippolytus

sexobject: Dionysus

sexobsessed: Apollo/Muses, Dionysus

sexually abstinent: Artemis, Orpheus

sexual boaster: Apollo/Actaeon

sexual nightmares: Apollo/Muses

sexually ambivalent: Pan, Dionysus

sexually attractive: Aphrodite

sexually confident: Dionysus

sexually frank: Hermes

sexually gentle: Artemis/Selene

sexually greedy: Aphrodite

sexually immature: Aphrodite,

Apollo/Actaeon

sexually independent: Artemis

sexually indiscriminate:

Dionysus/Centaurs

sexually innocent: Aphrodite/Adonis

sexually naive: Aphrodite

sexually potent: Aphrodite/Eros, Pan

sexually pure: Orpheus

sexually repressed: Aphrodite/Adonis,

Orpheus

sexually uncontrolled: Hermes/Heracles

sexually voracious: Aphrodite

sexual pushover: Aphrodite/Adonis

sex-withholder: Gaia/Demeter

sexy: Aphrodite

shaggy: Pan

shaman: Hermes

shameless: Apollo, Pan, Dionysus,

Hermes

shifty: Dionysus, Zeus, Hermes

shingles: Hermes/Heracles

shocked by own perversity: Aphrodite

short legs: Hermes/Odysseus

short term lover: Aphrodite

shy: Artemis/Selene

shy initially: Aphrodite, Apollo/Actaeon,

Artemis

simplistic: Zeus/Atlas

singer: Artemis, Orpheus

single-minded: Apollo/Aristaeus, Hermes/Odysseus

skilled with animals: Hermes

skilled with young boys: Hermes

skin problems: Dionysus, Hermes/Heracles, Zeus/Typhon

slave to women: Hermes/Heracles

slimmer: Aphrodite

slow to anger: Gaia/Demeter

slut: Aphrodite, Dionysus

smelly: Pan

snakelike: Zeus

sociable with other women: Artemis/Sirens

socially disruptive: Dionysus

sodomised: Apollo/Ganymedes

soldier: Apollo, Zeus/Poseidon/Ares

solid: Gaia, Zeus/Atlas

soother: Gaia, Orpheus

sorcerer: Dionysus, Hermes

sorceress: Artemis

soothing to men: Artemis/Selene

sound sleeper: Artemis, Dionysus, Pan

sparkling: Aphrodite

spellbinder: Artemis/Selene

spiritual: Apollo, Orpheus

spiritually aware: Artemis/Daphne

spiritually knowing: Gaia/Demeter

spiritual renewer: Apollo/Aristaeus

spontaneous: Aphrodite, Hermes

sportsman: Apollo, Hermes/Perseus

sportswoman: Artemis

stable: Gaia/Hestia

stern: Zeus

stiff: Zeus/Hades

stoned: Dionysus

stormy: Aphrodite, Zeus

storyteller: Hermes

stay-at-home: Gaia/Hestia

straightlaced: Orpheus

stranger to instincts and emotions: Orpheus

strength in numbers: Dionysus/Centaurs

stroke-sufferer: Zeus/Cronus

strong: Hermes/Heracles/Perseus, Zeus

strong opinions: Pan

strong subconscious urges: Artemis/Persephone

strong survival instinct: Hermes/Odysseus

strong unconscious urges: Gaia

strong willed: Hermes/Odysseus

stutterer: Apollo/Aristaeus

subjective: Artemis

subject to pederasty: Apollo/Ganymedes/Narcissus

sublimator: Apollo/Muses, Orpheus

sudden insights: Hermes

suffers from convulsions: Pan

suffers from panics: Pan

suicidal: Apollo/Narcissus,
    Zeus/Epimetheus

sunlover: Orpheus

sunbather: Apollo

superstitious: Hermes

supporter of own children: Gaia, Zeus

supporter of underdog: Zeus/Prometheus

suppresses own sexuality: Artemis,
    Orpheus

surly: Zeus

survivalist: Hermes/Perseus, Pan

survivor: Dionysus, Zeus, Orpheus

sweet tooth: Dionysus

sympathetic to living creatures:
    Hermes/Heracles

sympathetic to other women: Artemis

take-it-or-leave-it: Hermes/Odysseus

takes initiative: Apollo/Aristaeus

tall: Zeus/Ares

tantrums: Pan

teacher: Artemis, Dionysus/Centaurs,
    Hermes, Orpheus

teaser: Aphrodite, Hermes

technologist: Apollo

teetotal: Orpheus

telepath: Gaia

temper: Gaia/Demeter,
    Zeus/Prometheus/Typhon

tempter of providence: Hermes/Heracles

tender: Dionysus, Gaia

terrified: Pan

terrifying: Zeus

terrormonger: Gaia

terrorist: Hermes/Odysseus, Pan

theologian: Apollo

thief: Hermes

thinker: Zeus/Prometheus

thorough: Hermes/Perseus

thoughtful: Apollo

threatened by suffocation: Pan

threatening: Apollo, Zeus

tidy: Apollo

timid: Pan

tinnitus: Hermes/Odysseus

tolerant of cold: Zeus/Prometheus

tomboy: Artemis

tongue-tied: Apollo/Aristaeus

tormented: Zeus/Prometheus

totalitarian: Zeus

toucher and taster: Dionysus

tough: Zeus/Prometheus

toyboy: Adonis, Hermes

trader: Artemis

transcender: Orpheus

transformer: Hermes

translator: Hermes

transsexual: Aphrodite,

Apollo/Narcissus, Dionysus,

    Hermes/Theseus

transvestite interludes: Dionysus,

Hermes/Heracles

travel agent: Hermes

traveller: Apollo, Artemis, Hermes

treacherous: Hermes/Odysseus

trickster: Artemis/Medea, Hermes

troubleshooter: Zeus

troubled: Zeus

turbulent: Dionysus

turned on: Dionysus

two-faced: Artemis/Hecate,

    Zeus/Prometheus

tyrant: Zeus

unable to cope with unconscious: Apollo,

    Zeus

unable to retain partners:

    Aphrodite/Adonis, Orpheus

unable to settle down: Hermes/Odysseus

unattractive 'mask': Gaia/Demeter

uncertain: Hermes

uncompassionate: Zeus/Hades

uncontrollable: Pan

uncontrollable erections: Dionysus,

    Hermes

uncontrollable temper: Aphrodite, Zeus

uncontrolled: Pan

unconventional: Artemis/Amazons,

    Hermes/Heracles

undervalues women: Zeus/Prometheus

undisciplined: Artemis, Pan

unemotional: Apollo

unfaithful: Aphrodite, Hermes/Heracles,

    Zeus

unforgiving: Apollo

unifier: Zeus

uninhibited: Pan, Dionysus, Hermes

unkind to pregnant women: Artemis

unladylike: Artemis

unpleasant by turns: Artemis/Hecate

unpredictable: Artemis, Dionysus, Zeus,

    Hermes

unreliable: Hermes, Pan, Zeus

unrestrained: Dionysus

unruly: Aphrodite/Eros, Pan

unselfish: Dionysus/Dioscuri, Gaia

unstable personality: Dionysus, Orpheus

unsociable: Apollo/Narcissus

unsure of self: Dionysus

untidy: Pan, Dionysus

untrustworthy: Hermes

uses perfumes: Apollo

vacuous expression: Pan

vandal: Pan, Dionysus

variable: Artemis

vegetarian: Orpheus

vengeful: Apollo, Dionysus/Centaurs, Gaia, Hermes/Heracles, Zeus/Ares

versatile: Hermes/Odysseus

vigorous: Pan, Dionysus

vigorous instincts: Dionysus

vindictive: Apollo, Gaia, Zeus

vindictive to men: Artemis/Persephone

violator of rules: Hermes

violent: Dionysus, Hermes/Odysseus, Zeus/Ares

virginal: Artemis, Gaia/Hestia

virile: Apollo, Zeus

voyeur: Apollo/Actaeon

vulnerable: Aphrodite

vulnerable to homosexuals: Apollo/Ganymedes

vulnerable to own followers: Orpheus

vulnerable to abduction and rape: Artemis/Persephone

walks out under pressure: Gaia/Hestia

wanderer: Dionysus

warm: Gaia/Hestia

warrior: Zeus

wary: Zeus/Prometheus

watchman: Hermes

wears unattractive mask: Artemis

weatherforecaster: Zeus

wet blanket: Orpheus

wild: Aphrodite/Eros, Artemis, Dionysus

wild beast: Dionysus

wild dancer: Pan

wild driver: Apollo/Hippolytus

wilful: Artemis/Cyrene

winter depression: Artemis/Persephone, Gaia/Demeter

wise: Aphrodite/Eros, Dionysus/Silenus, Zeus

wise beyond years: Hermes

wise fool: Hermes

wise healer: Apollo/Asclepius

witch: Artemis, Gaia

womanchaser: Dionysus, Pan

woman's man: Hermes/Perseus

workaholic: Apollo

worker with animals: Hermes

works from hunches: Artemis

works well with adolescents: Apollo, Orpheus

works well with animals: Apollo

worldchanger: Zeus

worrier: Zeus/Prometheus

would-be rapist: Apollo/Actaeon

writer: Apollo/Muses

wrongfully accused of rape:

Apollo/Hippolytus

young at heart: Apollo

young outlook: Hermes

youthleader: Apollo, Artemis, Orpheus

youthworker: Apollo, Artemis, Orpheus

youthful: Dionysus

youthful good looks: Hermes

youthful outcast: Zeus

youthful prodigies: Hermes/Heracles

1

APOLLO – THE WAY OF THE MAN

Know then thyself, presume not God to scan;
The proper study of mankind is man.
Alexander Pope, An Essay on Man (II:1)

APOLLO is the god of many an inexperienced young man who is intellectually and/or spiritually orientated and wants his world to be organized, neat and comprehensible. Such a man may as yet feel uneasy in the presence of women, or of anything else that may threaten his feeling of control over that world or his sense of daily routine. Prolonged into old age, Apollo therefore threatens to bring with him rigidity and dogmatism, yet at the proper place and time the solar archetype can be the source of much youthful brilliance, understanding, artistic ability, athleticism and healing.

Characteristics of man and god

The sun is Apollo. Apollo is therefore brilliant. He is resplendent with the light of consciousness. No less than his human devotees, he simply has to shine. He is ardent (i.e. burning) too, and thus highly idealistic. He is steady, constant and regular. For that reason he is also reliable and predictable, a model of order and discipline. He it is who allows humanity to see and understand the world that lies about it, separating the miasmic landscape of the night into a plethora of distinct and identifiable objects, and so making possible the detailed work of the daytime. Reborn every day, he is ever-young, ever self-renewing, yet by the same token ever-dying too. His rays are healing, cleansing, antiseptic – so pure, indeed, that in time they can reduce even the darkest stains to purest white. Ever on the move, he is a natural master of movement, and especially of circular or parabolic movement. Ever aloft, or at least ever remote from things earthly, his unchanging celestial countenance seems to guarantee a transcendent immortality and the existence of a higher order of reality entirely.

Thus far Apollo's positive side. But Apollo, like all the gods, has an equally strong negative side, too – a negative side, inevitably, that is the exact mirror-image of his more positive aspect. His human acolytes, too, duly reflect this fact in their turn. Thus, his compulsion to shine and so to become the focus of attention inevitably tends to make him self-centred. The very brightness of his shining casts deep shadows, and so he all too easily falls prey to dualism, obsessively dividing up the world into light and dark, white and black, good and evil. At the same time he can become so obsessed with discrimination, understanding, learning and the acquisition of knowledge that he finishes up virtually dead from the neck downwards, cut off from all conscious experience of his body, his emotions and his deeper instincts. So intent is he on shining that he can turn into a mere show-off or know-all, using his knowledge as a kind of status-symbol to keep his less intellectual peers and counterparts firmly in their place (it goes without saying, after all, that when the sun is shining all the other stars are invisible). For much the same reason he tends to become an obsessive

---

Historical Apollonians

Numerous well-known people in history, whether in the spheres of war, science, medicine, the arts or sport, have exhibited the archetype of Apollo. Among them, possibly, are King David, Alexander the Great, Hannibal, Julius Caesar, King Richard I of England, Christopher Marlowe, The Earl of Oxford (possible leader of the group that wrote Shakespeare), Racine, Pascal, Isaac Newton, Mozart, Napoleon, John Keats, Gordon of Khartoum, Lord Baden Powell, Albert Einstein, Lawrence of Arabia, Field Marshal Bernard Montgomery, the composers Benjamin Britten and Michael Tippet, Arthur C Clarke, Wernher von Braun, Roger Bannister and Rudolf Nureyev, to say nothing of thousands of other dedicated scientists, doctors, artists, poets, musicians and sportsmen. Even Jesus of Nazareth could conceivably be counted among their number.

---

over-achiever whose ardent idealism makes him more concerned with the way things should be than the way things are, and thus a born moraliser as well. His burning passion for causes can become so intense as to blind him to the fact that other people may have different concerns and ideals entirely, and so he runs the risk of becoming something of a bigot into the bargain.

His mania for regularity, meanwhile, all too easily makes him rigid and inflexible, and a slave to routine. His determination to cast light even into the darkest corners can lead him to insist that darkness has no right to exist at all, and that what cannot be explained in the light of reason cannot be believed in, either. His perennial youthfulness tends to prevent him from ever growing up, so that – emotionally at least, and perhaps to some extent physically, too – he remains a mere child to the end of his days, even taking deliberate cosmetic steps to appear that way. At the same time the solar Apollo's periodic experience of apparent night-time mortality suggests that there is a natural term to all his activities – in other words, that they are best not persisted with for too long at any one time, and that a cyclic or serial approach to them is more appropriate if their continuance is to be assured.

Again, Apollo's powers of healing can become something of an obsession, with other people devalued into mere pawns for satisfying it. His concern with purity and whiteness can come out in the form of an exaggerated asceticism and a refusal to get his hands dirty, whether professionally or in the process of getting to grips with the seamier and soggier aspects of his own nature. As the sun, after all, he is inherently antagonistic towards all soggy patches, as well as naturally somewhat remote and consequently much more interested in spiritual ideals and eternal verities than with the nitty-gritty of daily life at the human level. His refusal to stand still can show up in the form of chronic over-activity, a mania for change, a constant restlessness which makes him ever dissatisfied with things as they are. In consequence, he may finish up living life on a constant, precarious knife-edge of physical risk and psychological insecurity.

Apollo's particular *bête noire*, however, is (very naturally) his polar opposite, the moon, symbol of all that is feminine. In fact he is determined to eclipse her at every opportunity. And since, in practice, there is no way in which he can do anything of the kind – since it is she who alone is capable of eclipsing *him* – he makes up for it by attempting to dazzle her, making her pale into insignificance and generally blinding her with science (or rather with his own particular form of *scientia*). Generally speaking, he can tolerate her – if at all – only at a distance, preferably in the opposite part of the firmament. And if their paths should accidentally cross in earnest, the most unholy disasters are likely to ensue (Latin: *dis-aster* = a derangement of the stars).

All of which has to mean that Apollo (and, by extension, any man who fully embodies him) tends to find women – as also his own inner, 'feminine' side – altogether too difficult and unpredictable to cope with, and so he is likely to seek most of his satisfactions either alone or in the company of other males. Thus, his inclinations may be purely narcissistic – i.e. those of the mythical Narcissus – his role essentially that of a loner. On the whole, however, he is more likely to be either homosexual or bisexual in orientation. This orientation may show up emotionally, physically, professionally or recreationally – or, indeed, in all four spheres at once. Professionally, for example, this may take the form of a tendency to place the company and approval of other males before all other considerations – which will often mean his putting his work before his home-life. On the leisure front, similarly, it may manifest itself in a marked reluctance to forsake either the sports-field or the male-dominated club, bar or pub.

In all this it is not difficult to recognise many of the characteristics and attitudes that not only were typical of Socrates and Plato themselves in their day, but continue to be typical of men in modern Western societies. Already, it seems, we have a remarkably clear and comprehensive portrait of a particular human 'type' – or rather of an *arche*type – which is evidently a fundamental aspect of human nature (and of *man's* nature in particular) and has clearly been so ever since man became truly man in the first place. To that extent it is neither 'good' nor 'bad', neither positive nor negative, but simply *there*.

No one archetype, however, *has* to be lived out for real, still less all the time or to the exclusion of all others. Nor do its negative aspects need to be to the fore. There is always some choice in the matter.

Exercising it, though, is not necessarily easy. The archetypes have a will of their own. Subjected to arbitrary, conscious choices on the part of a human individuals or societies, they have a way of striking back in ways that we may well experience negatively and certainly cannot hope to control. The best that we can do, therefore, is to go along with them. No doubt that is why Apollo's paradigm seems virtually inescapable at present for most Western males. It is, after all, culturally determined – determined, that is, by our whole Western philosophical tradition going right back to the ancient Greek philosophers.

Men *could* be otherwise, in other words. But this, as we shall see, would depend on their escaping their cultural conditioning sufficiently to accept not only the light of Apollo in all its multi- farious rainbow-colours (and not merely the approved ones), but also the equally valid ministrations of other gods entirely. It would depend, in other words, on their leaving behind the youthful pastures of Apollo and finally growing up.

The sources

The ancient written records of Apollo's myth duly go on to flesh out this basic paradigm (compare the titles listed in the biography: Campbell, Graves and Kerényi in particular give specific text-references). Thus, in reflection of his mastery of cyclic and parabolic movement, he is traditionally portrayed as the god of the dance, and thus also of music, poetry and the drama – for all four were at one time inseparably linked. With poetry from time immemorial a prime vehicle of spiritual revelation, and poetic frenzy indistinguishable from prophetic frenzy, he becomes the god of prophecy, too. And meanwhile he presides over the work of the fields and pastures, not only because the agricultural year is itself cyclic in nature, but because, as the sun, that is manifestly his proper function.

His constant youthfulness is axiomatic, and his inherent homosexual tendency is reflected in his perennial love and pursuit of adolescent youths not much younger than himself. True, his attentions tend, in the myth, to result in their premature 'death'. But then this seems merely to be symbolic of the fact that their relationship with Apollo acts, in effect, as a first initiation into the mysteries of adult sexuality – albeit, inevitably, of a purely 'Platonic' kind – and thus as a catalyst of maturation which thereafter places them, as well-adjusted young adults, forever beyond his reach. Henceforward, in other words, it is really *their role as Apollo's youthful paramours* that is finally dead and buried.

Not that Apollo shies away totally from heterosexual relationships. On the contrary, he is powerfully attracted to the more sylph-like of females, and especially to those of a somewhat boyish figure and disposition. To this fact, presumably, we owe not only the modern predilection of Western males for women who are almost unnaturally slim, but also the corresponding female urge to live up to this well-nigh impossible ideal.

Nevertheless, such heterosexual encounters tend for Apollo to be fleeting and non-committal, and never succeed in tying him down for long or turning him into the ageing, home-loving family-man who would be the very antithesis of his perennial youthfulness. He is ever on the go, ever on the lookout – indeed, ever the huntsman. His bow and arrows are therefore his constant companions. And if in the forest and in the field of love, then why not also on the battlefield? Here it is not only his natural skill in ballistics, but also his passion for order and discipline that place him firmly in the military camp. And when the struggle is over, it is rejoined anew in the sports-arena, where the discus is his acknowledged speciality.

At the same time Apollo's passion for learning and science, combined with a natural flair for things practical, maintains in him a keen interest in technology of all kinds, as well as in the mathematics that goes to support it. His natural idealism also draws him almost irresistibly (as Plato himself was to discover) into politics of various kinds, as well as – in conjunction with his healing bent and scientific skills – into specialist medicine.

In short, he can turn his hand with great brilliance to almost anything.

As ever, though, the myth also reflects Apollo's darker side. His totem animal, after all, is not only the dazzling white swan, but also the black crow – to say nothing of the wolf. Not unexpectedly, he turns out to be a born male chauvinist. He can be arrogant, shameless, bloody-minded, manipulative, jealous, hot-headed (what else!), rebellious, vengeful, sadistic. Lacking experience of the over-all range of human emotions, especially as experienced by others, he can be naive at the best of times. And thanks to his passion for cleanliness and hygiene he is (paradoxically perhaps) particularly vulnerable to infectious diseases, and thus liable to spread them to others too.

The surviving historical reports of Apollo's cult flesh out the picture even further. At Delphi, for example, it seems brutally to have taken over the former subterranean snake-cult of the Earth Mother, with its Pythian priestess and oracle, substituting for it a male-dominated regime that unashamedly used the former oracle as a tool for dabbling in international power-politics. At the same time the celebrated inscriptions that ornamented the Delphic temple reflected the more disciplined, restrained side of Apollo's nature. One of them is traditionally rendered as 'Know yourself', while the other is reported by Plato as reading 'Nothing in excess'. In the light of this latter, the real meaning of the first injunction is clear. In accordance with the known nature of Apollo, it is 'Know your limitations'. (Latter day esoteric speculations attaching a much deeper meaning to the phrase may, although well worth contemplating in their own right, safely be disregarded in this context.)

Also at Delphi, the presence of a magnificent sports stadium, cut into the mountainside (and slightly longer than its rival at Olympia), attests to the extremely competitive sporting side of Apollo's nature (as also to the fact that competitive athletics, like the drama, were a mandatory aspect of religious observance at most of ancient Greece's early cult-centres, only later degenerating into largely autonomous forms of public entertainment). At the same time Delphic tradition also insisted on the 'temporary' aspect of Apollo's rule, so that Apollo was held to desert the sanctuary for the snowy wolf-lands of the north during the two midwinter months of the year, in the meantime handing it over to the revels of the unrestrained and uninhibited **Dionysus**, to whom the site's magnificently-situated hillside theatre was consequently dedicated.

Discipline and restraint, in other words are all very well, but there need to be opportunities to 'let one's hair down', too, if the inner pressures generated by Apollo's inhibitions and emotional hang-ups are not to explode in disastrous and destructive ways.

The sacred sites

Sensitive visitors to Delphi will duly pick up on various of these themes from the surviving buildings themselves. The original site, it is evident, has its own autonomous magic. Its quiet, mountain seclusion, its lofty peaks and soaring eagles bespeak a closeness to the bosom of mother earth and a hushed proximity to the very threshold of the gods. But what is also self-evident is that the cult of Apollo has been superimposed upon it in the most shameless and arrogant way. His temple here positively exudes lordly transcendence and sheer masculine, political domination.

Moreover, this feeling is quite special to Delphi. By no means all of Apollo's temples give the same impression. True, at least one of the three – that of the Athenians – whose base-platforms still survive on the sacred isle of Delos, the symbolic hub of the Cyclades, seems to have an air of power-politics about it. But its neighbour, erected by the Delians themselves, picks up far more on the equally Apollonian (and, later, Aristotelian) virtues of moderation and restraint, as does Apollo's early temple at Corinth, whose monolithic columns also seem to reflect his basic concern for safe, measured stability.

By contrast, the precariously-sited temple of Apollo Karneios that looks out over the sea from the lofty mountain-fastness of ancient Thera – the rocky Spartan citadel that once dominated the south-eastern coast of the island of Santorini, and from it much of the Aegean – has a feeling about it of sheer pride of possession and resplendence and (small though it is) a confident air of 'this is the way things should be'.

As well it might, for, ensconced up here in this powerful and craggy eyrie, Apollo was very much in control, while on the nearby Terrace of the Festivals the naked youths (or *epheboi*) who were candidates for Apollo's initiation into manhood would annually perform the late summer dances known as the *Gymnopaediai* to the honour of the god and the delight of his exclusively male devotees – as so hauntingly set to music by Erik Satie in his latter-day piano work of the same name. Indeed, those spectators' admiring graffiti still survive on the adjoining rocks to this day.

Not all visitors to the various sites, of course, will find such impressions at all self-evident. Much will depend on their innate sensitivity to atmosphere. What *should* be evident by now, however, is the nature of the archetype that we call Apollo himself. And if of Apollo, then also of the basically Apollonian tradition to which we ourselves are heirs, just as Socrates, Plato and Aristotle were before us. Small wonder, then, that our society as a whole should display so many of his characteristics as set out above, and that Western males in particular should in so many respects continue to reflect the solar characteristics of the Greek god.

VITAL ACTIONS

With Apollo's characteristic attitudes and cast of thought long since endemic among Western adults, and now increasinglydominant in the rest of the world as well, one thing is clear. Apollo is no stranger to us. Yet because he is almost the *only* god that a good many of us know (and the men among us particularly), we fail for the most part to *re-cognise* him. He comes to us disguised in robes of established taboo and convention. He wears the impenetrable mask of sheer undisputedness. His presence among us is a matter of course.

And so we fail to see him for who he truly is. We fail to realise that we have been hijacked by a particular way of seeing and thinking, by a particular attitude to the world. Just as the ancient Greeks themselves assumed that their own language was the only true language, and that foreigners merely went *'Bar bar'* (whence the term 'barbarian'), so we in turn have become so mesmerised by the language of Apollo as to fail to accept that other tongues are even possible, let alone that they actually exist in our midst. And so we cannot even get Apollo's familiar tongue into its true perspective. We not only assume that it is what it is not – i.e. our only possible mode of communication with ourselves and each other. We also fail totally to appreciate it for what it is.

In Apollo's case, then, we are actually blinded by our over-familiarity. We are like the person referred to by Browning who does not know England precisely because England is the only country he knows (see the familiar lines quoted at the top of chapter 8). And so the task of getting to know this all-pervasive archetype presents special difficulties of its own.

Perhaps for this very reason, the task is one of special urgency for us. It addresses us at the point where we actually are. It impinges directly on the matter at hand. And so it is here that any attempt at remedial action needs to begin.

The following notes are offered as a guide to such action. They represent a possible first step along the path of getting to know *our selves*. And, in particular, they offer to all who would do so the chance to get to know the Apollo who lives and moves within us all.

1. Self-enquiry

The first step is to take time out to examine yourself, your attitudes and typical habits of thought.

(a) Accepted aspects

Do you prize logic, reason and the life of the head? Are you predominantly intellectual, rather than intuitive or emotional? Are you clear-headed, tidy-minded, methodical, analytical and a believer in moderation? If most or all of these descriptions apply to you, you are by definition a follower of Apollo. Especially if you are also devoted to science, mathematics or medicine, and/or keen on athletics, classical music, poetry, ballet or drama, Apollo is indubitably your ruling god.

Moreover, there is absolutely no cause for guilt or embarrassment in any of this. If you are a man, it is perfectly typical of many a cultured, Western male. If you are a woman, many a female, too, has found it natural to adopt such attitudes. In both cases the result may owe at least as much to circumstance as to nature, but the simple fact still needs to be recognised and accepted that *it is there*. There is no future in denying reality.

(b) Rejected aspects

Denial, however, may loom large in the next stage of our enquiry. For Apollo has his 'darker' side, too, and *re-cognising* it within ourselves is, for this very reason, often much more difficult. Indeed, the extent to which we *regard* it as 'dark' – or, indeed, are incapable of recognising it within ourselves at all – is itself an index of how far Apollo is posing problems for us.

Do not be surprised, then, if the next batch of questions arouses sudden feelings of anger or affront within you. Such reactions can themselves prove to be valuable tools for self-*re-cognition*. Do not be surprised, either, if – by contrast – they elicit neither identification nor rejection. If they seem to have nothing whatever to do with you, that, too, is entirely to be expected – and all the more reason for pursuing the enquiry.

For now you need to probe yourself rather more deeply and unmercifully.

If you are a man, do you have difficulty in coping either with your own emotions or with women? How far could you describe yourself as a male chauvinist? Do you socialise almost exclusively with men, whether at work or at play? Do you have bisexual or homosexual tendencies, whether secret or otherwise? Are you attracted, secretly or otherwise, to younger males in particular? Are you often prey to infectious diseases? Do you tend to put your work before your family? Do you detect a sadistic streak in yourself? Are you sometimes arrogant, confrontational or even hot-headed? Are you prone to over-react in ways that sometimes surprise you? Do you tend to be highly competitive and independent-minded, often manipulating others to fit in with your own point of view? Are you prone to secret jealousies? Are you a natural rebel? Are you sometimes unforgiving, vindictive or even threatening to others, however unintentionally?

Almost all of these topics, you are bound to admit, can be fraught with emotion – yet if they arouse strong reactions within you, this is actually a very helpful sign. Not because those reactions are necessarily justified, *but because they indicate clearly which aspects of yourself you have rejected as unacceptable.* In Jungian parlance, they form part of your *Shadow*. Moreover, they form a perfectly normal and standard part of *Apollo's* darker aspect, too. And so, to the extent that this is so, it is urgent that they now be *re-cognised* and accepted – for if you are rejecting them you are by definition rejecting large parts of Apollo himself.

And since Apollo is evidently so central to your life, as to most of us, this can only be a source of danger to you.

Much the same applies, indeed, if you find yourself reacting negatively even to the relatively 'positive' characteristics listed in section (a) above. If, in other words, you despise intellectuality, are incensed by logic and tidy-mindedness, and are determinedly uncompetitive, unmethodical and untidy in your own life, this is a clear sign that you are rejecting not merely *parts* of Apollo, but virtually the whole of his archetype, perhaps in a kind of exclusive deference to some other god or goddess – and specifically, perhaps, to the lunar **Artemis** (see next chapter). In which case the 'darker' group of qualities listed in this section may be all the more prominent in your make-up, though possibly transferred to the female context.

(c) Total non-recognition and projection

Potentially even more dangerous, however, is the case where you have failed to react to or identify with the listed characteristics at all. If this was so in your own case, go through the second list again now, and ask yourself whether you associate the qualities involved mainly with *other people*, rather than with yourself. Are there particular people, in other words, who really 'get your goat' precisely because they demonstrate some or all of the qualities listed? In particular, are you contemptuous of men who cannot control their feelings? Are you irritated by men who cannot cope with women and consequently prefer to have little or nothing to do with them? Do you despise, or perhaps even fear, bisexuals and homosexuals? Are you enraged at men who are attracted to adolescents of their own sex? If you had your way, would you have such men imprisoned, castrated, even exterminated?

There are many who take such attitudes, often in the most extreme degree. Most would seek to justify them in terms of morality or common decency. The very strength of feeling with which they advance such views, however, reveals the true reason. This has less to do with the actual rights or wrongs of the case than with the inner state of those doing the reacting. What the violence of their reaction actually reveals is that over the course of time they have come to reject the corresponding tendencies *within themselves* – generally as a result of severe parental or peer-group pressure – to the point of placing an absolute taboo upon them. So vehement is that rejection, in fact, that those concerned are unable any longer even to *re-cognise* them there. As a result, they are now involved in a truly desperate effort to foist them exclusively onto others 'out there', where they can duly be attacked and, hopefully, eradicated from the world entirely – so eventually appeasing the ever-nagging voice of parental or social conscience.

The phenomenon is well known to psychologists. It is an example of the apparently universal law that what we fail to deal with 'in here' eventually seems to descend upon us from 'out there'. It is called *projection*. Clearly, then, this is a mechanism of great potential danger for us. It has, after all, to be ultimately responsible for most of the wars and conflicts that the world has ever known. Yet it also has its distinct value for our present exercise. *For it follows that whatever irks us most about people 'out there' is, almost by definition, some rejected aspect of ourselves.*

In the present case, then, any failure to *re-cognise* Apollo's 'darker' aspects within yourself, and in particular any tendency to project them onto others, reveals a deep-seated rejection of a large part of Apollo's archetype, however devoted you may be in practice to other, more 'acceptable' aspects of it. *But at the same time it enables you to identify precisely those areas in which you need to become more flexible, and in which appropriate therapy may therefore lie.*

(d) Total acceptance

The eventual aim, of course, is to be able to accept *all* of Apollo's characteristics as essential parts of yourself, and consequently to be able to treat all the aspects of the god with equal honour and easy-going tolerance, even if you choose (not unreasonably – for how should Apollo be other than reasonable?) to avoid expressing some of them in practice. Just as no creature of the wild stunts its own development by being ashamed of its natural emotions and proclivities, neither do you need to do so. Just as it consequently becomes a supreme example of what it truly is, so, too, can you.

It may be, of course, that you have always been free of such problems. You will, in other words, have been able to identify yourself with both lists with complete equanimity, *re-cognising* yourself to some degree in both. If this was so, then Apollo is likely to be truly at home within your soul, and being at ease there, he will be disinclined to cause you too many problems of his own by over-emphasising his more 'negative' qualities. Nor is he likely to be jealous (as only Apollo knows how) when you invite in other gods, too, to share your life. In all probability, then, little in the way of Apollonian therapy is needed.

To most of us, however, even the familiar Apollo is welcome only selectively. We are more than happy with his 'sunnier' aspects, but much less relaxed about accepting the dark shadows that they inevitably cast at one and the same time both upon ourselves and upon the world in which we live.

At this point, then, some kind of therapy is called for – and fortunately the ancient myths give us ample and repeated hints of what forms it might take.

2. Invocation

The first stage in the process is simply to invoke the god. Deliberately welcome Apollo into your life in all his aspects. Start by naming him. Seek out images of him. Collect books about him. If possible, use your holidays to visit his main sanctuaries in Greece (Aegina, Bassae, Corinth, Delphi, Delos, Gortyn in Crete, Naxos, and Ancient Thera on Santorini), Turkey (Claros, Didyma), Sicily (both temples in Syracuse) and elsewhere in the Mediterranean. While doing so, buy at least one statuette of him. When you get home, consider setting up a 'shrine' to him in a corner of your bedroom. Meditate before it each morning and evening. Affirm your determination to accept his characteristics in their entirety, both in yourself and in others, and express your refusal henceforth to feel either guilty or ashamed at what in fact are perfectly natural and normal aspects of Apollonian humanity, and thus of your own humanity too.

But by far the most practical and effective way of invoking Apollo is also the most obvious one. For Apollo is not only the sunny side of your own nature. He is the physical sun itself. And if Apollo's therapy (Greek: 'worship', 'healing', 'service') demands that you let his gladdening light into every corner of your inner life, then the same inevitably applies on the outer level too. *As a disciple of Apollo, therefore, it is literally vital to allow yourself adequate exposure to the simple sunlight with which you are surrounded every day.*

True, that light is often weak, or diffused by clouds. Your therapeutic regime therefore needs to reflect that fact. At other times the sky is perfectly clear, and so once again your regime needs to reflect it. But at this point current medical wisdom intervenes by insisting that direct sunlight is bad for you. In latitudes where the Earth's ozone layer has recently started to break down, of course, this is almost certainly correct. Otherwise, however, even a moment's thought reveals the sheer wrong-headedness of the idea. Not only does it fly in the face of the manifest feeling of sheer physical well-being experienced by millions of sunbathers every year – or at least, by those of them who know how to sunbathe in moderation (which, as we saw, is a basic characteristic of Apollo himself). It also flies in the face of simple common sense.

Like the rest of the animal kingdom, the ancient human race evolved in sunlight, depended on sunlight, was constantly bathed in sunlight. Until the invention of clothes, there was no part of the human body that was not constantly exposed to it – apart, perhaps, from the palms of the hands and the soles of the feet. Inevitably, therefore, no branch of the human race can help but be potentially adapted *to the levels of sunlight obtaining in the geographical latitudes where it evolved into its present form.* To suggest otherwise is to suggest a failure of the evolutionary process – which would contradict the fact that humanity has manifestly survived and therefore, by definition, succeeded in adapting to its environment.

The invention of clothes was thus, in a sense, the beginning of a kind of Apollonian heresy, a denial of the light, an offence against heaven. In the name of order and decency, human beings started for the first time to keep parts of themselves in the dark, and specifically those parts that had to do with the 'messier' aspects of life that Apollo typically finds so difficult to cope with – in this case reproduction and excretion – as well as various of the associated erogenous zones. Moreover, what had started on the purely physical level soon started to happen on the inner, psychological level too. The long march of the Shadow had begun.

Opening ourselves up to Apollo, therefore, demands a fundamental reversal of that process. We need to let his heavenly light back in to dispel our self-imposed darkness. And not only on the psychological level, but on the bodily level too. True, we no longer keep our sexual and excretory functions mentally as much in the dark as once we did. Yet *physically* the associated organs are still kept literally almost as much in the dark as ever they were.

The basis of physical therapy, then, is both clear and almost absurdly simple. Invoking Apollo on the bodily level means exposing yourself to the sun – and not merely for a few days or weeks in high summer (which is clearly both unwise and dangerous), *but as nearly as possible all the year round.* (An ultra-violet sunlamp is unfortunately no substitute for the full-spectrum irradiation required.) Moreover, this needs to be done *regularly throughout the year* – for Apollo, as we have already seen, is by nature nothing if not regular. In this way the skin will be able gradually to adapt to the sunlight (which it is patently designed to do, as the backs of the regularly-exposed hands clearly demonstrate) as it slowly increases and decreases in intensity through the year, thus making both sunglasses and barrier creams unnecessary: indeed,

since both distort the natural interchange between sun and body –
with the eyes and skin the prime routes by which Apollo's pure
sunlight reacts with the organism – such adjuncts could well be
avoided altogether, *provided that you exercise sufficient moderation.*
Careful regulation of the length of exposure is of course necessary
(a couple of hours a day shared between front, back and sides is
probably more than enough for most people, and may even be too
much for those with very fair skin), but the main thing is that you
should remain sensitive and responsive to what your body is telling
you – and you should of course take full and careful account of your
family's racial and genetic origins, and hence of your skin-type, in
relation to the geographical latitudes in which you are now living.
(Take heed, too, of current scientific advice on the latest state of the
ozone layer at those latitudes: any serious local 'hole' in it could
render the exercise unsafe. If in any doubt because of your skin-type,
take medical advice.)

Meanwhile it goes almost without saying that *all* the body should
be exposed in this way – though the palms, the soles of the feet and
the already well-exposed head and face should perhaps not be
over-irradiated. A major object of the therapy, after all, is for those
with white skins to become, like the resplendently naked Apollo,
golden (though not necessarily brown, and certainly not sunburnt)
all over. Depending on the laws and conventions of the society
in which you live, therefore, the physical aspect of Apollonian
invocation may well involve you in finding – or establishing –
appropriate contexts in which to do so.

To sum up, then:

Sunbathe, if possible, all the year round on a daily basis, starting
no later than the early spring.

Expose no single part of the body for more than half-an-hour or so, and even less if you have very fair skin.

Protect from the sun those parts that are regularly exposed anyway.

Avoid the midday sun, especially during the summer: instead, sunbathe during the morning, preferably until not much later than about 11 am.

At all costs avoid sunburn, which is very dangerous.

Stop if you notice any harmful or unpleasant effects.

If you have doubts as to the wisdom of any of the above, seek medical advice.

In doing all this you will not only be performing your bounden duty to Apollo by deliberately casting light on aspects of yourself that you normally keep in the dark. Perhaps because you will at the same time be returning to the natural human state vis-à-vis the sun and the rest of the universe, and thus *seeing yourself in a new light*, you may well experience at the same time an extraordinary sense of well-being and peace with yourself. Such are the blessings that Apollo, once fully invoked to the point of being intimately known, can bring in his train.

3. Meditation

You are now ready to use your imagination and thought to intensify the process further – for that is what Apollonian meditation really amounts to. Unlike the form of virtual semi-trance with which the term is often associated in New Age circles, Apollonian meditation is much closer to what Christians have traditionally understood by the term (unsurprisingly, perhaps, in view of Christianity's obvious debt to Apollonian spirituality, as explained in chapter 8). Rather like the Hindus' *raja yoga*, it is, at basis, a process of intense thought and cogitation aided by the imagination.

And so, in the present case, the first task is actually to imagine the solar Apollo in all his radiance, and utterly resplendent both mentally and physically. Perhaps while doing your obligatory, but nevertheless moderate, all-year-round sunbathing, conjure him up in your mind – young, naked, muscular, supremely well-proportioned, his golden hair flying in the wind and crowned with a wreath of laurel. Arm him with bow and arrows, or grace him with the lyre. Recall and review all the basics of his nature as outlined in the current chapter. Imagine his presence within you. Then accept it there in all its aspects as being totally normal and natural for you.

Now you are ready to direct your meditation towards his prime symbols. The first of these is, of course, the sun itself. Recall once again its basic characteristics – its intolerable brilliance, its steadiness, its regularity, its reliability, its sheer heat, its cleansing and healing properties, as well as its propensity to cast deep shadows, to dry up all soggy places and generally to outshine not only the moon, but all the other stars as well. Recognise these characteristics within yourself, and accept them for what they are.

Now turn your attention to his lyre and its exquisite harmonies, from which the Apollonian Pythagoras was in due course to derive the mathematical and musical laws underlying the entire universe (see chapter 9). Could *your* life, too, do with some of that music and harmony, that general attunement to the laws of the universe? Are you totally in tune with the whole of yourself?

Think next of Apollo's bow and arrow and the hunting instincts that they serve. Is your own life sufficiently active and aggressive?

Are you, too, prepared to go all out for the things you need and want out of life?

Turn finally to Apollo's sacred beasts – above all, perhaps, the dolphin. Consider all its characteristics – its incredible intelligence, its insatiable curiosity, its physical agility, its boundless capacity for play and enjoyment, its sense of sheer delight in the presence of its fellows. Are you, too, managing to combine your intellectuality with a full measure of convivial fun, enjoyment, sport and recreation? Or are you paying too little attention to your natural instincts and the needs of your physical body? And what of your intellect itself – can it really be that your habitual way of thinking is the only possible one? Use your intellect itself to consider the question. Is it likely that the dolphin thinks in your own, familiar, logical categories? Does logic itself suggest that there can be no other form of intelligent cognition? Do the findings of neurology suggest that the left brain's characteristically reductionist and sequential way of thinking is the only way of thinking? And if not, can you relax enough to try some of the alternatives for yourself? In particular, you may care to experiment with so-called 'lateral thinking' techniques, as well as with analogical, rather than logical thought – as exemplified, perhaps, by medieval alchemy or traditional magic. Consider, too, the implications of the extraordinarily revealing linguistic idioms that received folk-wisdom has bequeathed to our language.

And what of the rest of Apollo's symbolic creatures? Can you allow yourself to be serene and even apparently narcissistic with the swan; warmly and emotionally sociable, as well as predatory and aggressive, with the wolf and the rest of the doggy tribe; proud, despotic and independent with the stag; determined and self-willed with the ram; instinctively thorough and persistent with the tortoise (as well as prepared to 'draw in your horns' and hibernate when the time is right); and direct and single-minded as the flight of the proverbial crow? And what of the sensitive and inquisitive mouse, ever investigating and exploring? What of the stubborn ass, the wilful goat, the cunning serpent? What of the migrating quail or goose, the soaring kite, the opportunistic white raven or vulture? Do the bountiful apple or olive tree, the stately palm or the leafy laurel have anything to say to you? Concentrate especially on any of these that appeal to you particularly.

In all these cases by far the best plan is to start by actually seeking out the physical presence of the symbol in question *with as many of your senses as possible* and observing it in its natural state – since the swan as we imagine it is, for the most part, only one particular aspect of the real swan as it actually lives and moves and has its being. Bear in mind that, in the very act of doing so, you are in some degree seeking out Apollo himself. Consider especially how the creature in question moves, grows and changes – for you, too, have plenty of all three to do.

In the light of this undoubted fact, finish by asking yourself the following specific questions:

Am I expressing my intellectual gifts adequately?

Am I finding opportunities to put my logical mind and natural clear-headedness to good use?

Am I expressing my taste for tidiness, symmetry, classicism and moderation?

Am I giving myself opportunities to learn, and to display my learning?

Am I living in the clean, ordered, masculine, even virile way that

I am really most comfortable with?

Am I acknowledging any bisexual or homosexual tendencies that I may have, and prepared to allow myself closer relationships with others of my own sex?

Ponder on your answers, and consider whether this is the moment to adjust your way of life to reflect them.

4. Remedial activities

We now come to a range of activities which, on the basis of the myths themselves, seem designed positively to encourage the development of the Apollonian aspects of the psyche. For this reason, you may care to consider taking up any of them that appeal to you, perhaps on a trial basis initially. Several of them pick up on themes that have been mentioned already. Feel free to add any further activities of your own that appeal to you and seem appropriate. For convenience, the activities listed are divided into two categories:

(a) Recreational and general

Wear white or light-coloured clothes. Adorn yourself with jewellery (preferably golden). Use perfumes and/or after-shaves freely. Consider taking up athletics, and especially discus, javelin, archery and other throwing-events. Take up classical music (especially stringed and essentially harmonic instruments such as guitar and piano). Study harmony and counterpoint. Take up dancing (especially classical ballet), poetry and/or drama. Actually try your hand at acting. Go hunting (in whatever form), if only with your camera – especially early in the morning. Cultivate adolescent friendships, while taking care not to become so involved as to transgress the rules of your society. Possibly involve yourself with youth-organisations, and help organise youth-camps of various types. If you are a man, join all-male clubs and societies. Give yourself plenty of opportunities for travel, moderate all-year-round sunbathing, swimming, snorkelling, scuba-diving and surfing. Subject to the laws of your society and considerations of medical safety, express yourself sexually in whatever ways you are most comfortable with. If you feel moved to reject marriage and/or remain celibate, by all means do so. Take up any monotheistic religion, but especially an idealistic, 'solar' one such as Christianity. Pursue philosophical, spiritual and intellectual studies of all kinds. Above all, live moderately.

(b) Professional

On a more long-term and thorough-going basis, you may even care to let your current inner needs influence your choice of career – indeed, it is quite possible that you have already have done so, however unconsciously. Particularly suitable areas for encouraging the growth of Apollo within you are: mathematics, science (including astro-nomy), technology, medicine (above all, specialist medicine), architecture, town-planning, the armed services (especially ballistics and artillery), music, ballet, drama, poetry and the other arts, the priesthood, teaching, youth-work, agriculture and work with animals.

SUB-PERSONALITIES OF APOLLO

Should any of the above analyses and therapies provide a less than perfect fit with your own case, you may care to consider the following variations, which may suggest alternative therapies that you feel to be marginally more suited:

ACTAEON

Possible symptoms

Voyeurism; would-be rape; sexual boasting; gossip; fear of women; irrational fears; paranoia; nightmares; psychological disintegration; accident-proneness; self-destruction

but also

Love of wilderness; attraction to female beauty.

Therapies

Name, imagine and welcome the ill-fated young hunter, and son of **Aristaeus** (below), killed by **Artemis** for peeping; dogs; wilderness; hunting (in whatever form); living by the sea.

Symbols

Stag; stag's horns.

Notes

Actaeon's myth is sparse, but he comes across as a shy young man who loves solitude but is troubled by unsatisfied sexual desires that too easily drive him to madness and even to self-destruction. Obsessed with sex, he adores women, yet is scared to death of being taken seriously by them. Among his friends he therefore tries to make up for this failing with brave talk. The wilderness, it seems, can be his salvation, provided that he can avoid human company, and especially the predatory type of female (the reflection, perhaps, of his own over-possessive mother) whose excitation of his animal instincts is likely to prove his chief danger. The syndrome seems likely to weaken progressively with age.

ARISTAEUS

Possible symptoms
Difficulty in self-expression; stutter or other speech-impediment; negative effects on women; drunkenness

but also
Dynamic leadership; initiative; single-mindedness; reliability; clean living; sense of justice; reforming spirit; enthusiasm for spiritual renewal; love; healing; prophecy.

Therapies
Name, imagine and welcome this thoroughly good-hearted and competent, but socially gauche stutterer who is always full of energy and idealism; agriculture; cheese making; beekeeping; olive-growing and pressing; animal husbandry; trapping; hunting (in whatever form); public health; emigration; colonisation; city-founding; swimming and subaqua diving.

Symbols
Sheep; fish; myrtle; Sirius, the Dog Star.

Notes
Aristaeus is perforce a man of action rather than words. Perhaps as a result of early parental (and especially maternal) neglect or lack of

attention – or merely as a result of having been sent away to school and subjected to a somewhat stern and military form of discipline – he sometimes appears sheepish, and quite often comes across socially as a fish out of water. But beneath his unprepossessing exterior he has a heart of gold, a will of iron and all the outgoing practical effectiveness of his Father Apollo. Since there is little to be done about the way in which he comes across to others, the obvious course of action for him to take is simply to get on with what he does best – preferably well away from the parental home. Possibly, indeed, he could take a leaf out of the book of Moses – very much his spiritual kinsman – and get himself a good public-relations officer.

ASCLEPIUS

Possible symptoms

Ambivalent attitude to healing powers; awareness that any cure can also have harmful side-effects; preparedness to kill; attraction to godlike power over others, whether for life or death; tendency to philosophical paralysis in the face of events; periodic 'seasons in hell'

but also

Healing powers generally; medicinal knowledge; awareness that even poisons can have curative effects; restoration of fertility; constant gentleness; philosophical holism; support from Apollo (i.e. civilisation and technology)

.Therapies

Name, imagine and welcome the Divine Healer with his gentle

hands, the beloved son of Apollo; lifesaving; healing or medical practice; first aid; dreams and dream-interpretation (after fasting); mistletoe (consult a reputable herbalist); hunting; light.

Symbols
Snake on staff; bitch; mistletoe; willow; pine-cone.

Notes

Right from birth, there seems to be something special about those who are taken over by Asclepius. Perhaps that birth was especially traumatic. Possibly they were exposed to the natural world at an unusually early age. At all events, the ever-helpful Asclepius turns out to be a natural healer. And because he is a true healer, and not merely a dispensing chemist, he has his share of worries and self-doubts, which are duly shared at various times both by conventional practitioners and by alternative healers. All of us, for that matter, act as healers and helpers at some time or other, and his myth speaks to us in our consequent dilemmas. The ever-present temptation to use healing as a tool for personal power is an obvious case in point. But Asclepius's particular problem is that he is only too aware that there can be no mountains without valleys, no light without darkness. He realises that organic diseases can be psychologically beneficial as well as physically harmful, that supposed 'cures' can be harmful as well as beneficial. He is fully aware that anything he does for his patients is likely to hinder them just as much as it helps them, even if this hindering may manifest itself in more subtle and less obvious ways. 'You don't,' in the popular phrase, 'get something for nothing.' And so Asclepius hovers, **Hermes**-like, perpetually between action and non-action, between intervention and non-intervention, knowing full well that the (literally) godlike powers with which he is popularly credited are largely illusory, and that the only person who can help the patient is ultimately the patient himself, guided by the symbolic intuitions and dream-insights of his own psyche. Perhaps it is appropriate, then, that his prime symbol has been transformed over the centuries into a staff which, like the *caduceus* of **Hermes**, bears *two* snakes instead of the original one – each opposing the other and so seeming to cancel out the power for 'masculine' action represented by the phallic staff itself.

GANYMEDES

Possible symptoms

Usurpation of women's privileges; tendency to stir up female jealousy; openness to homosexual advances by older men; subjection to pederasty and/or sodomy; liability to being kidnapped; aerial joy-riding

but also

Physical beauty; eternal youthfulness; love of flying; passive, easygoing disposition.

Therapies

Name, imagine and welcome the comely youth whose beauty and easy-going ways turn the head even of **Zeus**; catering; domestic service (or its commercial equivalent); passive homosexual relationships; wind-borne or wind-based sports; flying; sailing.

Symbols

The constellation Aquarius.

Notes

Ganymedes, like Adonis, is the spirit of arrested adolescence, the 'Peter Pan' or *puer aeternus* syndrome. In this case, however, his sexuality tends in the homosexual direction, and the syndrome is less likely to disappear with time. Nevertheless, provided that Ganymedes is fully accepted, and not suppressed, he is still capable of bringing with him a life of contentment and blissful fulfilment.

Astrologically, the Aquarian connection suggests that Ganymedes is above all a winter entity.

HELIUS

Possible symptoms

Over-eagerness; misplaced self-confidence; impracticality; carelessness; lack of observation; accident-proneness; tendency to draw the short straw / buy faulty goods / drop bread on the buttered side; inability to look after property; lack of control over own children; exaggerated conscientiousness; over-anxiety to please; doubtful dealing; tale-bearing; subordination to wife or mother

but also

Brightness; perspicacity; knowledgeability; acute vision; sudden insights; conscience; sense of responsibility; stamina; indefatigability; courtesy; purity; cleanliness.

Therapies

Name, imagine and invoke the brilliant former sun god as he drives his chariot confidently across the sky with less than due care and attention, eagerly looking anywhere and everywhere but straight in front of him; early rising; dawn; astronomy; astrology; intelligence work; spying; night-sailing; horse-driving; cattle-herding; supervisory activities; responsibility; fatherhood.

Symbols

Sun; cockerel; chariot drawn by four white horses or golden bulls; white cattle; poplar; alder; golden chalice; noon; sunset.

Notes

The bright-eyed Helius, historical predecessor of the solar Apollo, is something of a walking disaster-area, especially where property or children are concerned. He is a real trier, and full of goodwill – indeed, something of a 'Goody Goody Two-Shoes' – but at the same time he has an extraordinary inability to see what he looks at or to listen to what he hears. Yet he is quite prepared to broadcast it to others. And so this 'eager beaver' who is always on the go comes across as one with great knowledge who is nevertheless unwilling or unable to practise what he preaches, or as a father or husband who knows all the answers, but always manages to make a hash of things. Like Icarus, he is especially vulnerable to disaster if (in his incarnation as his son Phaëthon) he attempts to fly too high. The opportunity for relaxation and quiet contemplation provided by some of the therapies suggested could thus have a valuable role to play in redressing the balance between theory and practice, between intention and result. A study of holistic therapies might also help.

Somehow, it seems, the heat needs to be taken out of the situation. Some kind of 'step back' is likely to get things into less burning perspective and lead to calmer, more effective and competent action. Helius seems to have his female counterpart, too, in his daughter Helia.

HIPPOLYTUS

Possible symptoms

Incestuous attempts at seduction by mother or stepmother; subjection to wrongful accusations of rape; wild riding or driving; proneness to road accidents; narrow escape from death; exile; adultery

but also

Religious fervour and devotion; chastity; purity; severity; athleticism; marriage in second half of life; secluded and peaceful retirement.

Therapies

Name, imagine and invoke the energetic bastard son of Theseus, sublimated idealist, athlete and charioteer – and latterly adopted, for good measure, as a Christian saint; religious rituals; bachelordom; sport; athletics; driving; motor-racing and rallying; horses; hunting (in whatever form); retirement in the wilderness, well away from horses and other forms of transport; deliberate disguise or change of appearance.

Symbols

Olive; myrtle; the constellation Auriga (the Charioteer).

Notes

Hippolytus is sexually pursued (overtly or otherwise) by his mother – or at least his stepmother. His response is to seek refuge in sexual sublimation, whether religious or athletic (his particular devotion is in fact to **Artemis,** who generally supports him in a kind of platonic relationship). When matters finally come to a head he is forced to flee far from home, where the very wildness of his redirected passion nearly brings about his downfall. Only during the second half of life, possibly after his mother's death – and very nearly after his own – is he eventually able to settle down with a woman and find peace.

MUSES

Possible symptoms

Obsession with sex; promiscuity; orgies; sexual nightmares; proneness to lying

but also

Sublimation of sex-drive; aptitude for learning and training; artistic and poetic skills and discrimination; gift for producing both factual and fictional literature; oratory; acting; linguistic skills; healing powers; prophetic gifts; musicianship; astronomical knowledge; historical learning; good memory.

Therapies

Name, imagine and invoke the nine bird-like mountain divinities and sophisticated patronesses of the arts; music (especially singing and flute); dance; drawing and painting; sculpture; architecture; literature; art criticism; astronomy; teaching; public speaking; animal husbandry (especially sheep); divination using pebbles.

Symbols

Tablet and stylus; book; roll of paper; lyre; plectrum; flute; tragic and comic masks; club or sword; shepherd's crook; ivy-wreath; laurel-wreath; staff pointing at globe; bee(s).

Notes

The Muses are characterised by a deep inner contradiction. At basis they are intensely sexual beings, yet at the same time they tend, like both **Acteon** and Selene, to be frightened by the sheer power and ungovernability of the sex-instinct. Perhaps that is why they bear with them their own therapies, personifying the imposition of cultural values on a nature that is otherwise purely instinctive, wild and uncontrolled. The result may well be a person who is vigorous, healthy and at the same time a lifelong model of civilised virtues.

NARCISSUS

Possible symptoms

Possible subjection to pederasty, with special vulnerability to intellectual men of the Apollo type; incipient bisexuality or transexuality; self-love; admiration of own beauty; narcissism; egocentricity; auto-eroticism; fear of emotional or sexual rejection; rejection of love by others; unsociability; love of sound of own voice; love of the unattainable; lethargy; back-to-the womb feelings;

possible anorexia; death-wish; suicidal tendencies; self-destruction

but also

Eternal youthfulness; beauty; attractiveness to others of both sexes; silent admiration from gentle, passive women who are by nature afraid to make the first move; self-confidence; self-sufficiency; independence; idealism; quasi-sexual attraction to water.

Therapies

Name, imagine and invoke the beautiful, languorous youth of sixteen summers gazing morbidly at his own reflection in the water; auto-erotic practices; masturbation; reflection; self-examination; pursuit of self-knowledge; rivers and lakes; plunging into clear water; acting; public speaking and entertainment; teaching; the church

Symbols

Narcissus; lily-of-the-valley or iris; hyacinth (WARNING: NARCISSUS, LILY-OF-THE-VALLEY AND HYACINTH ARE POISONOUS: consult a reputable herbalist).

Notes

The spirit of Narcissus haunts most boys at puberty in one form or another. Like Adonis and **Ganymedes**, he is liable, if persisted with, to become in later years an epiphany of the spirit of arrested adolescence (the 'Peter Pan' or *puer aeternus* syndrome). In this case, however – possibly as a result of parentally-inspired fears of rejection – he is stuck at the very early auto-erotic stage. The result may well be difficulty in forming adult relationships. Though beloved by others of both sexes, he is unable to respond adequately, and while he has great idealism, he may well have to pay for it with a full measure of despair and heartbreak. If he remains unrecognised for too long, Narcissus is likely to prove a danger to the patient who identifies with him. Recognised, however, this troubled inner spirit tends to destroy *itself* – so, at least, the myth seems to suggest. Early and genuine self-understanding is therefore important, and any treatment that tends to lead to this, be it psycho-analysis or some other form of psychotherapy, is to be welcomed.

The associated story of the fifteen-year-old Hermaphroditus (son, as the name suggests, of **Hermes** and **Aphrodite**) meanwhile reflects a form of the syndrome with a more hopeful prognosis. In this case the subject's narcissistic fascination with water is so strong that he literally prefers plunging into it to plunging into sexual liaisons. Yet therein lies his salvation. For in so doing he does contrive to express his ambivalent sexuality, albeit in substitute form, and so achieves not only sexual satisfaction, but inner balance and emotional serenity too. There is even a hint in the story that he may eventually find happiness with a like-minded woman of a passive, soothing, domestic and above all totally dedicated disposition, and not at all like **Artemis**.

SUMMARY

The aim of all the above activities is to bring Apollo more fully and naturally into your life so that you may have life more abundantly. With Apollo sitting more easily within you, the solar divinity will be freed to get on with his job and, the task eventually done, to retire somewhat from the fray, thus leaving the field clear for other archetypes to move in and start their own literally vital evolutionary work within you. It is by accepting yourself as you are, in other words, that you free yourself to evolve quite naturally into who you could be. 'Normality' does not come into it. Nobody is 'normal'. A norm is a statistical concept, not an ideal – still less a live, flesh-and-blood human being.

Acquiring self-knowledge involves, in the first instance, *getting to know your selves*. But getting to know your selves necessarily makes you aware of *all* your potentialities, responsive to *all* your gods. It frees you to develop, to evolve. In the process you will become far from 'normal'. Accept the fact, then. Dare to be abnormal, eccentric, peculiar. Dare, in short, to be you.

2

ARTEMIS – THE WAY OF THE WOMAN

Varium et mutabile semper Femina.
Virgil: Aeneid (IV. 569)

ARTEMIS is the goddess of many a young (and not-so-young) woman who is uneasy about close relationships with men, and not at all sure about fitting in with masculine planning and logic. Her devotees are much given to listening to their own inner feelings and, like any self-respecting wild animal, doing whatever they feel like doing at any given moment, without respect to supposed 'masculine' values such as consistency. Energetic, but always independent, intuitive and hard to pin down, the Artemisian woman is very much a woman's woman, and a healthy – even necessary – counterweight to the overwhelming influence of Apollo in the world. The Artemisian man, by contrast, and partly for this very reason, is almost unknown.

Characteristics of woman and god

Artemis is the moon, symbol of all that is feminine. And, once again, in that luminous natural symbol her whole myth is comprehended.

Like Apollo, Artemis casts celestial light over a darkened world. But it is her own particular form of light, and very different from Apollo's. Prone though Apollonian commentators are to insist that

---

Artemis in history

History has no doubt seen just as many unwitting acolytes of Artemis as of Apollo, but because of her inherent demureness and the male-orientated nature of most historical societies, few of them are known to us. Perhaps the earliest was the Greek poetess Sappho of Lesbos. In the middle ages, Joan of Arc seems to have been a likely example, while England's virginal Queen Elizabeth I manifested the archetype almost to perfection. More recently, Artemis has taken to expressing herself through innumerable female explorers, single-handed sailors, poetesses, novelists, health-workers, counsellors, healers, occultists – and almost any woman with a dog.

---

her light is a *reflected* one, the ancients who invented the myth were patently unaware of the fact (significantly, Plato credited his own near-contemporary Anaxagoras with the discovery). Artemis's role is not to act as some kind of pale reflection of Apollonian masculinity, but to cast a magical and strangely deceptive light of her own.

It is a light, admittedly, that constantly varies. Yet it is a light nevertheless. And, like Apollo's, it is a light that casts shadows. Moreover, the brighter that light (i.e. that of full moon) and the darker, consequently, the shadows, the more those shadows are apt to be the identical ones that Apollo first illumines at his rising.

For the full moon, by definition, always appears opposite the sun in the sky.

What this means, consequently, is that the areas of human experience that are second nature (or rather, first nature) to Artemis are the very ones that Apollo most scorns, devalues and endeavours to mask and expunge – i.e. those of emotion, intuition and sheer, animal instinct. Those, by contrast, that are dark and impenetrable to her are the self-same ones that, to Apollo, are literally as clear as day.

Yet the shadows she casts, though sometimes deep, are also variable. Sometimes, depending on her current phase of development, they are hardly there at all. Her dualism is thus of a more flexible kind that is altogether harder to pin down. Indeed, her aspect constantly changes, her outlook continually alters. Her whole being is forever in flux, an analogue alike of the tides of the sea and the tides of the human psyche. She is the very essence of motion, and thus of *e-motion* too, but not to any conscious, intellectual end. She does what she does purely because she is who she is, and so acts primarily out of nothing more conscious and comprehensible than her own native intuition and instinct.

It is no surprise, then, to find that Artemis's characteristics are, in almost all other respects, too, the exact reverse of Apollo's. We have already referred to Apollo's brilliance, for example. The light of Artemis's consciousness, though magically and gorgeously resplendent in its own right, is more subdued, even wan: her intellect, in other words, is more diffuse, more restrained, more subordinated to her over-all needs as a being in course of continual change and development. Her logic, consequently, lacks Apollo's clear rules and defined regularities: it cuts corners, takes surprising twists, executes extraordinary leaps which simply leave him standing.

Where Apollo, similarly, is manifestly hot-headed, her light is cool, even cold – an indication, once again, that she is prepared to exercise her undoubted intellectual gifts quite coldly and dispassionately as a means to other ends, and without ever making the mistake of identifying herself too closely with them as Apollo tends to do. Where he is literally ardent, she is much less idealistic, much more concerned with things as they really are.

Again, where Apollo is a model of regularity, constancy, order and discipline, Artemis is clearly the reverse. Not only does her course through the heavens vary much more widely than his, not only is her aspect or outlook never the same for two nights together, but she waxes and wanes to a monthly rhythm which is directly reflected in the menstrual cycle of her female human acolytes. Once a month, in fact, she is liable to disappear entirely from view, and possibly to undergo a time of some darkness and distress. And in addition, at times that are very hard to predict, she is vulnerable to further periods of even deeper blackness when, eclipsed by the shadow of earth – and thus, perhaps, of physical experience itself – she is liable to find her heart eaten out by sheer despair, her very being cast as it were into outer darkness. Fortunately, such periods are only temporary; but at the time they seem to her more like the end of the world as she knows it. As, indeed, in a remarkably literal sense they are.

Artemis, then is not only essentially changeable. She is not only a creature of mood, of emotion and intuition. She is also a child of the unconscious, a denizen of humanity's inner night.

There is a further curiosity about Artemis, moreover. For the fact is that, although she shows only one face to the world, that face can display both light and darkness. Compared with bright Apollo, who typically refuses to admit to having a dark side to his nature at all, and so projects it constantly onto the world 'out there' instead, Artemis is able periodically to acknowledge her own darkness and suffering and so, in the process, actually *reduces* the degree of shadow that she casts upon the world. As a result, she is able at other times to keep her darker mysteries – her 'other face' – almost entirely to herself. (In direct reflection of this, it seems, far fewer women than men fall foul of the law or finish up in jail, while far more women than men attend doctors' surgeries with incapacitating depressions and psychosomatic disorders.)

Occasionally, however, the literally unthinkable happens, and the lunar Artemis collides head-on with the overweeningly intellectual Apollo. Contrary to what one might suppose, he stands no chance whatever in the encounter. His intellectuality is a fragile artefact, a house of cards which the very first breath of cosmic wind is liable to demolish. And so there follows a major eclipse of the human conscious mind, an upsurge of the irrational and the unconscious, a fundamental celestial set-to which the ancients from time immemorial regarded as presaging *dis-aster* on a truly cosmic scale. And who, in the light of the obvious symbolism, is to say that they were wrong?

There *are* circumstances, in other words, which virtually force Artemis to invoke her powers of darkness. It may be a collision of interests with those of Apollo, an attempt on his part to dethrone her or debunk her dark, feminine mysteries in the light of Apollonian reason and science. Equally, it may be the reverse. The total darkness of new moon may betoken an *over*-concentration on the things of the unconscious, a self-centred attempt on her part to elevate herself into the unrivalled Queen of the Night to whose dread power even the things of the daytime must learn to defer.

The dark side of the Moon

It is basically an unbalanced or confrontational situation, in other words, that tends to bring into manifestation Artemis's darker side, her alternative aspect. It was this aspect of her that the Greeks recognised under the name of *Hecate*, seeing her as the hag-like goddess of witches. In this role, once ingrained, Artemis becomes (by contrast with her usual nature) an almost crudely sexual being who is steeped in the world of the occult (i.e. of the 'hidden'), addicted to the esoteric, a mistress of all forms of magic, a psychic, a medium – yet for this very reason a potential psychological healer of great power, too. In this aspect, in fact, her knowledge is of a deeply mysterious and even apparently supernatural kind.

At the same time, like the subterranean deities themselves, Artemis-as-Hecate *demands blood*. For she, like them, is now a virtually permanent denizen of the underworld who emerges only at dead of night, and specifically within the human night-time consciousness. True to her lunar nature she is therefore pale and anaemic. And so blood is above all what she needs.

The results are inevitable. From now on, her demands on others (be they psychological, emotional or sexual) will be voracious, even insatiable. She will do almost anything to gain the attention that she craves. And so she will start to move in mysterious, occult ways, apparently exerting strange, magical powers over those around her in order eventually to become queen in her own esoteric kingdom – even though that kingdom, by definition, can only last the night, and must vanish like the dew at break of day.

Indeed, in severe cases she may take the syndrome even further, turning into a veritable sorceress of the stamp of Circe or Medea, intent on using drugs and potions to manipulate both her own animal desires and the world around her, or poisons to rid it of those aspects (or people) that seem to threaten her. As in the former Borgias, it seems, Medea is alive and kicking yet.

But the systemic anaemia that is characteristic of Hecate has other connotations, too. It is, for example, a natural and well-known characteristic of young girls at puberty. No doubt this is why Greek myth immemorially portrays the lunar Artemis as a girl of nine to about fifteen or so – a girl, moreover, who has distinct tomboyish characteristics. She insists, for example, on wearing boys' clothes, on playing in the wilds, on going hunting and generally doing her own thing. She resolutely declines to be tamed or civilised. She refuses point blank to be turned into a lady. And perhaps it is for this reason that the ancient Greeks also saw her as the archetypal She-Bear.

It is not merely that the words 'Artemis' and 'bear' (*arktos*) were seen as being possibly related in Greek. The she-bear, it is well-known, is both highly independent and ferocious when cornered. Indeed, she is reputed to be absolutely untamable. What better symbol, then, for the youthful, untamable Artemis?

In consequence, her young, saffron-clad, female temple-servants – who were in many respects the ancient Greek equivalents of the Brownies, Girl Guides or Girl Scouts – were known as the *arktoi*, or Bears. On ritual occasions they even dressed themselves in bear-skins, played bear-games, performed bear-dances. It was entirely in character, then, that during our own era at least one group of young precursors of the British Girl Guides, inspired by the foundation of Baden Powell's Boy Scouts in 1912, should have insisted on calling themselves 'the Bears', as though in direct response to the unconscious archetype, as well as in reflection of the corresponding male 'Cubs'. It was only later that these packs of young Amazons (the term, as we shall see, is quite apt) were granted an organisation of their own and given much 'nicer', if psychologically less appropriate names.

The ancient sources

The ancient myth of Artemis (see references in the Bibliography, and particularly the works by Campbell, Graves and Kerényi) duly goes on to reflect both this ursine symbolism and that of the moon. The Artemis of myth is essentially a loner, a lover of wild places, a companion of wild animals. At the same time, as befits the moon, she is, if not frigid, at least determinedly virginal. Perhaps for this reason, she is modest, shy and retiring (in male company, at least), and hates to be spied on. Highly attractive to men, she nevertheless ferociously rejects their advances. Shy she may be, in other words, but she is far from timid. She will tackle any physical challenge, wrestle with any beast of prey, use her deadly and ever-ready armoury of bow and arrows to shoot down anything that moves. At times of stress, particularly, she much prefers her hunting-dogs or other animals to human company. And if necessary she will also emasculate and destroy any man who threatens her highly-valued independence, virginity or peace of mind.

With women, by contrast, her relations are more ambivalent. Perhaps influenced by her own penchant for virginity, she tends to be bitchy to women who are pregnant, and merciless to mothers in childbirth. Yet, as a woman's woman, she is sympathetic to their plight, too. Thanks to this paradoxical mix of attitudes, she thus tends to make an admirable midwife, able to be both firm and gentle by turns. Moreover, she can make close and lasting friendships with other women. At times, especially when forced by male repression to combine with them to form roving hunting-packs of resentful, militant Amazons, such friendships can even intensify into fully-fledged lesbianism.

Meanwhile she is a natural sportswoman and athlete, a dancer, a lover of music, a born nanny or teacher. With young people – and especially young girls – she is in her element. She loves not only mountains and travel, but commerce and city-life too – provided only that she does not actually have to get intimately involved with people in the process, or with men in particular.

This wariness of men is, of course, merely the direct polar counterpart and mirror-image of Apollo's own well-established inability to cope with women. It is an opposition which to either of them in isolation no doubt seems fundamental. What it is all too easy for both of them to forget is that, seen from an only slightly 'higher' level, the two views are not so much opposite as complementary. The astronomical fact that the apparent sizes of sun and moon in the sky are exactly the same reflects the psychological fact that they are both equally important. The one simply has the task of enlightening the day, the other of illumining the night.

And so it is with human consciousness itself. Apollo's intellectualism has its valued place in our daytime consciousness; but we have a night-time consciousness, too, and it is Artemis who just as firmly and justifiably rules over it. Woe to those of us, then, who refuse to recognise or acknowledge our dreams! In the world at large, similarly, man has an essential role to play; but without the compensating light of woman his efforts must ultimately prove unbalanced, warped and ultimately self-destructive.

It is all very well to approve of day and disapprove of night, in other words, but this is merely a recipe for *dis-aster*. A planet that offers only eternal day or eternal night is a planet that does not turn, and the only possible result is death on both counts – in the one case through over-heating and sterility, in the other through sheer darkness and frigidity. It is only on the precarious boundary between the two that life itself starts to become possible.

Our consciousness, like the world itself, in other words, needs both day *and* night, both Apollo *and* Artemis. To defer to the one without the other must prove fatal in the end. Man needs to discover his 'dark', feminine, 'unconscious' side, woman her 'light', masculine, 'conscious' qualities. The two need to be integrated, made into a whole. Perhaps, indeed, that in large part what life itself is ultimately about. And, if so, we should do well to take account of the fact before we commit ourselves too eagerly to modelling either our world or our own psyche exclusively in Apollo's gladdening light.

It needs to be remembered, after all, that Artemis is traditionally the archetypal midwife. Apollo's twin she may be, but she is also the first-born, and it is she who draws Apollo into the light of day from the womb of his mother Leto in the first place. It is Artemis's dark world of instinct, emotion and intuition, in other words, that is actually the more fundamental: Apollo's intellect, to say nothing of his idealistic spirituality, is a later child of human evolution, and one which attempts at its peril to cut itself off from its primal roots. It is a tender plant which, for all its apparent 'goodness' and attractiveness, ultimately has its roots (as does *any* plant) in darkness. And without them it can only die.

The sacred sites

Apollo's birth is said to have taken place on the sacred isle of Delos, and so the latter duly became 'his' island, resplendent with no less than three temples in his honour. But the ancients were well aware of humanity's basic need for roots, for balance, for not putting all one's mythological eggs in one archetypal basket.

And so neither Leto not her daughter Artemis are forgotten there.

Artemis, in particular, (who, after all, was born on the island too) has two temples dedicated to her, each seemingly reflecting a different side of her nature. Thus, her elegant temple in the middle of the city has a comparatively generalised feeling of deep, benevolent femininity about it. It corresponds to the lunar goddess's 'light' side, her shining public face.

On the other side (significantly) of the island's central mountain, crowned with its sanctuary of Zeus and Athene, we have another Artemis entirely. Here, on a precipitous slope some distance below the summit, she is almost entirely alone. This primitive, secluded sanctuary is clearly that of the wild, night-time, hunting Artemis – the Artemis of dark, ill-understood emotions, of spontaneous intuitions and atavistic animal instincts.

The siting and disposition of the two temples, as was so often the case in ancient Greece, is thus perfect. The symbolism is entirely apt. So it is, too, at one of Artemis's much 'darker' shrines on the Greek mainland, on the eastern outskirts of the city of Sparta – a siting which thus once again suggests that it is dedicated to her in her wilder aspect. Visited by moonlight (the obvious light, it has to be said, to visit it by), this dark sanctuary in its gloomy grove has a distinctly 'spooky' feeling about it. Moreover, it is fairly obvious why. In front of the diminutive temple, Spartan youths were at one time ritually flogged – sometimes literally to death – until the altar was spattered with their blood, ostensibly as a test of endurance (though perhaps also as part of some kind of fertility rite). The remains can still be seen there of the viewing gallery which the Romans later erected around it in order to turn the occasion, in time-honoured Roman fashion, into an organised spectator-sport with sexual overtones.

The blood is the key. The only Greek divinities that regularly demanded blood-offerings as such were the naturally anaemic underworld deities. And from this it would seem to follow that, at Sparta at least, Artemis was being worshipped in her dread aspect as Hecate, goddess of witches and of the night. From which the site's 'spooky' atmosphere would then seem to follow as does (to use an entirely apt phrase) the night the day.

These are not, of course, the only sanctuaries of the goddess. In Anatolia there still survive scanty remains of the vast temple of Artemis at Ephesus, for example, which originally covered even more ground than a football field – extending as it did to some *four times* the size of the Parthenon at Athens. But visitors from the West do not need to go so far afield to experience the simple *genius loci*, the sense of atmosphere and place that are characteristic of even the smallest sanctuaries of the Greek godheads.

The gnosis of Artemis

What, then, is the special nature of Artemis's knowing, and how does it differ from Apollo's?

Once again we need to beware of the common assumption that there is only *one* way of knowing, one form of *scientia*, that merits the name. Conscious, intellectual comprehension is only one form of knowing among many. There are other forms of cognition too, and while Artemis herself has a perfectly adequate intellectual side to her nature, her real *forte* lies in other directions entirely.

For a start she displays, as we have seen, a strong intuitive knowledge – an 'all-at once' type of cognition (typically, that of the right brain) that seems to be able to arrive at firm conclusions long before there is very much evidence available of a more rational, Apollonian type to go on. There are dangers in this approach, of course. The process of undertaking intuitive leaps, of 'jumping to conclusions', can too easily be influenced by unconscious hopes, fears, preconceptions and wishful thinkings. But then those conclusions themselves should not then be judged in the light of cold – or, rather, strict – Apollonian reason.[1] Artemis's conclusions, once arrived at, need to be judged not as rational *facts*, but rather as the intuitive *truths* which they really are. For there can be no doubt about it – Artemis's intuitions and hunches *are* her intuitions and hunches. One may evaluate them as one will. But the fact remains that they are indubitably *there*, and therefore need to be recognised as such.

The distinction between these and Apollo's strictly 'scientific' conclusions is thus clear. Apollo's 'facts' are statements about reality that purport to be able to stand on their own two feet. They claim to be totally objective, and therefore not to need Apollo's continued personal presence to validate them (a claim which, as we have seen, turns out in practice to be distinctly dubious, merely reflecting Apollo's characteristic obsession with divorcing the world of the head from that of both body and emotions).

Artemis's intuitions, on the other hand, make no such claim to objectivity. They are essentially and unashamedly subjective. Artemis herself is and remains a basic part of the equation. Unlike Apollo, she does not pretend to be remote from what she observes.

---

[1] 'Cold' is a somewhat inappropriate word here: even Apollo's apparently rational conclusions are quite often arrived at in the heat of the moment or of personal desire, and so are just as susceptible to irrational preconceptions as Artemis's: the sole difference is that Artemis is generally conscious of her subjectivity, whereas Apollo is by definition unconscious of his. The fact that this subjectivity consequently becomes part of his rejected 'shadow' then makes him, thanks to the process of projection, particularly critical of it in others.

Her statements should therefore not be regarded as autonomous, immutable 'facts'. For the lunar Artemis, as we have noted, nothing stays constant for two nights together, and so what is true today is liable to be dismissed as false tomorrow. Her perception, her knowledge of reality, varies with her own state of being – for between the two, as she knows full well, there is no separation. She herself is intimately involved in all her perceptions. And so all statements such as 'This is so' need in her case to be interpreted to mean 'Artemis *currently feels* that this is so.' Here the words 'currently feels' should not be seen as some kind of Apollonian disclaimer or put-down – a suggestion that what is said is not 'really' true – for this, once again, would be to assume that Apollonian cognition is the only possible or valid form of cognition. Artemis's intuitions *are* true. They accurately reflect what she feels at any given moment. It is merely that, in her case, they reflect the elements of time and subjectivity that are present in any piece of human cognition, whereas Apollo's statements too often attempt to ignore these variables, so running the risk of subsequently invalidating themselves in the light of changing human nature and experience.

As, indeed, the lesson of Einsteinian relativity and its debunking of long-established Newtonian 'laws' resoundingly demonstrates.

Apollo's attempt to establish an absolute and eternal cognitive dispensation, a kind of 'knowledge of the gods', is all very well, but Artemis's form of knowing, with its inherent human variable, is actually nearer to the real nature of things as we, in our role as temporal beings, actually observe *and so condition* them.

The essential point, then, is that nobody should make the mistake of treating Artemisian *truths* (any more than purported spiritual or religious truths) as though they were Apollonian *facts*. For they are nothing of the kind. A 'fact' (Latin: 'done', 'made', 'established') is not a present realisation but a past conclusion, not an 'is' but a 'has-been'. It may once have been true for whoever established it at the time, but it is not necessarily true for anybody else at any other time. Anybody who takes the trouble to observe the average schoolroom science-experiment can readily confirm this point. Approached in the true spirit of Apollonian science, such experiments performed by pupils *en masse* invariably prove, if anything, that the scientific 'facts' and 'laws' which they are designed to demonstrate are statistically *un*true – however optimistically they may subsequently be written up for the official record. What the experiments do succeed in demonstrating, on the other hand, is the considerable influence that the experimenter himself or herself exerts over the eventual outcome and the way in which it is observed. The point, however, is generally ignored. In consequence, science students arriving at university frequently have to be de-educated out of their acquired habit of routinely falsifying results. This intrusive subjectivity presumably also has to lie at the basis of the scientific media-battles and academic slanging-matches which occur from time to time over such diverse topics as the incidence and mechanics of AIDS or the possibility of room-temperature nuclear fusion. True objectivity, it seems, is far from easy to attain. The laws of nature are by no means so obvious or so easy to get at as is popularly supposed.

But then perhaps this is not really so very surprising. For nature *has* no laws – nor does it need any. In its own terms at least, it is perfectly well behaved. Even within the confines of the professional laboratory, the supposedly objective 'laws of nature' so beloved of Apollo turn out to be no more than laws of man (and I use the word advisedly) – mere, man-made formulations, that is, of statistical probability, designed to tie nature down to a finite system of human preconceptions and expectations. Outside the laboratory the predict-abilities soon start to break down, as even Apollo's keenest disciples are nowadays increasingly prepared to recognise thanks largely to the advent of chaos theory. And in both contexts the very intervention of the observer adds – and has always added, had we but realised it – a further, crucial weapon to the devastating armoury of chaos.

True, orthodox academic circles have only comparatively recently started to recognise the vital importance of the interaction between observer and observed – indeed the actual *impossibility* of observing without taking the observer and his or her situation into consideration too. That science ever came to recognise the point at all was due largely to the inescapable impact of particle physics and the subsequent development of quantum theory. In the field of cosmology, with its inevitable links with relativity theory, the realisation has also lately begun to dawn. And in both spheres the resulting *scientia*, the emerging form of knowing, is essentially that of Artemis rather than of Apollo, of the woman rather than of the man.

We are moving, in other words, into an era of feminine, rather than masculine science. And not – it might be said – before time.

What goes for Artemis's intuitions goes for her emotions and instincts, too, of course. Except that in this case her 'knowing' is direct and personal, and therefore incontestable. Because Artemis, unlike Apollo, *re-cognises* her emotions and instincts, she is fully aware of what any given experience does to her internally, and is generally quite capable of expressing that knowledge in equally direct – if not necessarily linguistic – form. The process may at times alarm and terrify Apollo, who typically would rather that such things did not happen. But what he cannot do is deny them. Indeed, he excludes them from his own system of *scientia* at his peril, for any description of human experience (which is what any *scientia* basically is) is necessarily incomplete that fails to take both emotions and instincts fully into account.

True, it is difficult, even impossible, to tie them down. What is true at one moment is not necessarily true at the next. As a frustrated biologist was once heard to remark, 'Once all the conditions have been carefully controlled and predetermined, the experimental animal will react as it damn well wants to.' Perhaps the men among us could learn a thing or two from its unwitting example.

As for frogs and mice, so for Artemis. Her glory lies precisely in the fact that she recognises her animality, knows her humanity, feels her emotions, responds to her intuitions, is alive to her instincts.

Such is the nature and the value of the woman's proverbial 'knowing'. And the men among us, with Apollo, ignore it at their peril.

VITAL ACTIONS

Most women will find little difficulty in *re-cognising* Artemis within themselves. Those who have not been inveigled either by conditioning or by sheer self-interest into taking up an essentially masculine, Apollonian attitude to life will be well aware of their links with the moon, their essential changeability, their distaste for order and control, their inherent wilfulness, their ambivalent attitude towards sex, their closeness to their emotions and intuitions – and possibly, too, of their antagonistic feelings towards those men who are aggressively Apollonian in disposition. By the same token, however, most men will be totally unaware of any corresponding tendencies within themselves. Banished to the shadows, therefore – or rather to the Shadow – those tendencies are all the more likely to beaver away within them in secret, always ready to break out in a rash of violence which may be expressed either physically or emotionally – and certainly in ways that can poison their relations with the opposite sex. That violence may even manage to disguise itself (as is so often the way with the oppressed Artemis) under a veneer of logic and rationality.

For most men, then, Artemisian therapy is truly urgent. It is vital for establishing their inner balance. But it is equally urgent for all those women who still have residual feelings of guilt about being truly feminine, or who have been constantly pressurised by the men in their lives to adopt a 'man's outlook' and all the concomitant 'masculine' values of present-day Western society. Indeed, that therapy is sorely needed in the wider context, too, if our world itself is not to succumb to the disintegration and destruction which too easily follows in Apollo's train whenever he appears among us in isolation.

Unremitting sunshine, as we all know, leads only to drought, sterility and ultimately total desertification.

1. Self-enquiry

The first step, as with Apollo, is to take time out to examine yourself, your attitudes and feelings.

(a) Accepted aspects

Do you regard yourself as a creature of emotion, intuition and instinct? Are you happy to rely on these for guidance? Are you prepared to act quite independently on this basis, without the need for anybody else's approval? Are you prepared to revise your views, plans and opinions – repeatedly if necessary? Are you unconcerned about whether you are being logical or consistent? Do you love animals and young children – sometimes rather more, perhaps, than you do adults? Are you less than enthusiastic about sex? Are you drawn to solitude and wild places? Are you nevertheless also keen on dancing and social life? Are you an enthusiast for vigorous, individual, competitive sport and other personal, physical challenges? Are you energetic and always on the go?

If the answer to most or all of these is 'Yes', Artemis is undoubtedly your ruling archetype.

By the same token, however, all this is far more likely if you are a woman than if you are a man. Most Western men will vehemently dismiss a good deal of the above as 'unmasculine' – i.e. as other than they themselves 'should' be. Yet a man who reacts *negatively* to most or all of the above is in fact rejecting Artemis within himself – and will probably reject it in the women around him, too. Whereupon the stage is set for both inner and outer conflict.

(b) Rejected aspects

If Artemis's 'accepted' aspects offer some idea of the size of the inner task facing the typical Western *male* if he is to attain some semblance of inner balance, her additional, 'rejected' aspects may well make it seem well-nigh impossible. Even many women may find the following questions disturbing, or alternatively simply see them as having 'nothing to do with them'.

Are you repressed sexually? Are you love-shy, even prudish? If you are a woman, do you tend to bite men's heads off, or have a generalised compulsion to belittle them, undermine their confidence and if possible destroy them? Do you lead them on sexually and then back off when they take you seriously? Are you, too, sometimes catty towards other women, especially young mothers-to-be?

Whether as a woman or a man, are you aggressive, rude and/or opinionated, especially to anybody to tries to direct or control you? Do you sometimes make yourself deliberately unattractive, whether physically or otherwise? Are you always changing your mind? Do you find it impossible to be either settled or consistent for more than two minutes together? Do you despise all plans and so-called logic – while still being prepared to advance what purport to be 'logical' arguments to back up your basically illogical hunches and intuitions? Are you moody and sometimes bad-tempered? Are you subject to a continual series of alternate 'highs' and deep depressions? Are you anorexic? As a woman, are you drawn almost exclusively to the company of other women and young girls? Are you, for that matter, a lesbian, whether openly or secretly?

As in the case of Apollo, these rejected aspects may well prove difficult to admit to. Even if you are a woman, they may well seem to imply some kind of hidden criticism. You may find yourself resenting the implications as if they were some kind of personal attack.

Yet, once again, if you find that you react negatively to these 'rejected' characteristics there is actually cause for considerable hope. In a curious, negative way, after all, it means that you are still identifying with them, even though you have consigned them largely to your Shadow. You are thus, by this very token, indirectly admitting that they are an essential part of yourself. You may not choose to express them all in practice, but your very *re-cognition* of them means that you have not entirely dissociated yourself from them. Wholeness, consequently, is still re-attainable.

(c) Total non-recognition and projection

The situation is far more difficult, however, if the list of 'rejected' aspects – and perhaps even of 'accepted' ones – seems to have 'nothing to do with you', and therefore arouses neither your approval nor your disapproval. True, this disinterested reaction may merely indicate that Artemis is totally at home within you – in which case there is of course no therapy to be applied. Before this can safely be assumed, however, there is a particularly telling 'litmus-test' to be applied. This involves answering the following questions.

Do you associate the characteristics in the 'rejected' list – or even those in the 'accepted' one – exclusively with *other people*? Do you despise people who are continually carried away by their emotions? Are you incensed by people who act on intuition and hunch, or who determinedly follow their instincts rather than logic? Do you find other people's moodiness unbearable, and suspect their occasional depressions of merely being a deliberate act to annoy or frustrate you? Are you angered almost beyond measure by people who keep changing their minds, or who seem to agree on a course of action and then sabotage it, often apparently deliberately? Do you find people who despise all plans and logic virtually impossible to understand? As a man, are you frustrated, even hurt, by women who keep them-selves to themselves or who are prickly, touchy or downright prudish – and even more so by women who seem to lead you on sexually, then let you down? Are you contemptuous of people who are appar-ently more interested in animals and children than in other adults like yourself? Do you despise women who, though healthily vigorous and full of energy, are only happy in female company? Are you enraged by lesbians, especially *en masse* – perhaps even to the extent of feeling that they should be expunged from society altogether?

If so, then you are once again a victim of psychological projection. You are being (as most of us are) critical of your own hidden faults in other people. Alternatively, you are approaching other people exclusively from the viewpoint of Apollo, who in his negative aspect is always antagonistic to the Artemis within us – which, of course, ultimately amounts to saying much the same thing.

But at least you are reacting. And in that reaction there is always some hope, as long as you are prepared to undertake appropriate remedial action.

(d) Total acceptance

This, as we saw earlier, is the ideal state, signifying total inner balance – at least as far as the inner Artemis and her relationship to Apollo are concerned. If you have attained it, there is clearly no Artemisian therapy to be done. If, though, you are still not able to accept both of the lists above with easy-going equanimity, or to admit that most or all of the tendencies mentioned are characteristic of yourself (whether or not you choose to express them in practice), then the need for therapy is indicated.

And, once again, the ancient myths offer ample hints as to what forms that therapy might take.

2. Invocation

Once again the first stage is simply to invoke the goddess. Welcome Artemis into your life by naming her, imagining her, seeking out pictures of her and finding out all you can about her. If possible, use your holidays to visit her sanctuaries at Athens (on the Acropolis), Brauron, Delos (best visited from nearby Mykonos), Sparta and/or – in Turkey – Ephesus, Izmir and Sardis. Use your visit to see what 'vibes', what echoes of the nature of Artemis, you can pick up from the surviving ruins. If you can bring back a small statuette of her, make a 'shrine' around it in your bedroom and meditate before it morning and evening. Make up your mind to accept her in all her manifestations, and to start living your life accordingly, whatever the initial objections of those around you.

Great care needs to be taken, though, to distinguish between spontaneous responsiveness to your emotions and intuitions on the one hand, and sheer wilfulness and bloody-mindedness on the other. The distinction is not always easy to make. Fortunately, though, this is something that the more full-blooded forms of invocation will soon make a good deal clearer.

As with Apollo, after all, Artemis is present not only within you, but in the outside world. She is the moon and everything associated with it. She is the night-time world and all its uncertainties and terrors. She is the wild and the world of animal instincts. And it is by immersing yourself intimately in all of this that you are likely to encounter her most vividly and so eventually to learn to *re-cognise* her within yourself, too.

What is called for, then, is a kind of personal Outward Bound course to complement your equally vital *Inward* Bound course.

The time has come, in other words, to waterproof your walking-boots, get your rucksack and sleeping-bag together and set out for the mountains or the forest. Take a small stove, too, if you must – but leave your tent, radio and tape-recorder behind, for this is to be a journey into the wild, not into some alternative form of domesticity. By all means take your mobile or cell phone for use in case of emergency – but leave it turned off. Take plenty of warm clothing, waterproofs, a sharp knife, a First Aid kit, a sewing kit, a can-opener, some string, a box or two of matches in a dry plastic bag, a piece of clear plastic sheeting big enough to wrap yourself in twice over, a bare minimum of provisions for your trip (including a full water-bottle) and any essential medicines – together with a book on survival in the wild for reference. *Unless you are much more familiar with how to identify food from the wild than most modern, civilised people are, this last is particularly important.* If you have a dog, take that as well.

But next to nothing else.

The aim is to spend as many nights as you have time for alone in the mountains or in the depths of the forest. And I stress the word 'nights'. For the real purpose of the experience is to experience directly nature's unfamiliar night-time world – and thus, by the same token, your own too – and not just to spend all day sunbathing and all night tucked up in your nice, warm sleeping-bag. This will of course involve a certain amount of discomfort and cold. Above all, then, do not attempt this exercise in the winter: even summer nights can be quite cold enough. (It is also wise to let somebody know exactly where you are and when they should expect you back, just in case of unforeseen emergencies.)

You may choose to make this a walking expedition or simply a static camp. The former is possibly closer to the spirit of Artemis. Either way, though, you will need to choose one or more campsites with all due sensitivity to the natural circumstances currently prevailing. Where is the wind coming from? Is it likely to change? Do you have sufficient shelter from it? Do the clouds suggest that it is likely to rain? What will happen to the ground beneath you when it does?

Once you have established your bivouac, start to become fully aware of your situation here and now. Somehow you have to survive. This is not the time to think about 'ought' and 'should', of what is logical, of what is expected of you, of what other people will think. Still less is it the time to start thinking of what you have left behind – your job, your financial situation, your family problems. You have left them behind – so leave them behind! Right now you have quite enough problems of your own to be going on with.

And the main one is the sheer uncertainty of your predicament.

All of a sudden, nothing can be foreseen with any certainty. Your main need is to react appropriately *in the moment* to everything that is happening around you. And make no mistake, something *is* happening around you. Just sit there and become aware of it. The wind is no doubt blowing, the plants are moving, the insects and birds are going about their business. So – if only you will sit still long enough to spot them – are the animals, too. Somehow they are managing to survive out here without any assistance from civilisation. So why can't you?

Close your eyes for a moment and absorb the full feeling of the situation. Here you are, amid apparent abundance. Is there any reason why *you* shouldn't tap into it, too? Somewhere nearby – provided that you are nowhere near any human habitations, or downstream of any farmers' fields – there is probably clear, clean, running water (this is more likely in the mountains than in the forest: if it is not both clear and running, it is probably not clean). Can you make use of it? Smell it and taste it – that is what your senses of smell and taste are for. If it seems drinkable, feel free to drink it – only a little to start with, though, in case of reactions, and in any case at your own risk (if in real doubt, boil it, or seek another source). *After* you have had your drink, or at some point further downstream – always assuming that the water is deep enough – you may care to take a dip in it, too, whether naked or otherwise. Be careful to ensure that you are not observed, though – for the feeling of furtiveness and fear of being observed is inseparable from any wild animal that is in danger of being hunted, and must therefore be familiar, too, to the inveterate hunter who is Artemis.

The hunter who is not one with his prey, after all, rarely catches it either, as every traditional American Indian knows.

Which brings you to the matter of food. Once again, around you there must be food a-plenty. Most commonly-found roots, leaves, seeds and nuts are perfectly edible (though not, for example, those of bracken, buttercup, daffodil, foxglove, laurel, lily-of-the-valley, mistletoe, privet, ivy or yew), and so (with care) are quite a few common berries and fungi. Your senses of smell and taste can usually be relied upon to tell you which of them (or which parts of them) you can safely eat, especially in the raw state. That is what those senses are for: they are not just organs of pleasure. Except in a few comparatively unusual cases, what smells and tastes good is for the most part – astonishingly enough! – good to eat. Nevertheless, you should for obvious reasons try only very small quantities of each to start with. *To be doubly safe, use your survival book to identify positively those that are edible, and then eat only those that you are absolutely sure of.* More to the point, the animals, birds, grubs and less colourful insects around you are for the most part edible, too – and if they are not, your nasal sensors and taste-buds will again soon tell you. Can you catch any of them to eat? It's wonderful what you can do with a piece of string (once again, see your survival book). Set whatever traps you like, then, and settle down for the night.

Make a point, though, of not retiring to your bivouac for a few hours at least. Foregoing the seductive comfort of a fire, sit still in the darkness and listen. Contrary to what you might perhaps have supposed, the world around you is abuzz with frenetic activity. Small mammals are constantly on the move in the undergrowth or among the rocks. So, somewhere out there in the darkness, are the beasts and birds of prey. Moreover, next to none of them are any threat to you – not even the bears and wolves. (In countries where such large predators are present, though, you should of course take local advice – and it can in any case help to avoid unpleasant surprises on both sides if you start by marking out your desired 'home-territory' in exactly the same way as any dog would!). All this dark, unfamiliar world, far from being foreign and threatening, is as much a part of you as you are, reflecting directly those aspects of your inner being that you are so keen to keep in the dark. If there is a moon, then, sense the feeling of serenity that it and its light convey. Sense, too, the primeval stillness of the ancient stars. But at the same time contrast that stillness and serenity with the underlying turmoil suggested by the constant scurrying and scrabbling in the dark undergrowth around your and beneath your feet. Reflect on the extent to which you, too, have within you an apparently serene 'upper world' and an 'underworld' that is constantly seething and in turmoil. Sense within you the personal counterparts both of the prowling predators and of the frightened, furtive quarry. Then accept both as intimately and irredeemably *you*.

Your dog, if you have brought it along, will meanwhile serve an invaluable function. As one of Artemis's characteristic animals, it is fully up to the situation, even if you initially are not. If you are unsure of how to respond to the circumstances, simply take a leaf out of its book. Watch it during the day as it instinctively forages, hunts, explores and generally *goes wild*. Watch, too, what it does at night. Then think yourself into its skin, and imitate it – for going wild is precisely what this particular exercise is really all about.

And who knows, your four-legged friend may even help to feed you, in the true spirit of Artemis's primeval hunting hounds.

Meanwhile, another way of attuning to nature's changing moods and to *re-cognise* their reflections within yourself is to seek out the elements where they are perhaps at their most changeable – namely by or on sea. The tides, after all, directly reflect Artemis's changing rhythms, while constant changes of wind and weather once again ensure that nothing is fully predictable (despite the best efforts of the meteorological service), and that those human beings who are faced with the elements can do no more than be sensitive to them and constantly adapt and change in response.

Even regular swimming at given states of tide can help attune you to Artemis's inherent irregularities – for you will finish up by swimming at a different time each day or night. (If you can actually do it by moonlight, you will at the same time have an additional chance to contemplate her apparently at her most coolly serene.) Set up your bivouac on the seashore, and even your food-gathering will depend largely on her tides – since winkles, cockles, mussels, and limpets are available only at low tide, and clams and razor-shells only at the very lowest springs. (On Britain's wilder south and east coasts, you can often supplement them with copious quantities of sea-kale or sea-cabbage.)

But the most vivid way of invoking Artemis in the maritime

context is possibly to arrange to do some cruising under sail. Even if you have no suitable boat of your own, this is less difficult to arrange than you might think. If none of your friends has a cruising yacht or can be persuaded to take you along, simply approach your local yacht club, or apply to one of the national sailing associations such as Britain's Cruising Association or Royal Yachting Association. There are generally at least as many skippers looking for crew as there are crew looking for skippers. You may even wish to consider applying for an official training berth with one of the main organizations devoted to youth training under sail.

Where you have any choice in the matter, meanwhile, you should aim to ensure that your cruise includes a fair ration of night-passages, preferably without the help of auxiliary power, and using only a minimum of technological gadgets such as autopilots and satellite navigation systems. Thus, a small boat may well suit your purposes better than a large one. In this way you will be virtually forced to cope with nature at her most unpredictable. You will be largely at the mercy of tide, wind and weather – for ultimately there is no way in which you can now resist them. The best that you can do is go along with them, co-operate, go with the flow. By being canny and alert, you will eventually find that you can use even their unpredictabilities to your advantage. *Note, though, that wilfulness has nothing whatever to do with it: your responses will always need to be appropriate and sensitive, never based on uninformed will alone – for that way way lies only frustration and possible disaster.*

True, while sitting out the long hours of the night-watch with the boat beneath you plunging and tossing unpredictably to the waves as they bear down upon you unseen out of the darkness, you may soon find yourself longing for the stillness, warmth and safety of port and all the securities and certainties of Apollonian civilisation. But this, of course, is not where you are currently 'at'. What is important at this moment is to adjust to the situation as it is, and to accept that all of it – all this turmoil and movement and general insecurity – is a perfectly legitimate way of experiencing life in its own right, as the first gannet that soars majestically into view above the whitecaps next morning will soon remind you. There really is no point in wishing that you were somewhere else – in fact, to do so is merely a guaranteed recipe for deep and prolonged misery.

Fully accept the situation, however, and life can take on an entirely new meaning. One stormy night, as you contemplate the lunar Artemis soaring serenely above the scudding cloud-wrack and the crazily swaying mast, apparently supremely indifferent to the dark, watery chaos that she is helping to create here below – not least through the deep, submarine force of her tidal streams – you will start to sense the natural necessity of her inherent contradictions and of the hidden forces that their very polarities in turn release. As the gale rises, there is nothing to be done, you come to realise, but to reduce sail and batten down the hatches – i.e. to accept her in all her paradoxical unpredictability. And the result of doing so is paradoxically that instead of being tense, anxious and insecure you suddenly start to feel as at home with the elements as the gannet is and, by the same token, as at home with yourself. This, too, you now realise, is life of a sort – even life more abundantly.

On returning home – there can be not the slightest doubt about it – you feel renewed, more complete, more self-confident, more supremely you. This applies to both types of expedition, whether terrestrial or maritime – which is no doubt why Outward Bound organisations are so keen on both. You start to feel that you can cope with anything that life throws at you – even your own long-suppressed emotions, hunches and intuitions. For you have dared to invoke all the ferocity of Artemis and survived. And with her you have also started to face up to all those unknown aspects of yourself that you formerly kept firmly locked up in the dark for fear of what they might bring – and have lived to tell the tale.

3. Meditation

Unlike Apollo's form of meditation, then, that of Artemis has essentially to be a *feeling* meditation. It involves becoming aware of your feelings and emotions, your intuitions and hunches. But such things are not easy to do from your armchair, or merely by act of will, especially if you have hitherto tended to deny that you are subject to such things in the first place. Artemisian meditation needs to be practised mainly in practical, physical contexts which practically *force* you to become aware of your instincts, emotions and intuitions. The activities just outlined are ideal for this – and thus amount to a kind of invocation and meditation rolled into one. Daunting they may at first seem, but then the more they daunt you the greater your need for Artemisian therapy in the first place.

The essential is to *become aware* of what you are feeling at the time and, having become aware of it, fully to accept it as your present reality. Identify your emotions at each instant, locate the hurts, fears and joys within your body, then express them all in whatever ways seem most natural to you – and not merely in words. You can, for example, express them not only through outdoor pursuits, but through music, painting and physical activities such as athletics or intuitive dance, too.

Meanwhile Artemis's favourite sport of hunting, too, can

summon up all kinds of unfamiliar emotions within you that you could well benefit from savouring, familiarising yourself with and then discharging in the appropriate way: you may even start to become aware, almost by osmosis, of the corresponding emotions of the quarry. If you are on horseback, you may directly sense your mount's reactions, too – which is appropriate, for the horse is itself closely associated with Artemis in her incarnation as the shy and rather horsey Selene. But all this will of course depend on your own attitude to bloodsports, which may be strongly negative – to say nothing of the current laws governing them. This attitude may be fully justified – most attitudes, after all, generally are – but it in turn could lead you to consider how far any objections you have are really to do with questions of ethics and morality, and how far with fear of confronting and accepting your own feelings and emotions – i.e. those of your inner, ill-tamed Artemis. Could it, in other words, really be a matter of what fox-hunting does *to you* rather than of what it does to the fox?

All kinds of bloodsports, in fact, from big-game hunting to simple fishing, can provide suitable contexts for Artemisian meditation, aided by whatever experts you can rope in to help you such as gamekeepers or (at your own risk!) poachers. In all of them it is not primarily your instinctive responsiveness to the wild creatures concerned that is at issue, nor even the emotions that the hunt evokes, *but your awareness and acceptance of them at the time.* Watch, then, your reactions. Keep asking yourself not 'What am I thinking at this moment?' but 'What am I *feeling instinctively* at this moment?' *Then act accordingly.*

Once you have acquired plenty of active experience of Artemisian instincts and emotions in the context of nature in the raw, you will be in a better position to turn to some of Artemis's quieter, more purely contemplative therapies. In particular you may wish to start considering her typical symbols. Can you now be as brutal and aggressive, as self-assured and wilful as the she-bear? Are you prepared to go into virtual hibernation with her in the winter or when depressed – or, as a woman, at the time of your menstrual period? Are you also prepared, like the lioness, to express your more brutal, aggressive aspects as a member of a pack?

Alternatively, can you be proud and independent like the stag, relying entirely on your own instincts? Can you express those instincts completely naturally like the dog, making use of them to worry and ferret out what you really need from life? Can you share the instinctive joys and delights of the dolphin, combining your instincts, emotions and native intelligence into a seamless robe of almost transcendent consciousness? Can you be as slippery, free and uninhibited as the fish, and for that very reason – to change the simile – as busy, industrious and productive as the bee? Above all, can you now accept that you are naturally as changeable as the moon? Are you prepared to exercise all the instinctive and emotional powers that your lunar nature has bestowed on you in order to fulfil yourself as you truly are?

Consider these points, along with any other aspects of the creatures listed that occur to you. If possible, observe them with as many of your senses as possible in their natural habitat, noting how they move, grow, change and feed themselves. Identify with each of them in turn. Merge your identity not only with the moon, but with its reflection in still or gently moving waters. Then add to your list of possible symbols the guinea-fowl, the mythical gryphon, the ear of corn (see chapter 6), the date-palm, the cedar, the oak, the laurel or bay tree, the hazel, the willow, the oak, the flaming torch and the swastika, and consider them in turn. Finally, do not forget Artemis's bow and arrows: be prepared, if necessary, to shoot down anything that moves and to ask questions afterwards. It may not make you popular (the real Artemis, after all, is totally unconcerned about such things) – but it may help you to *come to yourself.*

Finish your meditation by asking yourself the following questions:

Am I feeling sufficiently positive about any taste I may have for celibacy or virginity?

Am I content to be emotionally and practically self-sufficient?

Am I prepared to be the wild person that I really am at heart?

Am I giving myself enough opportunities for uninhibited contact with young people of my own sex?

Am I attempting to be too consistent and logical?

Could I link my life less to clock and calendar, and more to the natural tides and seasons both of the world 'out there' and of my own psyche?

Am I fully alive to my dreams, my emotions, my intuitions and my unconscious generally?

After considering these points, consider whether this is the moment to adjust your way of life to reflect them.

4. Remedial activities

On the basis of the myths, there are a number of activities that seem designed positively to encourage you to develop your Artemisian aspects. You may wish to consider adopting some of them, perhaps on a trial basis initially. Several of them pick up on themes that have been mentioned already. Add any favourite activities of your own that seem natural to you. For convenience, as with Apollo, the activities listed are divided here into two categories:

(a) Recreational and general

Wear men's clothes in saffron (orange-yellow), brown and/or black according to your mood, or – if you dare – in animal skin (whether imitation or otherwise). Keep pets, especially dogs. Go horse-riding. Take up athletics (especially running), gymnastics, wrestling, hunting, archery, hill-walking, mountaineering and/or dancing. Take part in keep-fit classes and associated activities. Join Outward Bound courses of various kinds, and possibly help to organise similar courses for young people of your own sex. Join a single-sex community of some kind – possibly a religious one, or even a single-sex protest-group. Go out in the moonlight. Frequent moonlit rivers, pools and seashores. Swim regularly in the sea at high tide, or spontaneously – as the fancy takes you – in clear streams and rivers. Immerse yourself in music – especially 'natural' music such as that of birds, waterfalls, the wind and the Aeolian harp. Take up travel. Go sailing (possibly single-handed, once qualified and/or experienced). Observe your dreams. Study magic, the esoteric and/or the occult. Subject to the laws of your society and considerations of medical safety, express yourself sexually in whatever ways you are most comfortable with.

(b) Professional

Particularly suitable areas for encouraging the growth of Artemis within you are: child-care and/or youthwork, open-air work of all kinds (especially work with animals, ecology and nature conservation, botany, forestry, geology and other wilderness-orientated occupations), teaching, physical training, physiotherapy, nursing, midwifery, obstetrics, travel, tourism, dancing, commerce generally, religious orders, alternative healing, the occult and/or – for women – the women's armed services or any other uniformed women's organisation.

SUB-PERSONALITIES OF ARTEMIS

Should any of the above analyses and therapies provide a less than perfect fit with your own case, you may care to consider the following variations, which may suggest alternative therapies that you feel to be marginally more suited:

AMAZONS

Possible symptoms

Feminism; initial love-shyness; violent rage when treated as a sex-object; anti-male feelings; opposition to male chauvinism (see **Zeus**); warlike attitudes, possibly leading to violence; anti-domesticity; anti-monogamy; promiscuity; all-devouring love; emotional ups and downs; violent swings of mood; child-cruelty; self-mutilation; unconventional attitudes and behaviour; possible tendency to breast-cancer

but also

Fair dealing; basic human friendliness; independent-mindedness; psychological balance; matriarchy.

Therapies

Name, imagine and invoke the marauding army of determined, bare-breasted Amazons, bows and arrows in hands; horses; hunting; music (especially pipes, flute, woodwinds); matriarchal societies; women's groups; reversal of traditional sex-roles; colonisation; city-founding.

Symbols

Bull; date-palm; bow and arrow; double axe; the moon.

Notes

The Amazons, champions of femininity, are present whenever women combine to assert their collective rights in the face of male domination and exploitation. Perfectly feminine when allowed to be themselves, but highly negative when provoked or treated as mere sex objects, they represent the natural spirit of female aggression in combination with the spirit of comradeship – Artemis in collectivity. Their natural milieu is always on the fringes of society. Yet it is also in the nature of the Amazons eventually to over-reach themselves. They would therefore be well-advised to seek moderation and constantly to ask themselves what their real purpose is. In view of their roots in revolutionary protest, any attempt to hijack the establishment is almost bound to lead to their own self-destruction.

CYRENE

Possible symptoms

Hatred of household tasks; anti-domesticity; love-shyness; wilfulness; irresponsibility

but also

Love of the outdoors, especially water and mountains; tomboyish-ness; love of strenuous physical activity; acceptance of challenges; love of high living.

Therapies

Name, imagine and invoke this wild, untamable virgin Nymph with her passion for all kinds of physical activity; wilderness; animal husbandry; shepherding; cowboy-work; hunting; riding; wrestling; running; swimming and water-sports generally; marriage, possibly to an intellectually orientated husband (see **Apollo**); motherhood; high living; being pampered.

Symbols

Lion; horse; bee.

Notes

The spirit of Cyrene beats in the breast of every keen sportswoman and female athlete. All the while she can remain single, that spirit is likely to flourish. Within marriage it may represent a problem. Marriage may thus be seen either as a cure or as a threat. There may be a choice to be made, and correct timing will in this case be of prime importance, if made more difficult by the constant, wolfish attention of men of the **Apollo** type with a particular weakness for tomboys. It may well be advisable to send the children of any marriage away to boarding-school at an appropriate age – an action which may have some injurious psychological effects on the children, but is likely to pay off handsomely in terms of training, education and eventual all-round competence .

DAPHNE

Possible symptoms

Pursuit by unwelcome suitors; fear of sex; possible lesbianism; panic flight from men – especially intellectuals (see **Apollo**); constant washing; possible anorexia

but also

Spiritual awareness; sensitivity to nature; love of mountains and running water; devotion to Earth; love of female company; celibacy; virginity.

Therapies

Name, imagine and welcome the shy mountain nymph and priestess of Mother Earth who is amorously pursued by **Apollo**; ecology; gardening; geology and other earth-sciences; mountains; naked river-bathing; female company; flight and exile; laurel or bay-leaves (consult a reputable herbalist).

Symbols

Laurel tree; mare's head.

Notes

From a particularly sparse myth a picture seems to emerge of a sexually attractive and virginal young woman who has found her niche in nature and wishes above all not to be disturbed by sexual entanglements, especially with intellectual men. Such men, in other words, could be either her downfall or her salvation. Since the former seems more likely, keeping her distance may well prove the best policy. She may, however, experience problems – or alternatively be forced to overcome her sexual hang-ups – if she takes part in mixed geological or ecological work. Since her natural context is consistent with maintaining her inner balance, there seems to be no special reason for changing it. Far better that she should have the courage of her convictions and simply disappear into the bush.

HECATE

Possible symptoms

Possible upbringing as only child; immersion in the occult; witchcraft; magic; hidden, unconscious powers; two-facedness; bitchiness; crude sexiness; extreme unpleasantness at times

but also

Psychic gifts; mediumistic abilities; restorative powers; gift for sacralising the profane; good luck; wealth; multifaceted personality; charm and attractiveness at moments of her own choosing.

Therapies

Name, imagine and invoke the dark, winged, hag-like underworld Goddess of Witches in her gleaming 'Gipsy Rose Lee' headdress; shamanism; mediumship; counselling (especially of the dying and of pregnant women); midwifery; responsibility; supervisory duties; policing; road-walking; caving; the sea; the colours black, purple and mauve.

Symbols

Screech owl; snake; weasel; mare; cat; lion; she-wolf; dog; bitch; Sirius (the 'Dog Star'); the moon; flaming torch; junctions of three roads; triple mask; gleaming headdress.

Notes

Whether in men or in women, Hecate's most characteristic statement is 'I am psychic.' She is particularly prone to appear during the second half of life, possibly as a kind of mask – a way of coping with the temporary 'loss of identity' characteristic of the midlife crisis. Once installed, she is not to be driven out. With her she brings illusions of specialness and power over others that attract to her all the wrong kind of friends – basically, those who are prepared to bolster her illusions, and especially Persephone (below). Nevertheless, the genuine gifts she brings can have value in bridging the gulf between conscious and unconscious. Her main danger lies in the temptation to hijack the unconscious for the exclusive benefit of the ego. Should she insist on involving herself in magic and other occult activities, she may indeed be queen for a while in her own kingdom, but it is likely to be an illusory kingdom, a dominion of the dead, and unlikely in the end to bring her much joy. And the unconscious, it needs hardly be said, will always have the last word, eventually confronting her with the stark reality of what she is doing to herself.

MEDEA

Possible symptoms

Magic; witchcraft; deviousness; trickery; cruelty; poisoning; insane jealousy; bloodthirstiness; ambition for selected children; preparedness to destroy rest of family.

but also
Psychic gifts; healing powers; constancy; determination; support for own children.

Therapies
Name, imagine and invoke this cruel, archetypal witch and dark weaver of intrigues who murders her own brother and children to further her own ends; snake-charming; meadow-saffron (WARNING: HIGHLY POISONOUS: consult a reputable herbalist).

Symbols
Moon; winged serpent.

Notes
Medea's myth is sketchy, but out of it emerges the unmistakable picture of a woman consumed with personal ambition, which she is prepared to pursue with utmost ruthlessness – even by proxy through her own children or, if need be, at their expense. This trait she compounds with an unhealthy passion for the occult. Totally ruthless and calculating, this spirit of untamed female egotism is thus a danger to herself, her family and everybody around her. Possibly that is why the surviving records have little to say about therapies. Apart from suggesting that she confine her activities to relatively harmless contexts, the best that can be done seems to be to attempt to concentrate on purely positive applications of such gifts as she has. Weaving, basketry and tapestry-work could possibly help. On

the whole, the syndrome tends, if anything, to increase, rather than to disappear, with age.

PERSEPHONE = Proserpine, Kore

Possible symptoms

Gullibility; loss of innocence; proneness to abduction and rape; preference for female, rather than male company; possible frigidity and childlessness; vindictive attitude to men; possessiveness; strong unconscious urges; fear of snakes; winter depression; manic depression; periodic insanity; love of darkness; obsession with death

but also

Feminism; graciousness; complaisance; faithfulness; regenerative and restorative powers; mercy; admiration for real heroes; 'merciful' destruction of present circumstances; unwillingness to espouse death; ability to learn to love what she orignally hated; vulnerability to the spiritual or divine; eventual acceptance of death as a part of life.

Therapies

Name, imagine and welcome the lost, depressed daughter of Demeter and unwilling Queen of the Underworld; cosmology; self-transformation initiatives; self-development courses; weaving; agriculture; gardening; springtime; light; adoption; the moon; sacrifices of black rams and ewes; mint (consult a reputable herbalist).

Symbols

Black poplar; willow; aspen; pomegranate seed; narcissus; poppy;

green corn; the moon; iris; black ewe; bat; flaming torch.

Notes

Persephone, the feminine archetype of initiation, is the spirit of femininity in her most contradictory form, and may well reflect a decline from a former state of great energy, brightness and hope (see Athene under **Zeus**). Once she has discovered the dark side of her own nature, she can be creative or destructive almost at will. Her moods change unpredictably. The men around her rarely manage to cope with her tendency to blow hot and cold. Moreover, she herself suffers from her internal contradictions, to the point where she is sometimes unable to cope at all. At such times she is all too likely to fall under the baleful spell of Hecate (see above). Fortunately the natural world presents her with clear analogues of her inner tendencies. By directing her enormous energies into working with plants, soil, weather and moon she can start both to lower the internal psychological pressures and to objectivise her inner experience, realising as she does so that nature's contradictions, far from being arbitrary, have a valid place and significance within an overall cyclic plan. In this way balance and inner integration can gradually be achieved within a framework of ever recurring change.

SELENE

Possible symptoms

Gullibility, naïveté; insistence on knowing would-be lover's innermost secrets; revulsion against full-blooded sex; menstrual problems; periodic depression; manic depression; love of darkness;

possible alcoholism; spell-binding effect on men; elusive enchantment; shyness

but also
Beauty; sexual gentleness; keen observation; eventual regular menstrual periods; great fertility; re-emergence from depression (especially in the presence of **Dionysus**); cool skin; charm; spell-binding, soothing and healing effect on men.

Therapies
Name, imagine and welcome the winged Selene, the shy, retiring, virginal, original Moon-Goddess; darkness; veil; all-concealing clothing; male bodyguards; low public profile; activities involving careful observation; alcohol (WARNING: beware of addiction); orgies; sleepy or unresponsive men; childbearing; horse-riding.

Symbols
Chariot drawn by twin bulls or horses; mule; stag; twins; not-to-be-opened basket; veil; menstruation; torch; diadem; dark cave; the number nine.

Notes
Selene plays hard-to-get. Possibly the product of paternal over-protectiveness, she enjoys the sexual attentions of men, and is quite prepared to lead them on. But then she backs away in fright. Only very young men are likely to get past her guard, and then only by subterfuge, or with the aid of alcohol. In short, Selene is the spirit of female repression. She finds it difficult to let her hair down. In her

tightly-closed basket – her 'Pandora's box' – she bears all those aspects of herself that she is afraid to let out. And it may take many years and a great deal of loving gentleness (both of course preferable to the last resort of alcohol) to persuade her to release her hold and commit herself to the kind of relationship that she secretly most desires. The effort is worthwhile, however, for her real destiny is to be the mother of a large family. Should she, by contrast, reach midlife with her basket still unopened, severe complications could well ensue.

SIRENS = Harpies

Possible symptoms

Obsessive virginity; proneness to group-hysteria; group-seduction, and then destruction, of men; public broadcasting of, and saddling of others with, own emotional problems; cruelty; heartlessness; anaemia; fevers; reclusiveness; self-destruction if scorned

but also

Feminine charms; sociability with other women; attraction to life in a female group or institution; attractive voice; musical gifts; calming effect; good appetite; love of good food; foreknowledge.

Therapies

Name, imagine and welcome the two or more rapacious, bird-like female murderers who sing seductively as they lure sailors onto their fabulous island of flowery meadows (possibly Capri), only to devour them; isolation; living alone or in exclusively female company; singing emotional songs of love or death, especially in female groups; spiritual or religious music; plucked instruments and flute; prayer; membership of a religious order; good food and plenty of it.

Symbols

Spoonbill; stork; bee or wasp.

Notes

The Sirens are powerfully attracted to the opposite sex, but cannot satisfactorily relate to them. A collective and more dangerous version of Selene (above) with a touch of the Furies about them, they yearn for love, yet cannot accept it, preferring instead to indulge themselves with rather more food than is good for them. Somehow their childhood conditioning is in violent conflict with their natural urges. The result is a series of catastrophic personal relationships, for the most part sabotaged by an insistence on remaining a female group or gang.

Unable to give themselves to another physically, yet well able to express their emotions in other ways, their most rewarding course is therefore to give of themselves in one of their stronger, non-physical areas, and yet one which is closely associated with their gift for sexual allure – namely the human voice. All the while, of course, staying well away from intimate contact with men, which could prove disastrous if persisted with.

A particularly valuable and rewarding way of applying their talents may well be to devote themselves to spiritual or religious music, where their services are likely to prove of special comfort to the bereaved, elderly or dying. All of which suggests that joining a closed religious order with a good musical tradition is a possibility well worth considering.

SUMMARY

By learning to know your inner Artemis, you learn to *re-cognise* one further vital aspect of yourself . Yet, even if you are a woman, you may well find the process quite difficult enough after years of Apollonian conditioning by a male-orientated society. If you are a man, it may prove even more demanding a task – basically involving getting to know the feminine side of your own nature – than getting to know the inner Apollo can be for the more Artemisian type of woman. Hence the full-blooded, even literally brutal nature of the therapeutic exercises suggested. Artemis is not to be encountered in the refined atmosphere of the drawing-room. She needs to be encountered in the raw, in all her redness of tooth and claw.

Never fear, though. She can be survived. And it is in learning this in the 'outer' context that we gradually learn that we do not have to be afraid of the animal instincts and emotions that lurk within ourselves, either. We are designed to function as we are. We are perfectly adapted to nature. And if to nature, then also to that inner nature which we increasingly learn to know as we gradually *get to know our selves*, and Artemis in particular.

3

PAN – THE WAY OF THE CHILD

The child is father of the man.
William Wordsworth: 'My heart leaps up'

PAN is the wild, unrestrained god of childhood who is so often rejected with the onset of adulthood, and who therefore makes himself all the more felt in later life. Contacting and reconciling yourself with Pan, your inner child, can thus become a truly vital task, for it involves re-invigorating your very roots, the very substratum on which your whole being is based.

Characteristics of god and host

Pan is a terror. But then it is in his nature to be. Confronted with this demon-god who is neither wholly animal nor wholly human – nor, indeed, anything that most of us would gladly welcome into our familiar, civilised world – we all too easily fall prey to the condition which is his own peculiar trademark and speciality: *pan-ic*.

As well we might, for his very presence threatens all our reassuring boundaries, our neat pigeonholes, our fixed ideas about what can go with which. It undermines our sense of security, throws into question the stability of our ideas, our institutions, even our society itself.

In Pan we are faced with all the vigorous, primal, animal side of our nature that we had long thought discarded, forgotten, left far behind us. We are faced, in a word, with *the child*.

Not the *child archetype*, as so eloquently celebrated by psychomythologists such as Jung and Kerényi – a seemingly universal dream-image and construct of the human psyche embodying the eternal process of renewal, salvation and the re-attainment of psychic wholeness – but the *archetypal child* whose paradigm we have all lived out for real at some time in our lives and continue to carry with us, often unseen and unrecognised, to the end of our days.

As is now increasingly recognised, it was really this inner child whom the truly ancient Greeks chose – however unwittingly – to identify as *Pan*, and in recognition of his archetypal childlikeness they chose for him a living symbol. That symbol was the goat or kid. And to this day English-speakers refer familiarly to children by the latter term.

Not that the Greeks of later, classical times still made the connection. To them the pre-eminent gods of childhood were no mere goats, but the resplendent young Apollo, Hermes, Dionysus – even, perhaps, the prodigious infant Heracles. The literature, consequently, positively resounds with their precocious exploits. Yet all of these figures, clearly, are semi-magical, superhuman beings that have little or nothing in common with the nature of children as they actually are. Their stories are not factual but *mythical* – semiconscious, almost dreamlike representations (as we have only lately begun to realise) of deep, communally-experienced psychic realities whose function is to heal the human psyche, promote its renewed development and compensate for its inner imbalances. To regard them as representing the experience of literal, blood-and-guts childhood, with all its hopes and fears, its sudden joys and primal dreads, its veritable Aladdin's cave of newly-sensed sights, sounds, smells and feelings, would be to betray the fact that one has lost touch with childhood reality as it is and as it has to be.

As, indeed, every generation of adults is all too prone to do.

The Greeks of classical times, it seems, were no exception to this. And so, even though it was recognised that the great gods themselves had their own wild, childish, Pan-like aspects (there was an acknowledged 'Hermopan' for Hermes, a 'Diopan' for Dionysus and so on), Pan himself, as the representative of childhood in his own right, was largely lost to sight, left out in the cold, abandoned to the forests of the night which had always been his natural habitat. Black and hairy, he became not a child, but a goat-like denizen of the unconscious, a creature of the shadows, a demon of the rejected kingdoms of the psyche, where the later Christians were in due course to rediscover him still cowering and turn him into the Devil incarnate.

It is all very well to pretend that the animal in us is dead, to forget our primal instincts, our primitive emotions, our atavistic desires. It is understandable that we should wish to push far from us that darker being who preceded the development of our more civilised adult human-ness. In order that we should become truly human, after all, it was always necessary for Pan to depart, just as the wild beasts themselves had to be scared away from the caves and clearings alike before human civilisation could arise. But Pan's departure is not the same as his death. One extraordinary classical tradition notwithstanding, he is far from dead. Still he lingers in the shadows, the living, goat-like symbol of everything that we imagine we have left behind us. And we, too, need to become alive to his continued infantile presence there if we are truly to learn to know our adult selves.

The symbolism of the goat

As ever, the symbol sums up the myth as a whole. In the wild, the goat is a sensitive, timid animal. It lives in constant fear of predators, and so seeks out shelter, protection and the company of its own kind. It is especially drawn to high, wild, lonely, out-of-the way places, far from the developed, artificial world of adult human society. It may *look* vacuous and stupid, yet is actually highly observant and intelligent. It is also extremely agile, elusive and fleet of foot. Whatever it gathers, it gathers on the hoof. It is a voracious feeder, willing to eat almost anything. And so it will cheerfully lay waste the precious garden of delights that adult humanity has spent so much time and effort cultivating for itself.

It has other characteristics, too, especially where the male sex is concerned. It is obstinate and cantankerous. It is capricious (the word actually *means* 'goat-like'). It has an overpowering smell. It is renowned for its strong sex-drive. And yet at the same time the goat-tribe in general has (as vets and farmers will alike confirm) an extraordinary tendency towards hermaphroditism, and thus an inherent sexual ambivalence about it.

Pan, in short, represents all the stubbornly instinctive side of our nature that is so prominent in early childhood, and that our elders are traditionally so intent on training and (if necessary) beating out of us at the earliest opportunity in order to turn us into decent, civilised adults. No wonder, then, that the early Christians, conveniently forgetting their own gospel's injunction that they should become as little children, saw in him the symbol of our lower nature, and came to associate him with 'the world, the flesh and the Devil'.

Pan in the ancient texts

Pan's recorded myth goes on to flesh out the natural paradigm. Traditionally he is treated as inseparable from his Nymphs. He is surrounded, in other words, by the young, female representatives of rock and tree, cave and spring – of living nature herself in all her manifold guises. At the same time he is also accompanied by a whole bevy of *paniskoi*, or 'little Pans' – other wild, goat-like beings like himself. And their continual wild dances, their revels and orgies are irrepressible. As, indeed, is Pan's own sexuality; for, goat that he is, he is irretrievably and unapologetically *horny*.

To the ancient Greeks a herd of goats necessarily implied the presence of a goatherd. Moreover, it was axiomatic that the latter must become totally one with his flock. In effect, he must play the role of billy-goat (whence, no doubt, the rumours – which still persist even today – concerning the supposedly eccentric sexual practices of shepherds and goatherds alike.) At the same time the goatherd traditionally uses the flute or pipes – to say nothing of the human voice itself – as instruments of guidance and control, and perhaps of protection, too. And since one of the herdsman's prime functions is to guard his charges from predators at night, he traditionally sleeps during the daytime, and particularly around noon.

All these characteristics, consequently, are duly attributed to Pan himself. Forever in the company of his rude entourage, he is always on the watch. He is sexually indiscriminate. He continually plays the flute or Pan-pipes. He has a loud voice. He is unbearable if woken from his noontide slumbers. Moreover he seldom, if ever, washes, and so smells much the same as his animals, and just as strongly.

In the kingdom of Pan, it seems, the proverbial 'nymphs and shepherds' are forever one.

At the same time it goes without saying that the goatherd, like his flock, is afraid of the dark. At night he will pen them for safety in some small natural cave or grotto. For warmth he himself will join them. And cooped up there with his animals he is liable to suffer not merely from something approaching suffocation, but continual nightmares about what may be prowling about in the darkness just outside – nightmares from which he is liable to awake in the same animal *panic* as his charges should the nightmares actually turn out to be true.

All these characteristics, then, are likewise reflected in the myth of Pan. Almost all of Pan's sanctuaries, consequently, consist of remote, barely-accessible natural caves and grottoes that are redolent with a feeling on the one hand of relief and security, and on the other of sheer animal terror of the nocturnal world outside.

And Pan himself (Greek: 'pasture') is the resulting composite. The man standing among his herd of goats becomes a single being with a human body and goats' legs – the archetypal goat-man.

Child and giddy goat

And so what is the relevance of all this to our experience of early childhood? The sheer animal instinctiveness, clearly, is a *sine qua non* for goat and child alike. The sensitivity and timidity, the need for security, the urge to run away and hide, the natural gregariousness, the observant yet apparently vacuous expression, the characteristic of 'knowing more than it lets on', the ingrained obstinacy and cantankerousness, the determination to eat absolutely anything (except, of course, what it is given), the sheer destructiveness and lack of sense of civilised values – all these are thoroughly characteristic of young children, as everybody knows from experience. So are the natural dirt and smell, the disinclination to wash and the general sexual ambivalence.

The goatherd's qualities that are incorporated into the myth likewise have their direct relevance. The love of music, the continual noise, the loud voice, the tendency to sleep all day and wake all night, the fear of the dark, the occasional *panics*, nightmares and suffocation-fits – these, too, are features that are virtually inseparable from early childhood.

Which brings us to a handful of features whose relevance may at first sight seem rather less obvious. These are Pan's black, bearded, hairy appearance, his deceitfulness, his incipient madness and above all his legendary, rampant sexuality.

To take these in reverse order, it is a purely modern preconception that children are not sexual beings – a preconception that merely reflects 'nice' society's assumption that children *should not be* sexual beings. In fact, however, children are *intensely* sexual. Right from infancy, young boys in particular will play with their genitals, masturbate and experience pleasurable erections. Subsequently they will also go on to chase and terrify girls at every opportunity – indeed, to do anything and everything short of actually siring children, of which they are as yet incapable. *But, by and large, this is precisely what is recounted of Pan himself.* Thus, the Nymphs who surround him are at the same time in continual terror of him, and will do anything to escape his advances (compare the natural behaviour of females in any flock of grazing animals). *Yet, even when he catches them, no actual offspring generally results.*

Pan is intensely *sexual*, in other words, but not truly *erotic*. As a description of young children, the cap thus fits perfectly.

Again, Pan's apparent madness – including, perhaps, an incipient tendency to convulsions and epilepsy – is a feature that is perhaps a good deal more typical of children than we may at first realise. Very young children not only do not understand the adult way of looking at things: often they *will* not understand it. If the adults around them treat this refusal to share in the established outlook as a form of madness, and choose to treat it accordingly – whether with educational persuasion or with brute violence – then it will certainly not be the first time that this has happened in human history, even of the adult kind. And if this then results in tantrums and screaming to the point of convulsions and apparent fits, there will be nothing surprising about this, either.

By contrast, Pan's inherent deceitfulness is an attribute that is easier to fit to the average child than it is to the goatherd and his charges. But the point here is that goats, for their part, are past-masters at escape and avoidance of control, while the goatherd himself has to put the direct needs of his flock well before his own ideas of what day or time it is, or indeed of what ought to happen next. Both, in other words, are essentially children of nature, and by this very token creatures of instinct, too. And instinct, as we have already seen, scorns all our cherished ideas of regularity and discipline. Inevitably, therefore, both man and beast will be seen as elusive, even dissimulating – as, indeed, to the prowling predators, they have to be.

But what of Pan's legendary beard and hair? Beards, after all, are not features that we normally associate with children, even if they are perfectly natural features of both goats and goatherds. On the other hand, the general shagginess of both these latter *is* a token of their wildness and lack of conventional discipline. Besides, children left to themselves usually grow luxuriant heads of hair.

But in Pan's case it is far more than that. The old word for shagginess was 'horror', which in Latin meant 'bristling' or even 'shuddering'. Pan's general shagginess, in other words, can be seen as the direct physical embodiment of the primal fears and dreads that represent the dark side of childhood, as of Pan himself.

Hence, too, the young god's incorrigible blackness. Far from being a mere bodily characteristic typical of the Nubian goats of the ancient middle east, this is a symbolic attribute of great and revealing significance. Pan, it is evident, is essentially *a creature of the night*. And not merely of the outer night, but of our inner night, too. Representing as he does all the primal instinctiveness, the atavistic terrors, the animal urges and even bestial passions of childhood, he has been pushed into the shadows, consigned to the pit, banished to outer darkness. And all in order to preserve our own cherished adult values, our civilised norms, our bright, **Apollonian** ideals. Even where they half-surface in **Artemis** they are powerfully repressed by a male-dominated society and banished to the realm of semi-darkness. But when, in the child, they appear in all their naked savagery, they must be tarred with the dark brush of original sin, painted black as night, hidden totally from the sacred light of day.

No wonder, then, that Pan is black. He represents the greatest possible threat to everything that we believe in, to all our ideals, to all our notions of adult self-importance. He threatens to break free and trample into the dust our carefully-tended garden of rational order, to devour all our most delicate blooms of cultural achievement.

And so we pen him in all the more securely and even attempt to starve him to death – thereby ensuring that when, one day, he *does* break out again, the chaos and destruction that will follow in his wake will be all the more devastating and widespread.

The lesson, then, is obvious. Pan, too, needs to be *ac-knowledged*. If there is a Hermopan, a Diopan and so on, it is because he actually underlies all the other gods. He is their common substratum. His animal urges and instincts are absolutely basic to our human-ness in every form. And so failing to *re-cognise* them is merely a recipe for ultimate *dis-aster*, an ultimate sentence of death on our entire human enterprise.

Making contact with Pan

If we are truly to know ourselves, then, we need to know Pan, too. The one is simply not possible without the other. And Pan's way of knowing is of an absolutely basic and rudimentary kind. He knows by crude, physical contact – whether with rocks, trees, springs or other living creatures. He knows through the intimate feel of the animals that he constantly needs to have around him, just as a small child knows comfort and security through the feel of its mother or of its small, furry toys. He knows through music and dancing, through sounds and sights and smells. He knows by being alert to everything that his senses tell him. And not only his senses, but his gut instincts, too.

In short, Pan knows *directly*, and not merely at second-hand or via the intermediary of the intellect. His feet – his *animal* feet – are planted firmly on the ground. He is an inveterate materialist. What he gathers (as we saw earlier) he gathers *on the hoof.* His knowledge is *grounded* in sheer, physical experience.

If we are truly to know ourselves, then, it is a vital precondition that we should learn to know – or rather to re-acquaint ourselves with – this Pan-like aspect of our being. As in the case of **Artemis**, we need to *re-cognise* and admit to our natural and inherent materialism, and not to pretend, with the sky-borne **Apollo**, that we are somehow 'above that sort of thing'. We need to rediscover the child within, to re-establish contact with the natural world around us, as well as within us. We need wilderness, and we need to experience it on a regular basis. Short of actually living in the wilds, we at least need to spend regular periods there. This necessarily means respecting and getting to know our environment. It involves learning once again to respond directly to night and day, to sun and moon, to tide and weather and to the natural seasons both of nature and of the psyche, rather than merely to clock and calendar. It also means re-acquainting ourselves with our primal instincts, with natural foraging, group-living, music and dancing, as well as with a number of much less Artemisian aspects of our nature such as wild humour and the urge for nakedness and raw sexuality of every kind – for all the entirely reasonable (and thus Apollonian) restrictions and inhibitions that our society is minded to place on them. And in particular it means re-experiencing such primal emotions as fear and *panic* – for these, too, we need just as much as we need love and security, if our whole being is to be fully nourished and nurtured towards full maturity.

'Freedom from fear' is all very well as an ideal but, taken too literally, it can also mean freedom from growing up.

Some of our current enterprises duly recognise these needs. The value of wilderness, and of experiencing it directly, is becoming ever more widely realised. Gone are the days when 'nature reserve' meant 'reserved for naturalists'. Ventures such as the Outward Bound movement reflect our growing realisation that people's personal development benefits from contact with each other in natural settings which also demand that they give full rein to their survival-instincts and experience a full range of basic emotions, and not least primal fear.

Where we fail is in assuming that such things are for young people only, and that 'we adults' have no more developing or grow-ing to do. Thanks to the ministrations of **Apollo**, we are all too prone to insist that all the 'problems' (ourselves, no doubt, among them) are under control, that everything in the garden is lovely, and that nothing must therefore be altered. In actual fact, however, everything in the garden is *not* lovely – or, if it is, it is a garden which is patently out of tune with nature, and which nature will therefore eventually claim back for her own.

Small wonder, then, that even major business organisations (most of them redolent of **Apollo** in all his most aggressive, go-getting aspects) are nowadays starting to realise that something is missing from their world-view – something important, even vital. Their executives are sickening, wilting under the stress of a highly unnatural work-situation which can only destroy them in the end. And so they are being sent with increasing frequency on 'de-stressing' weekends and courses involving renewed contact with nature, with wilderness in the raw, and consequently with their own deeper, primal selves too.

As we have already seen, many of these activities are already thoroughly characteristic of the moon-goddess **Artemis**, too, and may thus justly be regarded as her own preserve. But in Pan they acquire an added intensity, an almost sexual connotation, a wild frenzy, a demoniacal laughter, a dimension of panic and horror that can literally make the hair stand on end. And it is in that instant that the ancient goat-god once more comes into his own. As, indeed, he has to if we are once again to become the whole beings that we are truly designed to be.

Childlikeness is far too important to be left to children. A sense of primal intimacy and wonder, an ability to see things afresh in the most vivid and startling colours, a direct, uninhibited familiarity with our physical bodies and primal instincts, a total openness to being scared and insecure, an almost atavistic closeness to the natural world in all its most basic, physical aspects – all these forms of knowing and experience are not only inalienable human rights, but essential prerequisites if ever we are to learn to become who we really are.

In the celebrated words attributed to Jesus of Nazareth: 'Unless you turn around and become like little children, you shall not enter the Kingdom of Heaven.'

VITAL ACTIONS

The urge to rediscover Pan within ourselves is something that most of us experience quite naturally from time to time. At weekends many of us instinctively seek nature in the raw, however much we may have sundered ourselves from it during the week. On holiday the 'things' that we seek do 'get away from' are generally the very things – our work, our domestic tasks, our financial worries – that separate us from nature. Many of us have an endless fascination with television nature-programmes, as well as with horror-films and videos that promise to put us in touch once again with all our primitive fears and atavistic panics. And we all still have buried within us – however deeply – the primal urge to 'play the giddy goat'.

The fact that the urge is there at all, then, is evidence – if evidence were needed – that Pan continues to demand his due. And we would therefore be well advised to take that debt seriously.

Proper therapy is therefore literally vital once again. And it needs to start with careful self-assessment and diagnosis.

1. Self-enquiry

Take time out, then, to examine yourself, your attitudes and feelings from Pan's perspective.

(a) Accepted aspects

Do you think of yourself as a very physical person? Are you strongly instinctive? Are you full of nervous energy, and always on the go? Are you an inveterate enthusiast? Are you inclined to be natural and uninhibited – even devil-may-care? Do you have a strong sex-drive? Are you musical – and perhaps especially keen on folk-music and/or country-and-western? Are you convivial, yet at the same time independent-minded? Do you have strong opinions and are you prepared to voice them? Do you enjoy dingy dives, noisy parties and all-night dances? Do you love to be among animals and young children? Are you a natural survivor?

If the answer to most or all of these is 'Yes', Pan is obviously alive and kicking within you.

However, Pan has other, less welcome, aspects – and these, too, need to be considered. Do not be surprised, therefore, if you find the following list of questions increasingly disturbing. If you find your-self angry or affronted at what they seem to imply, that is actually a very healthy and promising reaction, as we shall go on to see.

(b) Rejected aspects

Are you sometimes afraid of the dark? Are you prone to panics, nightmares and/or breathing-problems? Do you have a history of epilepsy? Do you sometimes suspect that you are mentally dis-turbed? Are you liable to go mad – in either sense? Are you in any way deceitful, unreliable and/or inconsistent? Are you constantly restless and unable to settle down? Do you often stay up so late that you have difficulty getting up in the morning? Does bright light bother you, especially in the middle of the day? Are you inclined to 'drop off' at odd moments during the day, and especially after lunch? Do you suffer from migraines?

Do others sometimes look down their noses at you for being devilish, noisy and/or riotous? Do they complain that you are obstinate, irrational, capricious or arbitrary? Have you ever been told that you are unkempt and/or smelly, or that you should wash more often? Are you always flouting the rules and regulations? Are you a secret nudist, or at least unconcerned about the wearing of clothes? Do you constantly feel randy or horny? Are you inclined to auto-eroticism and masturbation? Are you inherently bisexual? Are you ever tempted to violate others sexually? Do those to whom you are attracted tend to avoid you or run away from you?

Once again, most of these 'rejected' aspects of the archetype are potentially fraught with emotion. It would be unusual if some of them at least did not arouse strong reactions within you. At the same time, though, the very strength of those reactions has an extremely helpful function. It suggests that the characteristics to which you are reacting are, potentially at least, *rejected aspects of yourself.* They pertain, in other words, to your own darker aspect, just as they pertain to the darker aspect of Pan himself, and for that reason they are normally hidden from you – however obvious many of them may be to others. Indeed, much the same may even apply to the *positive* aspects listed under (a) above – in which case therapy is doubly urgent. (In practice, this probably means that you are so devoted to **Apollo** or some related god as to be unable for the moment to *ac-knowledge* the presence of any other archetype within yourself, least of all Pan.)

What is important now, therefore, is to learn to *re-cognise* and accept not only the first list of characteristics, but the second list too – for if you are rejecting them you are by definition rejecting large parts of Pan himself.

(c) Total non-recognition and projection

As ever, though, the most dangerous case is possibly where you have failed to identify with – or to react to – the listed characteristics at all. If this was so in your own case, go through the second list especially for a second time now and ask yourself whether you associate the qualities described mainly with *other people.* Do you find people who are unreliable and inconsistent – let alone actually deceitful – hard to tolerate? Do you constantly bemoan other people's unwillingness to settle down to a steady job or routine? Does unruliness and anarchy bother you in others? Do you find children hard to cope with, primarily for this reason? Are you contemptuous of those who stay up half the night at parties and dances and then sleep late into the morning?

Are you enraged by people who are irrational and capricious? Are you quick to condemn cheaters, scroungers and law-breakers? Are you uncomfortable, or even disturbed, in the presence of the mentally ill? Would you rather that they were shut away out of sight? Do you despise nudists? Do you condemn all bisexuals out of hand? Do you dismiss as warped, unnatural and despicable anybody whom you suspect of masturbating? Are you contemptuous – or even fearful – of people who find their sexuality difficult to control? Are you incensed beyond measure that rapists should even be allowed to live?

Once again, there are many who take such attitudes – often for reasons that they regard as perfectly logical, natural and moral. The very strength of feeling with which they do so, however, reveals that the characteristics concerned *are actually part of their own Shadow*. Having rejected those qualities within themselves, they are now (naturally enough) unable to *re-cognise* them there, and so are forced to project them onto other people, where they can now safely go on rejecting and condemning them to their hearts' content.

Which, of course, is a recipe not for healing, but for continued division – whether in the inner or the outer world.

In such cases, then, therapy is especially urgent.

(d) Total acceptance

As ever, this is the ideal. We all need to be able to accept Pan within ourselves not only in his more welcome aspects, but also in his darker manifestations. We need to be able to accept all the characteristics listed, in other words, with easy-going equanimity, *re-cognising* that they are at very least potential or latent within ourselves – even if, as autonomous adults, we choose not to express all of them in practice.

If you can already manage this degree of acceptance, in all probability little in the way of extra therapy is needed beyond what you naturally undertake as part of your normal life-routine. If you cannot do so, though, some kind of deliberate therapy is needed – and the ancient myths can as usual be relied on to suggest suitable measures to take.

2. Invocation

Start, then, in the usual way. Name the ancient goat-god and welcome him unconditionally into your life. Seek out pictures of him. If possible use your holidays to visit any of his caves or grottoes. Most of these – naturally enough – are to be found in wild and out-of-the-way places. On the Greek mainland there is one due east of Glifadha (just south of Athens's eastern airport), and another some miles west of the village of Marathon. A cultic cave on the north face of Athens's acropolis is now unmarked and inaccessible to the public. On the islands, there is a grotto on Thasos, and the ancient underground workings of the Marathi marble quarries on Paros have a carved relief at their entrance which suggests that they, too, were originally dedicated to Pan and his nymphs. Wherever you can find such a site, go inside and try to get the 'feel' of the place – preferably alone and in the dark.

If you have the chance, buy a statuette of him. (Be warned, though – its sexual frankness may shock you.) When you get home, consider setting it up in your bedroom and making a 'shrine' around it. Then meditate before it each morning and evening. Affirm your willingness to accept Pan's animal characteristics in their entirety, both in yourself and in others, and express your refusal henceforth to feel either guilty or ashamed at what in fact are perfectly natural and normal aspects of the Pan who is still alive and kicking in all of us.

Meanwhile, invoking the gods means deliberately giving yourself the chance to encounter their characteristics within yourself (however daunting the prospect may seem) and to recognise them for what they are. As ever, thanks to our *penchant* for projection, this means (among other things) exposing yourself to outer circumstances that reflect them. In Pan's case, these characteristics are primarily his highly physical, animal nature, his sense of fear and panic, his appetite for fun and his reliance on physical touch as his primary tool for learning.

In general, then, your first and most important task has to be to put yourself fully back in touch with nature. Young children who take off their clothes and run around naked in the woods are fulfilling this task to perfection – even to the vague sense of sexual excitement involved, which is of course typical of Pan. As an adult, you may find opportunities for such activities strictly limited, if not entirely lacking. What you *can* do, though, is subject yourself to a kind of land-based Outward Bound course, as already described above in connection with Artemis. This, then, has to be one of your first priorities – and so you should now refer to pages 107 to 112 with a view to taking appropriate action on your own behalf.

In this particular instance, however, you will need to concentrate even more than in the case of Artemis not only on smelling and savouring the plants and herbs around you (the sense of smell is, of all the senses, possibly the most primitive and thus the closest to Pan), but also on observing the animals – and especially the more secretive ones – from as close as you can. This will of course involve you in some pretty stealthy stalking. Deer, foxes, badgers and hedgehogs may well be among your initial quarry. As well as becoming aware of their sometimes literally awesome physical presence, try to sense (perhaps through your own currently inevitable sense of furtiveness) their natural feelings of insecurity and fear – but note at the same time that they seem to be able to turn it on and off in a moment, not letting it interfere with their evident enjoyment of what they are currently doing. If they have young with them, try to absorb some of the latter's sense of physical playfulness, too. Then, as you return to your campsite, see if you can incorporate some of these attitudes into your own way of living and surviving, too.

Naturally, you can see such things even more clearly on television. The fact that millions regularly do so possibly reflects their instinctive need to get in touch with Pan once again. Unfortunately, though, television alone is too remote to mediate the full flavour of the experience. In particular, the latter's physical content is lacking. Pan never could gain satisfaction merely from seeing – which is why taking young children on sightseeing tours by coach is, educationally, worse than useless. They need not only to see, but to hear, touch, taste and smell as well. *Especially* to touch.

Thus, you really need to be in the direct physical presence of the animals concerned to gain the full benefit of the exercise. Now is the time, then, to get your survival gear together and set off on your own Outward Bound expedition in search of them – as well as of yourself. In addition, numerous wildlife holidays exist to cater for your needs, from locally-based nature-rambles to African wildlife safaris. All of them offer you unmissable opportunities to experience the awe, the sense of the sacred, that attends the sheer physical presence of a whole range of wild creatures. And if, despite everything, you do miss them, try contacting your local gamekeeper or (at your own risk!) poacher.

Even then, however, you may not be able to get near enough to touch the animals concerned. High on the hills, the browsing sheep may well succeed in transmitting something of their sense of panic to you as you approach – but actual physical contact is highly unlikely unless you can find one that has become snared in brambles or caught in a wire fence. And so a visit to the zoo, the livestock market or a farm has to be the next item on your agenda. The less domesticated the animals, the better, though. If you can corner a full-grown sheep or goat, grab hold of it and sense the vibrant, animal energy, the instinctive animal force, the almost electric panic that surges through its body from moment to moment. So potent is it that the full-grown animal may well prove too much for you to handle. In this case try something smaller – a lamb or kid, for example.

Almost any semi-wild herbivore can help to put you back in touch with this primal experience. Perhaps that is one reason why city zoos and farms – and specifically ones that permit handling – are felt to be so important to the groups of schoolchildren who regularly visit them. The Pan in children always responds to animals. They are among the first things that they like to draw and model. The wilder and more primitive, the better. Hence, perhaps, the childhood popularity of the reptiles and dinosaurs.

Carnivores, admittedly, can mediate something of the same experience of physicality and animal energy. But the feelings of fear and panic are often absent, at least in the domesticated varieties. Thus, playing with your dog can be highly beneficial to both of you – indeed, it even incorporates a great deal of Pan's sense of physical fun – but always bear in mind that one important element of the jigsaw is missing. Much the same goes for romping with young children.

Nevertheless, by all means do so. For this is the direct human equivalent of the animal Pan-experience, and it is therefore what you will need to adjust to next. Deliberately seek out opportunities, then, for physical human high-jinks. These may occur at the rugby club after the game, in the service mess after – or even during – the social evening, or merely outside the pub after closing time. The rugby match (like its American football equivalent) itself represents a form of high-jinks involving a great deal of bodily contact, if in a rather more controlled context. All physical-contact sports – wrestling included – can be beneficial in this regard. So can many of the so-called 'growth games' promoted by the New Age movement, which tends to place a high value on sheer physical fun.[1] The fact that this latter is generally of a strictly non-competitive nature may appeal to you particularly if the competitive aspect of the various sports mentioned tends to put you off.

Even ordinary parties have their role to play, but here it is the informal, spontaneous, late-night get-together rather than the formalised social event that is likely to bring you the greatest benefits as you continue to seek the inner Pan. Playing the giddy goat is an essential part of the experience. If the activities additionally involve music – and especially live folk-music and uninhibited dancing in dark and dingy cellars and dives – so much the better. Activities involving singing and shouting are especially important.

Pan's original dark and dingy dives, however, were natural caves, grottoes and protective rock overhangs. And so actually sleeping out in such places – possibly as a member of a like-minded group – may

---

[1] See Lefevre, D.N.: Playing for the Fun of It (Element, 1984) and Lewis, HR. & Streitfeld, H.S.: Growth Games (Abacus, 1973).

help to give you some feeling for Pan's fearful, panicky aspect. Inside all may be warmth, light, friendship and human smells – but what, you wonder, can possibly be prowling about in the darkness outside . . . ? Savour the moment, for it is that *frisson*, that shiver running up and down the spine, that finally announces the arrival of the god. In the very instant when the hair rises on the back of your neck, you are in the awesome presence of Pan.

In these and similar ways, then, you can successfully re-invoke Pan and learn to *re-cognise* his presence within you. Indeed, it is literally vital that you should. Otherwise you will be missing out on the whole animal aspect of yourself, and your knowledge of yourself will forever be only partial. Pan is the animal substratum on which virtually the whole of the rest of yourself is based. His death, then, may be the birth of civilisation. But at the same time it can only be the death of you.

3. Meditation

Pan's typical form of meditation, clearly, has to be one that involves the physical instincts, bodily contact and the sense of touch, perhaps with a tinge of fear and/or panic about it, as well as possibly of sexuality. Thus, merely remaining aware of your physical sensations and your gut instincts and emotions during all the activities listed above is, in a very real sense, already a kind of meditation in itself. What is important is to *re-cognise* what is happening to you at these very basic levels – noticing both how it feels and where in your body you are feeling it – and then to accept it fully as your present reality. Finally, go on to express it freely in whatever way seems most natural to you, vocal or otherwise.

And bear in mind that all vocal *ex-pression* necessarily

involves... *breathing*!

Only when you have familiarised yourself somewhat with these possibly less familiar, physical aspects of yourself can the process of intensifying your awareness profitably begin. Only now is it appropriate, in other words, to consider some therapies of a more contemplative type. And prime among these must, as usual, be a consideration of Pan's typical symbols.

The first of these, inevitably, is the goat. But do not merely think about it. Actually go and find one. Observe it in the flesh. See how it moves, eats and reacts to whatever is happening around it. If possible, keep physical hold of it as it does so. Sense directly its instinctive movements, its panic reactions. Then attempt to locate and identify the corresponding reactions within yourself. If it has young kids, carry out the same exercise with them, this time additionally noting their inherent uninhibitedness and playfulness. Can you identify and locate the same tendencies within yourself?

Now repeat the exercise with a friend's pet hare or rabbit, and if possible with a donkey, too. In this last case you will have an even better opportunity to sense its instinctive reactions than with the goat: after all, you can actually sit astride it and attempt to ride it. In each case attempt to identify and locate the animal's reactions within yourself.

Pan's final symbolic creature is the bee. Once again, observe it as it goes about its daily business. Taking due care not to annoy it, see what happens if you get in its way, or attempt to control what it is doing in any way. Can you be as responsive to your gut instincts, as undisturbed by what anybody else expects of you?

Finish your meditation by asking yourself the following questions:

Am I finding sufficient opportunities to express my raw, nervous energy?

Am I finding legitimate contexts for dropping my inhibitions, my moral hang-ups and – where possible – my clothes?

Am I giving myself the chance to exploit my inbuilt survival-instinct – preferably in the wild?

Am I being physical enough?

Am I fully accepting my sex-drive as natural to myself?

Am I allowing myself sufficient social contacts with others of my kind, so that I can express my enthusiasms and my passionate views and opinions?

Am I feeling unnecessarily guilty about living and thinking independently?

Is there enough play, music and dancing in my life?

Ponder on your answers, and consider whether this is the moment to adjust your way of life to reflect them.

4. Remedial activities

On the basis of the myths, there are a number of activities that seem designed positively to encourage you to develop your Pan-like aspects. You may wish to consider adopting some of them, perhaps on a trial basis initially. Several of them pick up on themes that have been mentioned already. Add any favourite activities of your own that seem appropriate and natural to you. For convenience, the activities listed are as usual divided here into two categories:

(a) Recreational and general

Wear rough old clothes or – where appropriate – none at all. Seek solitude. Do your own thing. If you prefer to remain free of marriage-ties, feel free to do so. Give yourself opportunities to live rough, preferably out in the wilds. Become an animal- or bird-watcher. Go camping, hiking and/or caving. Visit naturist camps or communities. Enjoy nude swimming. Seek laughter and relaxation in convivial company. Visit dark dives of every description. Give yourself plenty of opportunities to play the giddy goat. Go all-night dancing. Feel free to be late to bed and late to rise. Insist on afternoon siestas. Be as determinedly chaotic and unpredictable as you like. Resist other people's attempts to control you and tie you down. Take up folk music and traditional wind instruments such as pipe and flute. Keep goats and/or other animals. Read children's books and animal stories. Watch horror movies. Recall and recount your dreams, either to others or in a notebook. Subject to the laws of your society and considerations of medical safety, express yourself sexually in whatever ways you are most comfortable with. And above all, *breathe*!

(b) Professional

Particularly suitable areas for encouraging the development of Pan within you are: farming, herding, work as a zoologist or naturalist, organising wilderness-experience or Outward Bound courses, adventure-training, outdoor-pursuits, exploration, any work involving physical contact with others or with animals . . . and sheer vagrancy.

SUB-PERSONALITIES OF PAN

Pan is primitive by nature – so primitive that he has not yet had a chance to develop any particular 'sub-personalities'. However, please refer to **Dionysus**, who represents the next stage on his journey...

SUMMARY

By learning to know the Pan within, you learn to *re-cognise* another vital aspect of yourself – and in this case an absolutely basic one. Once again, though, the process needs to be carried out in context, so that outer circumstances and inner realities can be brought into living harmony. The result can be a quickening of the life-force within you, a re-*ac-knowledge*-ment of the physical verities of which you are an inescapable function.

The self whom you would know – whatever else it may be – is nothing if not animal. *Re-cognise* that animal, then, and become more truly you.

4

DIONYSUS – THE WAY OF THE ADOLESCENT

In vino veritas
Roman proverb

DIONYSUS is the wild, unrestrained god of sex, drugs and rock 'n roll whom most teenagers unconsciously invoke whenever they 'let their hair down'. Formerly very much restrained and kept under control by Western societies, nowadays he is almost approved of, as incarnated by many a rock group. In the bar and at the football match he equally makes his presence felt, even if this time with less public approval. Re-contacting him is something that most adults need to do, not only in order to put themselves back in touch with their growing children, but in order to re-acquaint themselves with their own deeper selves.

Characteristics of god and host

The turbulent Dionysus is virtually impossible to pin down. Even he himself does not truly know who or what he is. In search of his real identity he is in a constant state of change. Semi-divine, horn-crowned infant of the stamp of Pan, persecuted child, sacred ivy, miraculous vine, subterranean bull, cosseted kid or ram, hunted animal, boy on a dolphin, effeminate youth, lion, panther, powerful magician, bearded sage, mad wanderer, returning king – there is no end to his transformations. He changes and changes again as though his life depended on it. He seems to want to be anybody except who he currently is. This, plus his youthful irrepressibility, is what marks him out above all as the supreme archetype of adolescence. And perhaps it is also why he is pre-eminently the god of *ec-stasy* – literally of 'standing outside oneself', of 'being beside oneself' and thus, by natural extension, of 'being out of one's mind'.

Certainly there can be no doubt that ecstasy is his most characteristic mode of being – that primal ecstasy that every new generation of adolescents discovers for itself as for the first time. Sex to the point of exhaustion; drink and drugs to the point of paralysis and unconsciousness; music and dancing to the point of frenzy and hysteria; meditation to the point of trance; trance to the point of possession; spiritual exaltation to the point of self-mutilation and self-sacrifice. To say nothing of irrepressible high-jinks, coarse humour and manic belly-laughter to the point of paroxysm and convulsions.

For Dionysus *is* irrepressible, as his characteristic symbols make clear. He is above all the erect phallus, symbol of rampant male eroticism, and thus of the irresistible life-force itself. This phallic symbolism is duly reflected in his *thyrsus* – his ivy-wreathed sceptre made out of a fennel-stalk and tipped with a pine-cone. He is also the bubbles in the wine – the *en-thusiasm*, or 'god within' – which will eventually cause the bottle of restraint to explode whenever its top is kept screwed down for too long. Yet at the same time he remains the vine, or ivy, so revealing not only a vigorous impetus to grow and mature, but also a tender, clinging side to his nature.

And true it is that Dionysus has a passionate need for other people. He especially loves the company of his own kind. For that reason he is constantly surrounded, in the myth, by other beings like himself. The *Satyrs*, or *Silenoi*, are wild, randy, almost Pan-like creatures with human bodies, but horns, tails and goats' legs, and a penis in a constant state of erection. The *Maenads* are the female equivalent – wild, screaming females in an almost permanent state of sexual madness and frenzy, who are quite prepared to tear their male sex-objects limb from limb.

And both are in reality Dionysus himself.

At heart, then, he is a sexually ambivalent, even bisexual being. Brought up (in the myth, at least) mainly among women, and for a time actually as a girl, he always retains an effeminate side, however much he may prefer to conceal it. Thus, Dionysus' characteristically exaggerated 'maleness' in adolescence and early adulthood, together with his lack of restraint and apparent 'devil-may-care' exterior, are really an elaborate blind concealing a much more private, sensitive side that he does not care to reveal to the world at large – to say nothing of the *real* 'devil' that lurks all unsuspected within him.

For the Maenads it is above all music and dancing that cause the inhibitions to drop. The throbbing of the drums, the clashing of the cymbals are sufficient to turn them on and impel them to let their hair down. Intoxicated and punch-drunk with sheer noise, they will turn like beasts of prey on their male victim. And that victim is generally Dionysus himself. He it is who is ultimately, like the Hindus' Shiva, the primal lord of the dance. He it is who, in his quest for sexual dominance, sounds the loud mating-call that presages the rut: he sings, plays the flute, beats the drum and sends the sound of the phallic guitar screaming to the rafters. And so it comes about that the would-be hunter becomes the hunted. For as a musician he needs to keep his wits about him, and with his wits about him he finds it far from easy to drop his own inhibitions and join in the wild dance.

If the male Dionysus is truly to be Dionysus, he needs another form of drug. And in his case that drug is primarily alcohol. With its aid he, too, can let go, 'let it all hang out', become the hidden being that he really is inside and so contrive to show himself in his true colours. And seen in the light of pure, unsullied Apollonian reason those colours are rarely pretty ones. No doubt that is why his skin is traditionally seen as being so dark: like **Pan**, he represents the atavistic, even bestial side of human nature that **Apollo** is always so keen to hide and suppress. For the drunken male Dionysus is a veritable animal, a giddy goat, an out-and-out lout, a hooligan, a vandal, a rapist, a looter and even, if the mood takes him, a group-murderer – just as, *en masse*, his female equivalent can be an alley-cat, a slut and a sheer wild beast.

But then that, in effect, is who Dionysus *really* is – even if, thanks to his drunken stupor, he himself remains blissfully unaware of the fact. Indeed, it is part at least of who we all are, did we but know it. It is the infant Pan in all his irrepressible, subhuman wildness, but now in more violent, more aggressive, adolescent guise. More violent and aggressive, possibly, because he has been repressed during the pre-adolescent years. No doubt it is for this very reason that the Maenads now need the music and dancing, and the male Dionysus his drink and other drugs, in order to tear down the arti-ficially imposed barriers of civilised restraint.

There is thus not the slightest difficulty in *re-cognising* Dionysus and his noisy, riotous train in the average adolescent. Teenagers typically are not at all sure who they really are. As yet unfamiliar with their new, adult bodies, they are often unhappy with who they think they may be, chronically dissatisfied with the way they look. As though their lives depended on it, therefore, they keep changing their appearance and are totally blown away by every latest wind of fashion. In many ways uninhibited, they often still lack the self-assurance to express that lack of inhibition openly. Only in the presence of their peers can the barriers eventually be torn down, and then primarily with the aid of music and dancing, drugs and alcohol. At which point all hell is let loose. The all-night rave or rock festival, the drunken binge or alcohol-assisted afternoon at the football-match produce unimaginable scenes of riot, destruction and sheer adolescent madness.

And it is that madness that is the pre-eminent sign of the presence of Dionysus.

Dionysus in myth

As the myth itself suggests, however, Dionysus is by no means all bad news. No more than Pan is he merely the Devil incarnate. As we saw earlier, he is the vine or ivy, and is thus essentially a very clinging being. A vigorous natural climber, he needs a mature tree to attach himself to. Thanks to his largely feminine upbringing, the myth suggests that that tree may well take the form of his grand-mother. Equally, it may take the form of a *Silenus* – an admittedly tipsy and randy, but nevertheless lovable old ass of an academic and/or tutor who is prepared to take him under his wing.

Again, Dionysus has a distinct and growing idealistic side to his nature. He has a highly-developed sense of the mystical. He is responsive to his dreams and intuitions. He is resilient and, as the life-force incarnate, has almost magical powers of self-healing, recuperation and survival. He needs to have – for his role, as is already starting to become apparent, is to act as both priest and offering in the worship of *himself.*

Meanwhile, in his aspect as the wine itself, Dionysus is enthusiasm personified, even if each enthusiasm in turn, in the nature of things, tends to be succeeded in very short order by another. And the very nature of *en-thusiasm* (from Greek *en-theos*) means that he is by definition 'infused with divinity'. (It may be far from irrelevant that wine generally goes with 'spirits', too!) There is, in other words, something truly godlike about him – a divine 'something' which will merely get bottled up inside him if his true nature is repressed, and so will never have the chance of truly *ex-pressing* itself.

In fact, of course, the lid cannot be kept on for ever. As we have seen, Dionysus' *en-thusiasm* – originally the bubbles in the fermenting wine – will eventually burst apart whatever tries to contain it. And that explosion will inevitably mean that the god will not only emerge all at once, but in essentially negative and destructive ways. Possibly that is what has already started to happen in the case of his typical adolescent riotousness and hooliganism. Possibly the fermenting wine has already been kept corked for too long.

Provided that the growing pressure of the wine is constantly given the chance to release itself, however, something quite different happens. The wine quietly matures. Dionysus turns into a rounded adult of outstanding taste and quite resplendent qualities. In the myth, he returns from his wild pilgrimage to India and, finding the stricken Ariadne abandoned by the bull-slaying hero Theseus on the island of Naxos, settles down with her there to a life of indescribable joy and bliss. The revels go on, but now as part of the approved, responsible, established way of doing things. The wildness is institutionalised; humanity's animal nature is accepted as an inseparable part of life.

Dionysus, in short, represents our last chance to accept ourselves as we truly are before the specialised gods, the fixed, unchanging **Apollo**s and **Artemis**es of adulthood, threaten to overwhelm us and take us over. He is our true, over-all self, begging for one last time to be *ac-knowledged*.

The sacred sites

The sacred sites of Dionysus duly reflect various of these aspects of him – and in ways that are, as ever, appropriate to their surroundings. The theatre of Dionysus close beneath the south side of Athens's soaring acropolis was not only the stage on which the plays of Aeschylus, Sophocles, Euripides and Aristophanes were first performed, but also, in its original version, possibly the prototype of all Greek theatres. And its function was at that time purely sacred. What took place within it in those early days, as within all theatres, was in essence a dramatic mystery dance/play/recitation/chant in honour of the god. Only later did more 'arty' Apollonian elements start to enter the *drama* (Greek: 'action'). Their function was to provide an allegorico-tragic counterbalance to its more basic Dionysian elements, which included a fair ration of riotous and highly suggestive slapstick comedy in the form of the so-called 'satyr-plays'. And to this day the *orchestra* of this particular theatre – originally the ritual dancing-floor – is immediately surrounded by the carved, stone thrones of the Dionysian cult's high priest and of other religious and civic dignitaries.

Yet the site still manages to retain an intimate, friendly

atmosphere. It also has an air of innocent, animal enjoyment about it that reflects the drunken – i.e. the *true* – Dionysus' lack of shame about the way he is. It breathes acceptance – the acceptance by a psychologically wise agreed morality that Dionysus, with his reassuring and comforting popular cult of drugs, ecstasy and gross humour, has his rightful place in the scheme of things, that our animal nature deserves to be celebrated just as much as our more civilised, intellectual one, *and that it, too is sacred.* Spirit, in other words, is not to be confined to mere spirituality, to intellectually-sanctioned theology, to the world of pure, Apollonian ideals. It is our inherent birthright. It is immanent in all of nature, and in human nature in particular. Humanity, in other words, is godlike in *all* its aspects.

Yet in life, as in the theatre, Dionysus needs to be counter-balanced. As ever, there is no future in attempting to serve one god in isolation. Our current adult world, for example, is (as we have seen) plainly overbalanced in favour of the restrained, intellectual **Apollo**. But overbalancing in favour of the unrestrained, animal Dionysus is clearly just as dangerous. We can no more afford to be humans who forget our animality than we can afford to be animals who forget our humanity. To attempt either is to be false to ourselves as a whole.

Much the same goes for art without artiness, or ecstasy without true spirituality. Much the same, indeed, goes for Shakespearean history without Shakespearean comedy, for Prince Hal without Falstaff, or even for the spiritual message of Christmas without the uproarious festivities and gross physical self-indulgence that traditionally go with it.

Thus, just as Dionysus' theatre at Delphi counterbalances the overwhelming power of Apollo's lordly sanctuary, so on Dionysus' own island of Naxos Apollo duly keeps careful watch over his uninhibited revels. On the very same offshore islet where Theseus is alleged to have abandoned Ariadne, and the returning Dionysus to have discovered her and made her his queen, the massive west portico of a former temple of Apollo, its axis aligned with the larger island's *kastro*, or citadel, as well as with its central mountain-range, still keeps a beady eye on Dionysus' questionable goings-on – a lonely outpost of Apollonian light, as it would seem, amid a threatening world of dark instincts, murky motives and sheer, black mischief.

At ancient Thera, on the island of Santorini, on the other hand, it is the restrained and restrictive Apollo who is firmly in control. Here, consequently, the base-platform of Dionysus' now only fragmentary temple seems to exude a dark, brooding power as of some barely-repressed force which is only waiting to break out and devastate both the city itself and the Aegean world beyond.

On the sacred isle of Delos things are different yet again. Here it is quite clear that *all* the gods are welcome, even though the island is pre-eminently Apollo's. And so Dionysus' sacred shrine, which has its honoured place in the centre of the city, has a comparatively light and airy feeling about it not dissimilar to that of his theatre in Athens. The two prominent, erect phalluses on their pillars before its west front suggest a total lack of shame, an unquestioning confidence in the acceptance by society at large of Dionysus' rampant teenage sexuality and vigorous natural instincts. On Delos, it is clear, *no* way of knowing is taboo.

And no doubt there is a lesson in that for all of us.

The gnosis of Dionysus

This brings us directly, then, to the specific nature of Dionysus' way of knowing. As in the case of Pan, clearly, direct physical experience lies at the root of it. Touch, taste, sound and smell are very much to the fore. But sight, curiously, seems to be much less prominent than in the case of the sharp-eyed goat-god, almost as though Dionysus were in some sense a *blind* god as well as (as his name originally suggests) a 'lame' one. Certainly, his rages are *blind* rages, his ecstasies *blind* ecstasies. When he is drunk he is *blind* drunk, and when he awakes the following morning he may well have a *blinding* headache. Even as a spiritual seeker, he is *blindly* devoted to his cause or guru. His eyes, like his skin, are dark. He constantly closes them to the way others see him. He is totally unaware of everyday reality as it is. Which is why, when Apollonian society wants to cure him of his madness, it does so most characteristically by trying to *open his eyes to the folly of his ways*.

It is all so much wasted effort, of course. Dionysus does not want to be shown his folly. He wants and needs to *experience* it. And so he once again *turns a blind eye* to Apollo's views.

There is method in his madness, however. Dionysus' 'blindness' is a sign that his gaze is starting to turn inwards (later on we shall be noting the same characteristic in the sage **Tiresias**). Possibly rather more than Pan, he is directly aware of his emotions, conscious of how to stimulate them via the senses. And in this way he is starting to effect – albeit in crude, rudimentary form – some kind of synthesis of conscious and unconscious, some kind of psychic reconciliation. To **Apollo**, of course, all this is necessarily anathema. It represents a threat to his purely head-orientated mode of cognition. And so he will attempt to strangle it at birth. Sex must be controlled, even banned; drink and drugs must be rationed or abolished; loud music must be turned down and crude, popular music refined; meditation must be 'guided' or systematised, trance avoided, possession tarred with the dark brush of the 'occult'; even religious exaltation must be kept firmly under the control of sound theology. And coarse humour and loud belly-laughter must be firmly excluded from polite society.

Only in the matter of idealism does Apollo share in the typical outlook of Dionysus, though even here Apollo's idealism is much more organised, consistent and *willed*. Natural instinct, it is clear, has little or nothing to do with it.

Much the same goes for Dionysus' innate spirituality. Clearly, it is not the same as Apollo's. There is nothing pure or ethereal – still less, organised – about it. It is not remote. It does not involved asceticism or self-denial (even though full-blooded self-commitment and even self-immolation may well play a part in it). For all his passionate escapism, his quest for *ec-stasy*, Dionysus' path is one of immanence rather than transcendence – an all-at-once, down-to-earth spirituality which *real-ises* that spirit and matter were never separate in the first place and which *re-cognises* that heaven and earth are eternally one if only their point of common contact can be discovered.

But then that point of contact was never in doubt. It lies forever within ourselves. And so it is that Dionysus finishes up by worshipping *him-Self*.

Thus it is that, in the course of his quest, Dionysus plunges deep into physicality, plumbs the entire gamut of human emotions from exaltation to darkest despair, sounds the depths of all his instinctive urges without the slightest qualms that doing so might be 'unspiritual', and despite everything that polite Apollonian society may say about it. Reason and sanity have nothing to do with it. Dionysus is quite prepared to go mad.

And we, if we are to learn to share in his *ec-stasy*, need to go mad with him.

But Dionysus, once again, has good cause for this madness. He does not stimulate his emotions purely for emotion's sake. To him they represent a key to eventual escape – not merely from himself, but from the physical limitations and restrictions which prevent him from *real-ising* him-Self. They are paths to ecstasy, routes to nirvana. No wonder, then, that his wanderings eventually take him to India. Not that the ancient subcontinent needs to be taken too literally. Dionysus will head anywhere, set out in any direction to seek his goal, which is essentially *difference*. He wants to be 'somewhere else, man', in some realm far beyond the oppressive confines of Apollo's kingdom. Anywhere, in fact, but here.

And so Dionysus constantly runs away from himself. He is, as we saw earlier, continually 'beside himself', even to the point of 'going out of his mind'. Yet, curiously enough, what he eventually discovers at the end of his long flight from himself is . . . *him-Self.* That same Self to whom his entire self-sacrificial evasion has, in the event, merely turned out to be a protracted form of worship.

He who would save his life, as Jesus himself pointed out, must first be prepared to lose it.

True, it is a long journey, and the young Dionysus is only at the beginning of it. Thus far he only knows where he does *not* want to be. With the aid of his sex and drink, his music and dancing, his meditation and trance, his divine possession, his religious ecstasy and his riotous sense of humour he admittedly has some vague presentiment of what may lie at the end of the road. So, too, may we if we care to join him. But the end of a journey presupposes the journey itself; and the whole of the journey except the last step is spent, by definition, not at the goal but at some relatively unpromising point in between. Dionysus knows this, but does not care. Apollo knows this, too, but is more inclined to use it as a weapon for attacking him. The horned god is a 'lout', a 'hooligan', a 'drop-out'. And so, indeed, he is. But, once again, to treat dropping out as a crime is to suggest that what one drops out of is the only possible way of doing things, the one royal road to personal and communal bliss. Apollo, if he cares to think about it, knows that the suggestion is untrue. Nevertheless he still makes it. Dionysus, for his part, does not know what to think, but merely carries on regardless.

In Dionysus, then, we see aspects of our total knowing that are largely missing and repressed in Apollo, but which still survive to some extent in **Artemis**. These are the **Pan**-like aspects of our childhood selves which adult society is generally so keen to weed and uproot – and if necessary beat – out of us at the earliest opportunity. But what all too easily results, especially during adolescence, is not so much a love of what is imposed as a knowledge that 'this is not where I want to be'. And so in place of Pan's total knowledge of the here-and-now there develops in Dionysus a strangely present sense of the hereafter, a longing for Eternity Now, an unselfconscious and sometimes naïve idealism which may well lead him up some very strange paths indeed.

Yet whereas Apollo's idealism is often dashed by too clear and definite a vision of his goal, together with his very insistence on fulfilling it by purely rational means, that of Dionysus, being less clear-cut and less defined, is less easily disappointed. Somewhere at

---

Dionysus in the modern world

The adolescent idealism of Dionysus has always been recognised by society. From joining the nearest monastery or enlisting as a cadet in the army or navy, ready to be slaughtered on far-flung battlefields, right through to the uninhibited love-festivals of the sixties and the obligatory pilgrimage to India, his myth has always been acted out for real, by Western youth at least. His cult of ecstasy has nowadays become literally the cult of Ecstasy. And now his idealism and taste for self-sacrifice is finding a new outlet in non-Western societies: Muslim youths all across the Middle East are increasingly prepared at the drop of a hat to immolate themselves for the cause in which they believe. Mad it may seem to wiser adult heads, but then that is how Dionysus has always seemed to those who have long since forgotten that they themselves once gave unquestioning allegiance to his sacred myth.

---

the end of the road still lies the rainbow, even if the yellow brick road never quite seems to reach it. And so Dionysus becomes, all unwittingly, the agent of all our spiritual searching, the living symbol of our inner quest. Setting out for the grail, he begins to discover that it is none other than himself. By learning, little by little, what he is not, he eventually comes to know what he is.

The rainbow arches into clear air, then comes back down to earth again.

To the extent that we, too, are *enthusiasts* for any kind of general spiritual quest, then, it is for us to give ourselves opportunities to follow not only in the measured, orderly steps of Apollo, but in the much wilder ones of Dionysus. Allowing ourselves, however briefly, to become adolescents again, we need to play, to sing and dance, to laugh and make merry, to commit ourselves to all manner of exotic meditative and spiritual practices, to intoxicate ourselves with a whole range of unashamedly physical experiences in order to be 'taken out of ourselves'. For, once 'out of the body', we are given a god-sent chance to see ourselves more truly as we are.

The result may well be a let-down. In fact, in the last resort it inevitably will be. But that letting-down is actually a precondition for finding our feet again.

We may not finish up where we think we are going. But we shall certainly finish up where we are.

And the end of all our journeying (to paraphrase Eliot) will be to return to the point where we started, and to know the place for the first time.

VITAL ACTIONS

Getting to know the inner Dionysus means, as ever, getting to know the outer Dionysus as well. Both involve us in rediscovering the adolescent who lies buried in all of us. Just how deeply he is buried will determine the precise extent to which therapy is needed – though, in a highly Apollonian society such as ours, the need is likely to be both considerable and urgent.

As usual, the process needs to start with careful self-assessment and diagnosis.

1. Self-enquiry
Take time out, then, to examine yourself, your attitudes and feelings

from the Dionysian point of view.

(a) Accepted aspects

Are you an active, energetic person? Do you have a sense of humour? Are you an optimist? Do you have a capacity for tenderness and joy? Are you musical? Do you like dancing and pop music? Do you enjoy parties and pop festivals? Are you fond of mass spectator-sports such as football?

Are you fluid and adaptable? Are you an enthusiast for new ideas? Do you follow the latest fashions? Are you fond of animals? Do you relate well to your grandparents, or to an older person outside the family? Are you attractive – and attracted – to the opposite sex, even if not always successful with it? Are you sexually confident? Are you prepared to trust your emotions and intuitions? Are you totally uninhibited? Are you an idealist? Are you interested in spiritual matters, even if not necessarily in established religion?

If the answer to most or all of these is 'Yes', Dionysus is truly alive within you.

However, Dionysus has other, less welcome, aspects – and these, too, need to be considered. Do not be surprised, therefore, if you find the following list of questions increasingly disturbing. If you find yourself angry or affronted at what they seem to imply, that is actually a very healthy and promising reaction, as we shall go on to see.

(b) Rejected aspects

Do those around you keep telling you to shut up and settle down? Are you prone to dream up fanciful schemes that those around you dismiss as pie in the sky? Are you restless, even shifty? Do others see you as unreliable, and as altogether too fond of playing silly pranks? Are you undisciplined, clumsy, irrational and/or untidy? Are you over-excitable – possibly even manic or hysterical at times? Do you suffer from migraines, skin-problems or psychological difficulties? Are you over-confident of your own abilities – possibly dangerously so?

Are you a cult-freak or guru-hunter? Are you over-susceptible to people who are a bad influence on you? Is your behaviour not just uninhibited, but sometimes positively dissolute? Are you addicted to loud music, perhaps with a tendency to impose it on others too? Are you over-fond of the bottle? Are you prone to dabble in drugs? Are you possibly over-sexed? Do you constantly feel randy? Do you flaunt your sexuality as a compensation for inner insecurity and fear of sexual failure? Are your true inclinations (when you think about them) really bisexual or transsexual rather than purely heterosexual? Do you have sado-masochistic tendencies? Are you a secret body-organ fetishist – or even an open one? Do you nevertheless put on a show of conventional butchness, even of male chauvinism? Are you socially disruptive? Are you prone to act as a vandal or hooligan, especially in the mass? When in that frame of mind, are you a positive danger to others who are not involved?

Once again, most of these 'rejected' aspects of the Dionysian archetype are potentially fraught with emotion. It would be unusual if some of them at least did not arouse strong reactions within you. At the same time, though, the very strength of those reactions has an extremely helpful function. It suggests that the characteristics to which you are reacting are in fact *rejected aspects of yourself.* They pertain, in other words, to your own darker aspect, just as they pertain to the darker aspect of Dionysus himself, and for that reason they are normally hidden from you – however obvious they may be to others. (Hence, of course, Dionysus' traditionally dark skin, or 'outer' aspect.) Indeed, much the same may even apply to the *positive* aspects listed under (a) above – in which case therapy is doubly urgent. (In practice, this probably means that you are so devoted to **Apollo** or some related god as to be unable for the moment to *ac-knowledge* the presence of any other archetype within yourself, least of all Dionysus.)

What is important now, therefore, is to learn to *re-cognise* and accept not only the first list of characteristics, but the second list too (whether or not you actually put them into practice) – for if you are rejecting them you are by definition rejecting large parts of Dionysus himself.

(c) Total non-recognition and projection

As ever, though, the most dangerous case is possibly where you have failed to identify with – or to react to – the listed characteristics at all. If this was so in your own case, go through the second list especially for a second time now and ask yourself whether you associate the qualities described mainly with *other people*. Do you find people who are excitable and always on the go difficult to cope with? Are you exasperated by people who are irrational, unreliable, undisciplined and untidy? Are you annoyed by people who are always joking and playing silly pranks?

Are you resentful of those around you whom you suspect of leading dissolute or immoral lives? Are you enraged by people who play loud pop music? Are you contemptuous of those who over-indulge in alcohol or drugs? Are you incensed by those who flaunt their sexuality, and deeply disturbed in the presence of those whom you see as sexual deviants? Would you have them removed from society, imprisoned, even castrated or sterilised? And what of hooligans and vandals? Would you have the authorities seek them out, birch them, imprison them, even string them up?

Once again, there are many who take such attitudes – often for reasons that they regard as perfectly logical, natural and moral. This is because most of them, consciously or otherwise, are devoted disciples of **Apollo** (*q.v.*). The very strength of feeling with which they express such views, however, reveals that the characteristics concerned *are actually part of their own Shadow*. Having rejected those qualities within themselves, they are now (naturally enough) unable to *re-cognise* them there, and so are forced to project them onto other people, where they can now safely go on rejecting and condemning them to their hearts' content.

This, as we saw out earlier, is a recipe not for healing, but for continued division – whether in the inner or the outer world.

In such cases, then, therapy is especially urgent.

(d) Total acceptance

As ever, this is the ideal. We all need to be able to accept Dionysus within ourselves not only in his more welcome aspects, but also in his darker manifestations. We need to be able to accept all the characteristics listed with easy-going equanimity, *re-cognising* that they are at very least potential or latent within ourselves – even if, as autonomous adults, we choose not to express all of them in practice.

If you can already manage this degree of acceptance, in all probability little in the way of extra therapy is needed beyond what you naturally undertake as part of your normal life-routine. If you cannot do so, though, some kind of deliberate therapy is needed – and the ancient myths can as usual be relied on to suggest suitable measures to take.

2. Invocation

Start, then, in the usual way. Name the young, horned god of the vine and welcome him unconditionally into your life. Seek out pictures of him and his Satyrs and Maenads – though be warned, they may shock you by their sexual frankness. If possible, use your holidays to visit his theatres and temples in Athens (just below the south side of the Acropolis), on the isle of Delos, at Delphi, atop the high ridge of Ancient Thera on Santorini (though you may prefer to spare yourself the long climb, whether by taxi from Kamari or on foot from Perissa beach, as only the ruined base is visible – and/or – in Turkey – at Claros, Pergamon and Sigacik; also Dionysus' own island of Naxos (even though no specific Dionysian remains survive there).

If you have the chance, buy a statuette of him. When you get home, consider setting it up in your bedroom and making a 'shrine' around it. Then meditate before it each morning and evening. Affirm your willingness to accept Dionysus' basic characteristics in their entirety, both in yourself and in others, and express your refusal henceforth to feel either guilty or ashamed at what in fact are perfectly natural and normal aspects of the adolescent that is hidden within us all.

Meanwhile, invoking the gods also means deliberately giving yourself the chance to encounter their characteristics within yourself and to recognise them for what they are – and, as ever, thanks to our *penchant* for projection, this means (among other things) exposing yourself to outer circumstances that reflect them. In Dionysus' case, these characteristics are primarily his lack of inhibition (whether sexual or otherwise), his addiction to boisterous group-activities, his natural and infectious idealism and his general quest for ecstasy.

The first of these is in a very real sense the key to all the others. Most of us have long since become so buttoned up and tied down by the strictures and expectations of Apollonian society as to find it remarkably difficult to let go and 'let our hair down' in a way that almost every modern adolescent knows how to do virtually instinctively. Somehow we have to learn to drop our familiar inhibitions – at least when it is appropriate to do so. Yet few of us can do this purely by act of will.

It is no use telling people to *try and* relax. The very trying prevents the relaxation.

And so you may well need to call in any one of a variety of external aids. Many of us do this quite naturally, though for the most part only in certain very specific contexts. When we join any one of a variety of local sporting teams – football, hockey or whatever – we are, in a sense, already invoking Dionysus. Submerging our carefully-preserved personal identities in that of the group – sacrificing ourselves, in other words, to the common ideal – we suddenly find that we have lost many of our inhibitions too. As a result, we discover that we can bring enormous amounts of previously untapped energy to bear on helping to satisfy that ideal. Setting out on our various marauding expeditions to other clubs, we now realise that we are quite prepared to be loud, boisterous, boastful and even loutish in ways that we would be decidedly unhappy with were we still dressed in our city clothes. Especially at major matches, singing and rhythmic chanting are the order of the day. Whether we win or lose, the game gives us an enormous feeling of personal fulfilment – but if we actually win, the resulting experience borders on sheer ecstasy. The subsequent traditional drinking bout merely completes what is, in effect, the modern equivalent of the ancient Dionysian ritual.

Unless you have already done so, then, consider taking up such activities on a regular basis. Try a whole range of them for size. Consider, too, joining any one of a number of New Age personal development groups, where the dropping of personal inhibitions in a safe, group context involving plenty of physical contact and boisterous group fun tends to have much the same liberating and energising effect. One particular experience of this kind – the Experience Week regularly offered by the Findhorn Foundation in Moray, Scotland – is particularly recommended in this connection.

Always bear in mind, however, that the ultimate aim of true Dionysian therapy is *ecstasy* – i.e. 'standing outside yourself' or even 'being beside yourself', and thus, in some sense at least, 'going out of your mind' (if not actually 'going mad' in either sense of the expression). As history repeatedly demonstrates, this is nearly always much easier to do as a member of a group than as an isolated individual. Political or racial group-hysteria can after all lead, as we all know from bitter experience, to whole nations apparently *taking leave of their senses* – which is another perfectly good definition, by the way, of what Dionysus is really about.

And so (always keeping a weather eye out for the obvious dangers) you should now consider letting group-activities generally take up a good deal more of your life than may hitherto have been the case, and especially where they tend to involve the dropping of the 'I', the letting down of hair, the releasing of long-established inhibitions. It is by now traditional for the young to do this with the aid of loud pop music. If you feel able to join them in their pop concerts and rock festivals, then, you should seriously consider doing so. Do not merely listen, though: allow your whole body to move with the music – and, if you cannot, ask yourself why not. If the pop radio stations and record industry can then help you to keep in touch with the feeling of general excitement and uninhibited bodily involvement, by all means enlist their aid.

For girls and young women particularly, insistent, rhythmic music of this kind, especially in a group context, is often sufficient totally to break down the barriers of restraint without the need for any further artificial aids. For Western teenage boys and young men, however, the inhibitions are often harder to uproot – as one might perhaps expect in a predominantly Apollonian society. It is at this point, consequently, that the taking of a variety of foreign, and often noxious, substances starts to play an increasingly important role.

There is, of course, absolutely nothing new in this. Drink was always inseparable from the cult of Dionysus. But it needs to be pointed out that originally the drink in question specifically took the form of *wine*. The carousing did not involve spirits, and beer played a role only in a number of parallel cults in somewhat more northerly societies. Narcotics and hallucinogens, similarly, were not specifically part of the cult, and even if used unofficially (as they undoubtedly were) would by the very nature of the times have been largely limited to relatively dilute, 'soft' plant-drugs.

Thus, though the whole panoply of modern mind-altering drugs might be thought to represent a natural extension of Dionysus' natural alcohol – and indeed, they have long been treated as if they do – neither in their intensity nor in their effects can they be regarded as true tools of Dionysian therapy in the original sense of the term. You would therefore be well advised to stick to simple wine or beer – and even then only if, on the basis of experience, you find that you are unable to 'unwind' without them. Indeed, if you do not already have that experience, it might well be better for your health if you avoided them more or less altogether.

Clearly, with this as with all the other activities listed in this book, you alone must be the judge of what is appropriate for you. Always bear in mind what the true purpose of the exercise is. Dionysus's aim is not to produce artificial mental 'highs' or 'lows', nor yet either to deaden the mind or to induce contrived, chemical hallucinations – even though exalted moods, dreams and visions are very much his province – but simply to release his inhibitions. Once that has been done, the sheer boisterousness of his companions and the magic of the music can normally be relied upon to do the rest.

His aim, after all, was always to be natural, not artificial.

Whether you can successfully relate to all this, however, may well depend on your age. The *older* Dionysus is much less of a disorganised anarchist and noisy lout, and much more of an idealist with spiritual inclinations. If, then, you find this aspect of his character easier to relate to, you should instead seek your therapy in the context of spiritual or religious communities. With their constant singing, dancing, hand-clapping and even virtual spiritual possession, for example, the pentecostal and evangelical churches are positively pervaded by unacknowledged Dionysianism. If you prefer rather more 'fringe' forms of spirituality, all manner of communities and cults from the Findhorn Foundation to the Hare Krishna and Rajneesh movements are equally rife with the spirit of Dionysus, and are capable of mediating it to you in the most vivid ways, both physical and psychological.

Moreover, organisations such as these have the positive advantage that they encourage you to take up Dionysianism as a full-time way of life – which, after all, has to be your aim if you are truly to spend the rest of it *ac-knowledg-ing* your inner Dionysus.

In these and similar ways, then, you can successfully re-invoke Dionysus and learn to *re-cognise* his presence within you. Indeed, it is literally vital that you should, however daunting the prospect may seem. Otherwise you will be ignoring the perpetual adolescent who is hidden deep within you, and your knowledge of yourself will for ever be only partial.

3. Meditation

Merely by 'being fully with' the activities already mentioned you are, of course, already participating in an appropriate form of meditation. True Dionysian meditation, however, is what might be termed 'ecstatic meditation' – or what Christian mystics generally refer to as 'contemplation'. Not only does it contain a strong devotional element. It involves taking some suitable sacred object or icon, immersing yourself fully in its reality and becoming totally one with it.

Which means, of course, that the time has come for you to consider Dionysus' characteristic symbols, remembering especially that Dionysus himself is regarded as *actually taking the form of* many of the creatures concerned.

Thus, if Dionysus can appear as horse, stag, lion or panther, can you release enough of your inhibitions to act with all the devastating animal strength and force that all these animals naturally display? As the familiar boy on a dolphin, can you trust yourself totally to the sea of the unconscious, to your submarine urges, to your hidden instincts and intuitions? As the horned serpent, are you ready to rely on the animal wisdom and native cunning that lies, however unsuspected, beneath your civilised exterior? Can you become both the wine and the drinker, able to become totally intoxicated with your own reality? Even more to the point, are you, as the sacred bull, foal, kid or ram, prepared to sacrifice who you think you may be to who you really are?

Turning to Dionysus' less animate symbols, can you, in your role as a spiritual devotee, be as clinging and as persistent as the ivy? Can you learn to be as firmly rooted in the nether world – the world of dark, ill-understood, vegetative urges – as any tree (try actually meditating with your back against one), and consequently as fruitful in the upper world of sunshine and daylight as the proverbial vine? Can you indeed, as the ripe apple, become fruitfulness itself? Can your flesh, its vital task done, then become as the wood of the yule log, idealistically sacrificing itself on the fire for the birth of a new dispensation? Is that wood prepared to fashion itself into a phallic staff with a pinecone-tip, ready in symbol to propagate itself energetically for the sake of an unknown future? Can it become a toy in the hand of God, a mere dice or ball at the mercy of the infinite, a spinning-top or bull-roarer trustfully allowing itself to be whirled amid the winds of the cosmos in order to give voice to the word of truth?

Are you, in short, prepared to let go?

Do not merely *think* about these things. Seek out their physical presence wherever you can. Use as many as possible of your senses on them. Then allow yourself to *become* them, each in turn. Merge your identity with them. Immerse yourself in their essential reality.

Finish your meditation by asking yourself the following questions:

Am I, as a man, acknowledging sufficiently my hidden, feminine side – or, as a woman, my masculine one?

Am I giving myself sufficient outlets for my enormous energy, sexual or otherwise, without feeling guilty about it?

Am I being sufficiently fluid and adaptable?

Am I managing to express my passionate enthusiasm and my basic humour?

Am I responding sufficiently to the admiration I seem to inspire in people of the opposite sex?

Have I tried sharing my problems with my grandmother, or with a much older academic or tutor of sympathetic disposition?

Am I acknowledging and responding to my natural interest in things spiritual?

Ponder on your answers, and consider whether this is the moment to adjust your way of life to reflect them.

4. Remedial activities

On the basis of the myths, there are a number of activities that seem designed positively to encourage you to develop your Dionysian aspects. You may wish to consider adopting some of them, perhaps on a trial basis initially. Several of them pick up on themes that have been mentioned already. Add any favourite activities of your own that seem appropriate and natural to you. For convenience, the activities listed are as usual divided here into two categories:

(a) Recreational and general
Wear whatever style of clothes is fashionable, or seems to suit you at the moment. Vary your hair-style constantly, as the mood takes

you. Take up dramatics, especially comedy and farce. Explore all kinds of humour. Allow yourself plenty of opportunities to let your hair down and generally behave outrageously. Frequent your local club, bar or pub. Take up a variety of team-sports. Participate in New Age games. Take regular holidays – or, better, irregular ones. Go hiking, camping and mountaineering with your friends. Attend pop festivals, rock concerts, raves, all-night parties and wild beach-barbecues. Let yourself be carried away by the music. Then listen to more of it at home. Subject to the laws of your society and considerations of medical safety, express yourself sexually in any way that seems comfortable to you (Dionysus traditionally favours out-and-out communal sex-orgies, but you will naturally choose what seems right *for you*). Go swimming, surfing and/or sailing, preferably as a member of a group. Undertake communal feats of daring or endurance such as adventure-trips and expeditions. Immerse yourself in computerised 'virtual reality' games. Maintain contact with your grandmother or a sympathetic older tutor-figure. Try a variety of meditation methods and trance-inducing techniques, including music, dancing and specialised forms of breathing. Use alcohol if you are unable to release your inhibitions in any other way – but preferably only in the form of wine or beer, and then only if you are already used to it. Even if you already familiar with the 'softer' plant-drugs, use them only if you absolutely must – and even then at your own risk (bear in mind that, while Dionysus is certainly prone to sacrifice himself to himself, self-destruction cannot possibly serve the long-term interests of the self that it destroys – let alone of the other gods that help to make up that self). Join a variety of Christian sects of a pentecostalist or charismatic nature, or sample various alternative spiritual groups or cults. Visit at least one New Age community, such as Findhorn in Scotland. Go on communal group-pilgrimages to sacred sites such as Chartres, Iona, Glastonbury or Stonehenge, to say nothing of India itself and the great Eastern and Middle-Eastern cult-centres. Seek out the world's most charismatic gurus and throw yourself at their feet. Finally, once you have got it all out of your system, consider settling down and getting married.

(b) Professional

Particularly suitable areas for encouraging the development of Dionysus within you are: exploration, travel, the armed services, marine occupations of all kinds, acting (preferably in comedy or farce), life as a professional comedian, team-sports, energetic physical activities of all kinds, adventure training and, in later life, religion, law, administration and government.

SUB-PERSONALITIES OF DIONYSUS

Dionysus has only a limited number of sub-personalities, but you may still wish to consider their appropriateness to your own case, especially if the above seems a less than perfect 'fit':

CENTAURS = Satyrs (originally)

Possible symptoms

Herd-instinct; group-aggression; mass militancy; mass-hysteria; communal erotic orgies; indiscriminate sexuality; inability to hold drink; drunkenness; vengefulness; vulnerability to Heracles; collective Titanism; possibility (if persisted with) of a long final illness involving pain (e.g. arthritis) or poisoning in the legs

but also

Psychological balance; instinctive healing powers; strength in numbers; military effectiveness; individual wisdom and learning; ability as teachers and instructors.

Therapies

Name, imagine and welcome the wild, animal Centaurs, fabulous creatures that are half-horse (or goat) and half-man, and always on the warpath; imagine, too, their wise old king, Cheiron, with his healing skills and his painful and incurable poisoned knee or left foot, caused by a stray arrow from the bow of Heracles; sexual activities of all kinds; life in the wild; group-hunting (in whatever form); horse-riding; bull-fighting; cattle-herding; military service; individual healing; medical practice; self-sacrifice; alcohol (WARNING: beware of addiction).

Symbols

Horse; hobby-horse; chaplet of grass; darts of fir; the constellation Centaurus.

Notes

The Centaurs are a slightly older version of Dionysus and his Satyrs, with whom they were at one time considered to be virtually identical. Consequently they represent the emergence in the mass of instincts and urges which have long since been repressed by society in the pursuit of civilised living. Rather than drive them underground again, by far the best policy therefore seems to be to provide contexts, especially military ones, in which they can safely be given free rein. However, this approach cannot be applied forever: at some point the fighting has to stop. Soldiering is traditionally an activity for the first half of life, and many a soldier then takes up a second career.

In the particular form of the myth represented by the old healer and Centaur-King, Cheiron, however, it is an incurable illness caused by an accidental wound that eventually calls a halt. He, it seems, has pursued the military path for too long. Yet his suffering at least has the positive aspect that it allows death (see **Zeus** as Hades) to be welcomed as a friend. Or possibly it is Centaurism itself that eventually becomes so painful that it realises that it 'hasn't a leg to stand on', and welcomes its own death for the sake of the posterity of Prometheus, who represents human civilisation itself. (The agonised Cheiron, in the myth, consents to his own death in order that Prometheus may become immortal in his stead.) Which, if so, would suggest that the Centaur syndrome tends in time to disappear of its own accord, provided only that it is allowed to do so. Its obvious Sagittarian symbolism suggests that it may be experienced most acutely in early winter.

Meanwhile, at the individual level, Centaurism also has its immensely positive, direct healing aspect. Soldiers, for obvious reasons, need to learn to cope with wounds. But the more general healing gift (so it seems from the myth) tends to surface at some point *after* the wilder manifestations of group militarism, and at about the same time as the unexpected emergence of a deeper, intuitive wisdom whose presence has hitherto been scarcely suspected. Midlife seems, on the whole, the most likely time for this development. Yet here the image is primarily of the 'wounded healer'. The implication seems to be that any healing undertaken by a 'Centaur' is likely to be at the price of the healer's own health, i.e. as a result of his actually having taken on himself the patient's symptoms. Admirable and self-sacrificial this may be – and an intriguing example of the scapegoat-phenomenon in practice – but it is an initiative that needs to be adopted, if at all, only after the most careful consideration of the likely consequences, lest the healer, too, should eventually discover that he 'hasn't a leg to stand on'.

DIOSCURI = Castor and Polydeuces (Pollux)

Possible symptoms
Cattle-rustling; gangsterism; group-mischief; plotting; dissimulation; ambushes; murder; insults; taunting; danger of sudden death; possible homosexuality

but also
Comradeship; *esprit de corps;* unselfishness; self-sacrifice; forgiveness; courage in combat; military expertise; energy; persistence.

Therapies
Name, imagine and invoke the inseparable and ever-adventurous Heavenly Twins; soldiering; horse training; boxing; athletics; war games; martial music; wearing of helmet; short hair or shaven head; uniform; work as military instructor; coastguard and rescue work; physically demanding activities; challenges of endurance.

Symbols
White lamb; white horse; sparrow; wild pear tree; spear; white tunic; purple cloak; eggshell cap; the constellation Gemini; double

pillars linked by two transverse beams; Roman figure 'II' (the astrological sign for Gemini); double amphorae entwined by two snakes.

Notes

The Heavenly Twins are the spirit of youthful comradeship which, whether by land, sea or air, takes young fighters off to war. Both Castor the horseman and Pollux the infantryman know that the one may live while the other dies, yet both know, too, that the other will willingly give his life for his friend. Deprived of suitably constructive means of expression, however, both are equally liable to turn to other outlets for their urge for shared adventure – from membership of suitably helmeted and uniformed motor-cycle gangs to actual group crime. Whatever the context, their passion is to do or die together. Danger and excitement are their stock-in-trade. And since nothing can quench this youthful enthusiasm, it is largely a matter of luck whether they or the passion die first. Dioscurianism, in short, is an almost inevitable characteristic of young men of martial age, and there is nothing to be done about it but to allow it suitable outlets, ensure that they have good equipment, and trust that their natural instinct for survival will take care of them until they have finally grown out of this phase.

Astrologically, the Heavenly Twins are closely associated with Mercury (i.e. **Hermes**), and their prime time is early summer.

SILENUS

Possible symptoms

Lewdness; randiness; uncontrollable erections; debauchery;

drunkenness; fatness; female characteristics (e.g. women's breasts); laziness; sleepiness; romancing; inability to tell truth from falsehood

but also

Well-integrated personality; lack of inhibition; easy going nature; love of pleasure; musical gifts; abilities as a dancer; good humour; wide experience; general knowledge; raconteur; profound wisdom; prophetic gifts.

Therapies

Name, imagine and welcome the fat, good-natured, tipsy, rumbustious old Satyr and tutor of Dionysus, half-goat (or horse) and half-man; hills and mountains; teaching; music; wild dancing; humour; comedy; fiction; alcohol (WARNING: beware of addiction).

Symbols

Goat; horse; ass; hobby-horse; wreath of ivy, vine or fir.

Notes

For all his dissolute and lazy behaviour, Silenus is in fact the very symbol of the well-adjusted human being. Totally at home both with his animal nature and with his intellectual abilities, he is unfailingly friendly and good-natured. Wherever he finds himself, and in whatever circumstances, he is completely at home. In the academic sphere, he excels without apparently ever doing any work. And while he has his fair share of human weaknessess, notably his continual randiness and his addiction to drink, this mythical Falstaff more than makes up for them with considerable strengths. An ideal companion for the young, whose Dionysiac tendencies he can understand and sympathise with, the knowledgeable Silenus – almost the archetypal university don – is thus hardly a problem at all. It is sufficient to allow opportunities for his positive characteristics to manifest themselves, and he will serve as a valuable, life-long friend.

SUMMARY

Of all the gods, Dionysus is probably one of the most difficult for adult Westerners, with their long Apollonian tradition, to get to know. Apollo and Dionysus were always in competition with each other and, where co-existence proved impossible, arrangements had to be made for one of them to take a holiday every so often in order to allow the other a look in. The lesson is worth bearing in mind. All work and no play does not merely make Jack a dull boy. By robbing him of his inner adolescent it also makes him only half an adult.

Knowing yourself, inevitably, has to mean knowing *all* of yourself. In particular, then, knowing your inner Dionysus is vital if you are truly to come to terms with the adolescent who, contrary to general supposition, did not just disappear in your late teens but is still hidden deep within you, only awaiting his or her chance finally to break out once again. Indeed, he inevitably will, sooner or later – and in uncontrolled form, at that, if you have not by then learned to cope with him and finally made him your friend (see **Hermes**).

5

APHRODITE – THE WAY OF THE LOVER

Love still has something of the sea
From whence his mother rose.
Sir Charles Sedley

APHRODITE is the very embodiment of passionate sexual love, attractiveness and seduction. She haunts most girls at puberty and continues to accompany them until marriage. Through her various masculine counterparts she haunts most boys as well. She is quite literally irresistible – so it ill behoves anybody to resist her when she comes. Co-operation with her, however, is what ensures the survival of the race – and thus the survival of yourself.

Characteristics of goddess and host

Just as Apollo is the sun and Artemis the moon, so Aphrodite ('foam-born') is quintessentially the sea, the source of all life. Out of it she is born, in it she has her infant being, from it she sails enticingly into the world of young women and men alike.

Unlike the two great celestial divinities, however, she is not traditionally the *goddess* of her element. That honour is reserved for powerful, marine deities such as the fishy goddess Thetis, while Poseidon the earth-shaker is its great, presiding lord. They symbolise the whole of it; she one aspect only.

For while Aphrodite has the sea for her symbolic element, her real domain is the kingdom of sexual love – for its part, the source of all *human* life. Which of course means, in time-honoured fashion, that she *is* sexual love.

Sex, then, is the sea: the sea is sex. The link is far from surprising. For the two have been associated with each other since the earliest times. And not least by those who daily ride its waves.

Thus, fishermen traditionally treat their boats, their prime interface with the sea, as lovers. They call them 'she'. By day they care for them, pamper them, adorn them and beautify them. They go out with them all night. And their tiny craft duly respond by bringing them safely home to port again as dawn returns.

And so Aphrodite becomes immemorially associated with Venus, the morning and evening star, which among the Greek islands is never far above the sea, and which either rises from it in the early morning or sinks back into it each evening as darkness draws on. She is, in other words, the true *Stella Maris*, the 'Star of the Sea' after which so many fishing-boats are actually named, if ostensibly in honour of that other vesperal 'Queen of Heaven', the Virgin Mary. (How ironic, then, that the early Christians, with their characteristic fear and even hatred of sexuality, should have identified the literally *aphrodisiac* planet as Lucifer, Lord of Darkness, and thus as the Devil in person!) For fishermen know full well, however unconsciously, that their little barks, their frail cockleshells, are the very vessels of Aphrodite, who is said to have first come ashore among the Greek islands in a cockleshell – or rather a scallop-shell – of her own, far back in the mists of time.

Through the movements of his craft, the mariner can sense and feel the sea in all its moods. To him its movements are not far from being sex itself. It rises and falls, it twists and turns. Even in the Aegean it has its seasons, its high and low tides, be they never so small. At times it rages furiously, at others it lies almost still, scarcely breathing. The sound of its ripples as they kiss the bow can rise from a murmur, through a chuckle, to a licking of the lips and eventually an alternating series of gasps and sighs. Far out on the bosom of the deep, the rounded forms of its swells and billows can seem bewitching, even enticing. Its foaming whitecaps seem to embody primal, living, submarine forces that can scarcely be contained. It can buoy the boatman up or, equally, suck him under. It has both its roaring shallows and its silent, unimaginably profound depths. Yet of the two, curiously, it is the shallows that are most dangerous, while in stormy times the depths are much safer and more reassuring. Yet reaching them demands that the mariner first *get himself into deep water*, and this may involve something of a struggle against the sea itself.

Seen from the shore, equally, the sea rolls and tumbles, advances and withdraws, sends its tongues of white foam spurting up the beach, sucks the unwary back into its enfolding arms. It first repels the swimmer, then welcomes him into its liquid embrace. Intimately it fingers him all over. Then it alternately bears him up and threatens to smother and suffocate him. For a brief while he is living on a knife-edge between joy and terror, between life and death – the 'death' that likewise symbolises the ecstasy of love.

Small wonder, then, that film-makers without number have turned to the breaking sea as a symbol for the sex-act when to represent the latter directly on screen was taboo. The symbolism needed no explanation. It was obvious to everyone.

And so it is, too, where Aphrodite's myth is concerned.

The myth of Aphrodite

The story of Aphrodite's birth comes in various versions. In one she is born from the sea-foam issuing from the severed genitals of her father, the Titan Uranus ('heaven'), when his son Cronus castrates him as he is about to perform his nightly re-insemination of Gaia, the earth. And thereafter the cosmic love-making has to stop.

The advent of sexual love, in other words, marks the final cutting-off of earth from heaven, almost as though sex represents an ecstatic, physical compensation for the loss of some former state of mystical union on the psycho-spiritual level. The primeval Dream

---

Aphrodite the sex-goddess

The modern media make no bones about applying the term 'sex-goddess' to any woman in the public eye who embodies Aphrodite or Venus. Usually the term is applied to female film-stars, particularly of the blonde, blue-eyed kind. Obvious cases in point are Jayne Mansfield and Marilyn Monroe. But the archetype has been very much in evidence all through history, right back to the Greek courtesan Phryne (4th century BC), who actually posed for Apelles' famous painting entitled *Aphrodite Anadyomene* ('Aphrodite Rising from the Sea'). The Venus de Milo is another famous representation of her. Boticelli's even more famous painting *The Birth of Venus* depicts her coming ashore complete with her usual symbols of fair hair, blue eyes and scallop-shell.

Time of autonomous and all-inclusive emotion, intuition and instinct, it seems, has finally come to an end.

Or possibly it is simply that the former, titanic version of the masculine 'tyranny of the spiritual' – i.e. what we earlier identified as the top-heavy, cerebral dominion of **Apollo** – is undermined and brought to an abrupt and far from untimely end by the overpowering advent of the human sex urge. As, indeed, Apollo always fears it will be and experience repeatedly shows that it is.

Other, less allegorically pretentious versions of Aphrodite's birth are more in the nature of simple folk-tales. In one story she is born from a cockle, in another her first lover is one. She subsequently arrives naked in her seashell on the ancient shores first of the isle of Cythera and then of Cyprus, whereupon Eros ('lust') becomes her constant companion. She is variously named Anadyomene, 'the emergent', or Pelagia, 'she of the sea', as well as being identified with Dione, the water-goddess.

At once acknowledged as mistress of all girlish whisperings, of laughter, practical jokes, sexual desire, love and gentleness, she is next clothed in gorgeous red and then brought before the gods. Her impact is devastating. Fair-haired and blue-eyed (i.e. foam-capped and blue-watered), she is, after all, the archetypal sex-goddess – a veritable Marilyn Monroe in antique garb. To a man, therefore (as the entirely inappropriate expression has it), the gods fall for her. And to the end of her days she remains both a charmer and a seducer, not only free with her favours, but a demanding mistress into the bargain.

Fired by the burning arrows of Eros, she herself falls first of all for the youthful Adonis ('Lord' – the Greek version of the Babylonian sun-god Tammuz), a beautiful, innocent youth over whom she constantly quarrels with her apparently older rival, Persephone. But Adonis does not last long. His symbol is the ephemeral pot-garden that is watered once only and then left to die. Perhaps he himself is the flowers that Aphrodite herself loves to grow and care for so tenderly. But she, as the embodiment of the sea-foam, is likewise only a passing phenomenon. True, she bubbles and effervesces, but she is also inherently ephemeral. And so, having loved the young Adonis to death, she quickly moves on.

Her subsequent path, as befits a child of the sea, is a stormy one. She can be ruthless, exploitative, possessive, jealous, greedy, bloody-minded, foul-tempered, depressed, negative, destructive and just plain cruel. Anything is allowed, no holds are barred, where sexual desire and its satisfaction are concerned.

At the same time she can be lovable, irresistible, passionate, devoted, generous and caring. And always she is adorable and beautiful.

If Aphrodite is to be grasped at all, then, she has to be grasped in *all* her manifestations. Sex, like the sea, has to be accepted and coped with in all its infinitely varied moods. It cannot be tamed or ordered. It cannot be fenced in. Even the strongest sea-defences last only a short while before they must be either rebuilt or abandoned to the waves.

Whatever barriers are put in her way, Aphrodite will always find a way around them, however devious, underhand or simply bizarre that way may seem at the time. The sea always wins in the end.

Such, then, has ever been the career of the great love-goddess, as she moves from love to love, from affair to affair, from partner to partner. The process may last for many years. Until in the end she settles (in the myth, at least) for an uneasy marriage with, of all people, the deformed smith-god Hephaestus – the traditional marriage of dazzlingly beautiful woman with distinctly unattractive man – while at the same time carrying on a long-running affair with the altogether more handsome war-god Ares.

Sex-object, floosie, wife and mistress, then, the bejewelled Aphrodite in her characteristic red is the embodiment of sexual love in all its most uninhibited forms. And as the planet (and Roman goddess) Venus she also gives her name to the so-called 'venereal' diseases which, alas, are all too apt to follow in her train.

The gnosis of Aphrodite

With Aphrodite, then, a new form of knowing enters upon the stage of human experience. In the light of **Apollo** we have gained knowledge of the world of the head; in that of **Artemis** knowledge of the realm of the heart, of the emotions, intuitions and instincts. In **Pan** we gain direct, physical knowledge both of ourselves and of the world about us; through the ecstasies of **Dionysus** we start to re-discover our identity in the very act of trying to escape it. And now, in Aphrodite, we know for the first time the joy of self-giving and self-abandonment, in much the same way as the swimmer knows the joy of surrendering his or her body to the sea. But this time it is a self-abandonment not to some numinous and ill-defined unknown, as in the case of Dionysus, but to a known and quite specific *other*.

It is 'knowing' in the full, biblical sense of the term.

Where previously individual experience was all, with communal experience merely roped in to facilitate and intensify it, *mutual* experience is now of the essence. What was formerly two has now become one. 'I' and 'you' have become forever fused. Or so, at least, it seems at the time.

The fact that the personal 'I' is quite likely in due course to re-assert itself on both sides of the equation is neither here nor there. What is important is that fusion has occurred, however briefly. For that one short moment in time the 'I' has given up its 'I'-ness, only to discover that what resulted was not so much its own death as the birth of a new and infinitely more alive 'we'-ness. The puritanical, head-orientated Apollo in us may not survive the encounter, for Aphrodite is by definition *Androphonos*, the man-killer. Yet such 'little deaths', we now start to realise, actually have the effect of granting not only that we may have life, but that we may have it more abundantly.

A mere first step though it may be, the lesson is a literally vital one. In due course it will lead on to other lessons of more enduring import. However unexpectedly, the letting-go of ourselves which Aphrodite induces, the brief descent into coarsest physicality, has opened the door to an even greater and more enduring *as*cent. What puritan Christians may in the past have seen as a descent into hell has merely provided the basis for an ultimately glorious ascent into heaven.

Taking one's feet off the bottom may be a difficult step, but it is the ultimate pre-requisite for finally learning to swim.

Letting go with Aphrodite

Letting go, however, especially of oneself, is an act of supreme generosity. It demands both trust and openness. Perhaps that is why these are the very qualities that seem to emanate not merely from Aphrodite herself, but also from her minuscule but exquisite temple on the sacred isle of Delos. And the way in which its irregular marble blocks have been fitted together seems to be directly expressive of the 'wearing down of rough edges' that all love-partnerships necessarily involve.

Yet there are dangers, too, in being open and generous. Others are all too apt to take advantage of us, not merely for sexual purposes, but in pursuit of sheer personal power. Ares the brutal war-god, consequently, has his due ration of children by Aphrodite. Such are the risks that openness incurs. Nevertheless, there is also an old proverb which runs: 'Nothing venture, nothing gain.' Refusing to give oneself up, certainly, is a recipe for stability, for preserving the *status quo*. But it is also a recipe for *rigor mortis*, for what amounts to a living death. That which is dead cannot be self-aware. And so, if we would be truly alive to ourselves, we need to be open to change, open to the 'other' – and so open, too, to possible abuse.

True self-knowledge, consequently, is simply not available to those who cannot love. Finding ourselves demands that we first lose ourselves. It is only those who are wounded who can become whole.

Such is the brief but literally seminal lesson of Aphrodite. We all need at some stage in our lives to open up our personal frontiers and to dismantle the protective barriers of the 'I' in order to allow in the 'other'. It is only out of that interpenetration that something new can germinate within us – something which previously has never existed, whether within our personal universe or outside it. (Perhaps, indeed, it is the very advent of Aphrodite and the opening up of personal barriers that she represents which will eventually start to teach us that there is ultimately no difference between the two apparently separate universes.) And certainly it is a 'something' in which, with luck, we shall at last be able to *re-cognise* the fruits of our own being.

Aphrodite may not *seem* particularly 'spiritual'. Her

ministrations may seem to have little to do with anything as lofty as the quest for self-knowledge. Yet her advent brings with it the seed of a mysterious new birth. What that seed will grow into we cannot yet imagine. Yet unless we are prepared to take steps to allow her into our lives, the birth can never take place, and we shall forever remain sterile. We shall lack all progeny in which to *see our Selves reflected*.

'Love,' wrote the great Sufi poet and teacher Jalal'uddin Rumi, 'is the astrolabe of heavenly mysteries.' It is also the key to the door of self-knowledge – or at least to that of its ante-room. And it is certainly, in every sense, the sole guarantee of our posterity.

VITAL ACTIONS

Aphrodite, then, is to be encountered above all via the sea and via heterosexual love. To *ac-knowledge* her is to give yourself without reserve to the totally other, and not merely (as in homosexual love) to more of the same or (as in auto-eroticism) to nobody but yourself. Where she is truly present, consequently – in other words, where conditions are truly Aphrodisiac – neither impotence nor frigidity has anywhere to lodge.

As ever, though, the extent of the need for therapy deserves first to be carefully assessed.

1. Self-enquiry

Take time out, then, to examine yourself, your attitudes and feelings from the point of view of Aphrodite.

(a) Accepted aspects

Are you a loving, even passionate person? Are you attractive to others of the opposite sex, both sexually and otherwise? Are you in turn powerfully attracted to them and/or to others like them? Do you have a strong sex-drive?

Are you capable of long-term caring and tenderness? Are you good with children? Do you have a healthy sense of fun and humour? Do you love the summer and the sea? Do you nearly always speak your mind honestly and candidly? Are you spontaneous and original? Do you have a constant longing for the new, whether in relationships or in other contexts?

If the answer to most or all of these is 'Yes', Aphrodite is likely to be alive within you.

However, Aphrodite has other, less welcome, aspects – and these, too, need to be considered. Do not be surprised, therefore, if you find the following list of questions increasingly disturbing. If you find yourself angry or affronted at what they seem to imply, that is actually a very healthy and promising reaction, as we shall go on to see.

(b) Rejected aspects

Are you a flirt? Do older people of the same sex chide you for being youthful, inexperienced and altogether too sexy? Are you sexually rather naïve and unwilling to grow up? Are you easily wounded emotionally? Are you over-concerned with your own appearance? Are you so concerned with staying slim as to be virtually anorexic? Are you often depressed or melancholic? Are you prone to shut yourself up in a dark room at such times?

Are you constantly on the go, even hyperactive? Do you find it difficult to cope with long-term relationships? Are you prone to exploit your sexuality quite ruthlessly to get what you want? Are you prone to jealousy, even a deliberate trouble-maker where other people's relationships are concerned? Are you irrational, negative and sometimes foul-tempered? Are you always changing partners? Are you constantly liable to run off with the latest heart-throb? Are you over-erotic, even promiscuous? Do you nevertheless sometimes wish that you were still a virgin?

Once again, many of these 'rejected' aspects of Aphrodite are potentially fraught with emotion. It would be unusual if some of them at least did not arouse strong reactions within you. At the same time, though, the very strength of those reactions has an extremely helpful function. It suggests that the characteristics to which you are reacting are in fact *rejected aspects of yourself.* They pertain, in other words, to your own darker aspect, just as they pertain to the darker aspect of Aphrodite herself, and for that reason they ar normally hidden from you – however obvious they may be to others. Indeed, much the same may even apply to the *positive* aspects listed under (a) above – in which case therapy is doubly urgent. (In practice, this probably means that you are so devoted to Apollo or some other god as to be unable for the moment to *ac-knowledge* the presence of any other archetype within yourself, least of all Aphrodite.)

What is important now, therefore, is to learn to *re-cognise* and accept not only the first list of characteristics, but the second list too (whether or not you actually put them all into practice) – for if you are rejecting them you are by definition rejecting large parts of Aphrodite herself.

(c) Total non-recognition and projection
As ever, though, the most dangerous case is possibly where you have failed to identify with – or to react to – the listed characteristics at

all. If this was so in your own case, go through the second list especially for a second time now and ask yourself whether you associate
the qualities described mainly with *other people*. Are you disturbed
by people who are not consistent, or who are constantly in search of
the new? Do you despise people who apparently go through partner
after partner without any sense of commitment? Are you surprised
and suspicious when they unaccountably settle down into a long-
term relationship?

Are you contemptuous of people who are always 'tarting themselves up'? Do you suspect them of malingering when they say they
are depressed? Do you despise flirts? Are you incensed by people
who are apparently sex-mad, even nymphomaniac? Do you loathe
and detest those who are openly promiscuous? If somebody suffers
from AIDS or venereal disease, do you take the view that it serves
them right? Do you even secretly gloat about it? Do you resent or
even fear strippers and prostitutes, and wish that a law could be
passed to suppress or even abolish them? Would you exterminate
them on sight if you had your way?

Once again, there are many who take such attitudes – often for
reasons that they regard as perfectly logical, natural and moral. The
very strength of feeling with which they do so, however, reveals that
the characteristics concerned *are actually part of their own Shadow*.
Having rejected those qualities within themselves, they are now
(naturally enough) unable to *re-cognise* them there, and so are forced
to project them onto other people, where they can now safely go on
rejecting and condemning them to their hearts' content.

This, as we saw earlier, is a recipe not for healing, but for
continued division – whether in the inner or the outer world.

In such cases, then, therapy is especially urgent.

(d) Total acceptance

As ever, this is the ideal. We all need to be able to accept Aphrodite within ourselves not only in her more welcome aspects, but also in her darker manifestations. We need to be able to accept all the characteristics listed with easy-going equanimity, *recognising* that they are at very least potential or latent within ourselves – even if, as autonomous people, we choose not to express all of them in practice.

If you can already manage this degree of acceptance, in all probability little in the way of extra therapy is needed beyond what you naturally undertake as part of your normal life-routine. If you cannot do so, though, some kind of deliberate therapy is needed – and the ancient myths can as usual be relied on to suggest suitable measures to take.

2. Invocation

Start, then, in the usual way. Name the young, beautiful, seductive sex-goddess and welcome her unconditionally into your life. Seek out pictures of her (or, failing that, watch plenty of movies featuring Marilyn Monroe and other screen sex-goddesses). If possible use your holidays to visit her temples and sanctuaries on the isle of Delos (not far from Mount Kynthos: best visited from nearby Mykonos), on Rhodes and/or at Aphrodisias in Turkey, as well as on her native island of Cyprus – and especially her beach not far from Paphos. If possible, swim from it.

If you have the chance, buy a statuette of her. When you get home, consider setting it up in your bedroom and making a 'shrine' around it. Alternatively, substitute any small statuette – or even just a picture – of a beautiful, naked, seductive young woman. Then meditate before it each morning and evening. Affirm your willing-ness to accept Aphrodite's basic characteristics in their entirety, both in yourself and in others, and express your refusal henceforth to feel either guilty or ashamed at what in fact are perfectly natural and nor-mal aspects of the loving, sexual being who is latent within us all.

Meanwhile, invoking the gods also means deliberately giving yourself the chance to encounter their characteristics within yourself and to recognise them for what they are – and, as ever, thanks to our *penchant* for projection, this means (among other things) exposing yourself to outer circumstances that reflect them. And so your next task has to be both to renew your acquaintance with the sea and to allow yourself the chance to experience true, sexual love.

As soon as the summer arrives, then, the time will have come to pack your towel and swimming-gear and head for the nearest beach, preferably with at least one companion of the opposite sex (actually, Aphrodite at her most basic prefers to forget the swimming-gear, but this will obviously depend on the circumstances). This could either be during the day, or at night in the context of a beach-barbecue. Swimming and sporting in the waves is, of course, a *sine qua non*. But there is a particular exercise which can help you to invite Aphrodite into your life. Essentially, it involves simply *floating*.

Remembering that at the very basis of Aphrodite's nature is the experience of total self-giving, what you need to do is actually to *give yourself to the sea*. Not to conquer it, nor to resist it, but simply to go along with it. And so, once you have taken a few slow, deep breaths, try letting yourself float face-down in the water with your eyes closed for as long as your breath allows without undue discom-fort. If you have a snorkel, you can prolong the exercise for much longer. Notice the sense of disorientation that quickly sets in as the waves toss you about, turn you around and generally use you as a plaything. To start with there may be a feeling of anxiety, even panic, as you realise that you have lost all sense of where you are. Then, as you relax, you will start to accept that it doesn't *matter* where you are. You are here, now, in the embrace of the sea, and it is comfortable, soothing and relaxing. Enjoy the experience, then, for as long as it lasts – anything up to a minute or so, say, in the first instance. Feel the sea moving you, caressing you, fingering every part of your body. Hand yourself totally over to Aphrodite. Then repeat the exercise as many times as you wish. (A similar, though possibly rather less dynamic, experience is available commercially on dry land, generally via courses in Rebirthing: this involves self-immersion for anything up to a few hours in a womb-like flotation-tank. Participants report powerful recuperative psychological effects.)

Needless to say, you should attempt the exercise described above only if you are a moderately confident swimmer, and even then you should stay well within your depth. It may be advisable, too, to seek local advice on the tidal currents off your particular beach before taking to the water (few people are even aware of the fact that the sea *has* currents!), and in any case to ensure that you are accompanied for safety. Try the exercise only for quite short periods at first. If, on re-surfacing, you find that the depth has increased, this is likely to mean that the tide has started to carry you out to sea – in which case seek another beach, or try the exercise at a different state of the tide. For similar reasons, while the option of trying the exercise on an airbed or in a rubber dinghy *seems* attractive, it is actually highly dangerous, since in this case you are likely to be affected not only by the tidal flow, but by the wind as well (once again, few people are actually aware of wind-direction: often the wind is blowing offshore, even where the waves are still advancing towards the beach). This can carry you a long way out to sea even in a few minutes, as numerous people have discovered to their cost – and the obvious remedy of getting somebody to hang on to a rope attached to your airbed or dinghy clearly defeats the object of this particular exercise.

You can, of course, also practise the exercise while floating on your back, but in this case it is perhaps rather too easy to do it for too long – with the obvious dangers which that can involve – as well as to 'cheat' by opening your eyes and checking on where the sea is taking you. Theoretically it is even possible to fall asleep . . .

Another obvious Aphrodisiac therapy is to go sailing or, better still, to spend a gentle summer afternoon simply drifting just off the beach in a small boat (once again being careful to take full account of tidal streams and offshore winds). If you know an experienced fisherman of other qualified mariner, you could even arrange to spend all night far out at sea. In each case the object is to learn to surrender totally to the situation in which you find yourself, to sense the continual, living movements of the sea and to allow yourself to become one with them.

The sea apart, though, Aphrodite's prime realm is that of heterosexual love, and so encountering her necessarily means exposing yourself to it. Naturally this depends not only on your personal sexual orientation (those who are strongly homosexual, for example, may need to rely on alternatives such as the marine exercises mentioned above, as may those whose orientation is either exclusively auto-erotic or even asexual), but also on the current state of your interpersonal relationships – for sexual violence has nothing whatsoever to do with Aphrodite. Consequently your encounter with her is not something that can easily be planned, as her own nature makes quite clear. Nevertheless, you can hold yourself ready for the opportunity when it comes. And then the time will have come to let go and let yourself melt totally into your partner . . .

Contrary to what Christians in particular have long tended to suppose, heterosexual love and sex in no way constitute a kind of 'fall from grace'. On the contrary, the act of love gives you the chance to *ac-knowledge*, in Aphrodite, what is possibly the most passionate and living aspect of your own being. And, given that it is so basic to *yourself*, it has to offer one route – and a very powerful one, at that – to *your Self*.

Which in turn brings us to the subject of meditation.

3. Meditation

Merely by 'being fully with' the activities already mentioned you are, of course, already participating in a kind of meditation. The 'floating' exercise, for example, involves being fully aware of all the sensations involved – and much the same applies to the sex-act. The object has to be not merely to participate in it, but to become fully aware of everything that is happening to you during the course of it – your physical feelings, your emotions, your culminating ecstasy, and especially your total oneness with your partner during the whole process.

Remember, though, that it is the giving, rather than the taking, that is the ultimate aim of the exercise – the surrender, the self-merging, the giving up of the 'I'. It is for this reason that the sex-act has a long and honoured role in the practice of many of the most ancient religions. Even in the so-called 'religions of the book' – Judaism, Christianity and Islam – ecstatic union with the Beloved is the specific goal of a number of fringe sects, even if that Beloved is exclusively identified with God or the divine, rather than with any human partner. In their ancient Eastern counterparts, too, the concept remains, but here the agent, or catalyst, of the mystical union is often an ordinary human being, often in the form of a guru or spiritual master – even though it is nowadays comparatively rare for actual sexual intercourse to play any role in the process.

Nor is all this entirely illogical, for just as we cannot love other people if we cannot love ourselves, so we cannot possibly love God if we cannot love other people. Theological purists will insist, of course, that spiritual love (Greek *agape*) is quite different from sexual love (Greek *eros*) – as, indeed, one would expect them to claim – but there has to be more than a suspicion that the would-be distinction merely represents a typically Apollonian attempt (or even an Orphic one – see chapter 8) to separate what is essentially inseparable.

It is on the basis of this complex of ideas that the whole oriental concept of *Tantra* seems originally to have been based. Here, contacting the divine is to be achieved not (as in the Vedas and other forms of idealistic, scriptural religion) by 'running away from the dragon', but by confronting it – by directly contacting the deepest aspects of ourselves, and not least our sexuality. The Dionysian therapies outlined in the foregoing chapter may already be seen as a form of Tantra (the concept is of course by no means limited to sexual experience), and much the same clearly applies to those of Aphrodite.

Thus, under the terms of Buddhist Tantra, the object is for the married couple to become not merely physical consorts, but spiritual ones too, each working through every activity – and not only their love-making – to deepen their spiritual awareness and understanding. In Hinduism, similarly, the object is to *re-cognise* and ultimately merge with the divine in the very depths of carnal physicality – and it has to be said that, in this case, some of those depths turn out in practice to be very murky indeed.

Readers seeking further insights into Tantra will find a number of published books devoted either wholly or partly to it. Both Arthur Avalon and Bhagwan Shree Rajneesh have had much to say on the subject. Da Free John's 'Heroic Way', as described in his *Dawn Horse Testament*, represents yet another version of it. The various sexual techniques of Taoist yoga likewise merit serious attention. But one particular sexual technique may perhaps recommend itself to you.

Since the chief object is to become fully aware of the over-whelming sense of union and the total surrender and commitment that are involved, the technique in question consists in prolonging coitus so as to extend your opportunity for letting that awareness grow. The result is the so-called 'valley orgasm', in which both partners move and stimulate each other only sufficiently to maintain full penetration, while putting off the climax for as long as possible, if not altogether. In practice this form of coitus can sometimes last literally for hours. A variety of techniques can assist in this, many of them fully described in the available Tantric and yogic literature. Whereupon a kind of shared meditation has a chance to develop – one that truly deserves the name of 'communion'. It involves becoming totally sensitive to each other's needs from moment to moment, and so entering a state of physical and emotional oneness that is virtually unknown in other areas of human experience.

Perhaps it is no accident that the word 'communion', with all its connotations of interpenetration and shared physicality, likewise has its honoured place in the vocabulary of established religion . . .

Meanwhile, more purely contemplative activities also have a role to play in the meditation of Aphrodite. Which means, of course, that the time has come to consider her characteristic symbols.

As might be expected, these include a fair ration of marine creatures. The fish and the dolphin both invite you to consider whether you have yet learnt to feel totally at home in the ocean of your sexuality. The mussel, cockle and scallop-shell ask you whether you are fully attuned to its tides and seasons, and prepared to accept being alternately left high and dry and plunged deep into its raging waters. The shells of all three, too, challenge you to set sail in your frail craft on its stormy billows and trust yourself to its unfathomable deeps. And all three demand that you use your sexuality to seek the precious pearl of your own reality that lies hidden deep within all these experiences.

Turn now to the swan. Are you truly at home in your watery element, serene and beautiful in your sexuality, yet at the same time prepared to leave sexuality behind from time to time and take wing into the clear air and the sunlight? Are you prepared, with the humble frog, to emerge from the waters and set out across the dry land, confident that you can return just as soon as your partner – any partner – calls? Are you prepared to become one of a pair of proverbial cooing doves, always prepared to take wing, yet knowing full well that you can return to your love-nest with unerring accuracy just as soon as the occasion demands it? Can you become at home almost anywhere like the sparrow, and self-assured in your sexuality like the roving buck? Are you prepared, like the ephemeral rose, to flaunt all your beauty and allure, knowing full well that neither can last for ever? Red as the seeds of the pomegranate though your love may be

– to say nothing of the red, red rose – can you also be cool and changeable like the planet Venus itself, as well as prepared like her to take full advantage of the late evening and the last hours of the night? And what of the oak, the myrtle, the cypress, all with their roots planted firmly in the earth – do they, too, have anything to say to you?

Such questions are not, of course, for answering. They are merely for asking, then immersing yourself in the natures of the entities involved. Seek out their physical presence. Use as many as possible of your senses on them. The more you can become one with them, the more the answers will emerge of their own accord – and even then only when you stop thinking about them. Sleep on them, then.

Meanwhile, finish your meditation by asking yourself the following questions. This time attempt to answer them too:

Am I finding sufficient opportunities to express my sense of fun and humour?

Am I allowing myself to be the loving and caring person that I truly am?

Am I expressing my passion fully enough to my current partner?

Am I being open and generous to all, and yet at the same time devoted to the person I love?

Am I making the best use of my physical and sexual attractiveness?

Am I giving myself the chance to get to know a whole variety of people of the opposite sex, and so of gaining more mature judgement in matters of love?

Am I leaving sufficiently open the option of parenthood, and making full use of my natural skills with young children?

Ponder on your answers, and consider whether this is the moment to adjust your way of life to reflect them.

4. Remedial activities

On the basis of the myths, there are a number of activities that seem designed positively to encourage you to develop your Aphrodisiac aspects. You may wish to consider adopting some of them, perhaps on a trial basis initially. Several of them pick up on themes that have been mentioned already. Add any favourite activities of your own that seem appropriate and natural to you. For convenience, the activities listed are as usual divided here into two categories:

(a) Recreational and general

Wear fashionable clothes (preferably red) and expensive jewellery (preferably gold). Use perfumes and/or after-shaves at will. Invest in make-up and/or expensive hair-styling. Take time to admire yourself in the mirror. Luxuriate in warm, leisurely baths and gentle massages. Seek out suitable opportunities to practise nudity and naturism as the fancy takes you. Enjoy sea-bathing and boating. Collect and eat seafood. Indulge in humour of all kinds, as well as a variety of teases and hoaxes – including friendly strip-teases where appropriate. Before settling down and having children, gain experience with a number of partners. Study love-making skills. Enjoy suitably protected sex, especially at midsummer. Experiment with a range of aphrodisiacs. Listen to love-songs and romantic music generally. Beautify your home. Indulge yourself with home comforts. Take up gardening, and especially flower-growing (annuals for preference). Keep pets, especially soft, cuddly, gentle ones.

(b) Professional

Particularly suitable areas for encouraging the development of Aphrodite within you are: child-care, work with animals, modelling, acting, show-business generally, gardening, flower-selling, interior design, sex-counselling . . . and becoming a full-time life- or marriage-partner! (Other traditional areas of employment which accord fully with the archetype, but are not necessarily by any means attractive to everybody, are participation in strip-shows and prostitution.)

SUB-PERSONALITIES OF APHRODITE

Aphrodite has only a limited number of sub-personalities, but you may still wish to consider their appropriateness to your own case, especially if the above seems a less than perfect 'fit':

ADONIS

Possible symptoms

Retarded or long-unexpressed sexuality; sexual naïveté; over-susceptibility to erotic advances (especially by older women or mother-figures); resulting proneness to emotional wounding; immaturity; inability to develop lasting relationships; hyperactivity; manic depression; unwillingness to grow up (the 'Peter Pan' or *puer aeternus* syndrome); vulnerability to the predatory female (see **Artemis**) and to the lure of combat (Ares)

but also

Adolescent beauty; sexual innocence; prolonged youthfulness; capacity for constant change; taste for activity; enthusiasm for the new; refusal to accept old, rigid dogmas.

Therapies

Name, imagine and welcome the exquisitely-proportioned young god who so symbolises male beauty and desirability in the eyes of women that they feel driven to sacrifice their femininity to him, yet who at the same time is all too liable to fall foul both of the predatory type of woman and of the martial instinct; self-involvement in a variety of sexual relationships involving both extraverted and introverted (and possibly older) women; non-sexual interests, and especially aggressively masculine activities; myrrh (consult a reputable herbalist).

Symbols

Dove; fish; myrrh tree; red anemone; red rose; pomegranate; ephemeral pot-gardens containing seed that is watered once only.

Notes

The young and beautiful Adonis – one of a number of Middle Eastern corn-gods who die and rise again each Easter – comes to most males at about the age of puberty. Whether he is to be welcomed or helped on his way is a matter for personal choice. Society needs its share of Adonis types. Yet maturity is the natural aim of each individual, and it cannot be achieved while Adonis remains in control. Provided that he is kept in balance, the normal maturing process will eventually leave him behind.

Normally speaking, the seductive Aphrodite can be trusted to spark this process off – though the initial relationship is likely to be a dark and secret one. It is a truly initiatory encounter with Persephone (see under **Artemis**), however, that is most likely finally to take the lid off Adonis's adolescent sexuality. True, his subsequent path is unlikely to be a smooth one. It is almost bound to be marked by emotional ups and downs, rivalries, conflicts and even mortal hatreds. Taken too seriously, these could even destroy him. If, consequently, he is to attain full maturity, he will need to learn to take the rough with the smooth, and to realise that adult married life can never be all sweetness and light. Nevertheless, all the while the archetype remains prominent, spring and summer will tend to be joyful, heady times, full of warmth and passionate love.

EROS = Cupid

Possible symptoms
Lust; inflamed passions; auto-eroticism (see Narcissus, under **Apollo**); bisexuality or transexuality; incest; wildness; ungovernability; irresponsibility; immaturity; loud voice; cruelty; cunning; cheating; dishonesty; inability to hang on to wealth or property; seduction by mere glitter; fire-raising

but also
Energy; sexual potency; sexual attractiveness; creativity; spirit of self-sacrifice; idealism; wisdom; ardent love; ability to 'live lightly'; resonant voice.

Therapies
Name, imagine and welcome the young god of primal sexual desire in all his winged, but self-willed beauty, the son (and thus younger version) of Aphrodite; sex; seduction; matchmaking; nocturnal wandering; sleeping out; hunting (in whatever form); activities

involving the making and feeding of fire; late-night barbecues; torchbearing; flowers; beautiful surroundings; idealistic and self-sacrificial initiatives; magic; pursuit of wisdom and truth.

Symbols

Rose; bull; ram; goat; lion; hare; cock; serpent; bee; goose; dolphin; cuttlefish; phallus; torch; bow and arrow; whip; axe.

Notes

Eros personifies most of the bitter-sweet hallmarks of newly discovered adolescent sexuality and physical maturity in both sexes. In him, too, emerge all those aspects of the psyche which were hidden during childhood. Yet these emerge only because they need to emerge, and so Eros must simply be put up with until he grows up a little more. Human development is not to be hurried, much as we may wish it otherwise. Nor, in the case of Eros, does it need to be, for he carries within him enormous potential for future development.

SUMMARY

To deny the presence of Aphrodite within yourself is to deny one of the most basic urges which go to make up our human nature. *Ac-knowledg-ing* her presence within us is therefore vital if we are ever to *get to know our selves*.

Learning to surrender to love in all its aspects is an essential prerequisite for learning to love ourselves. What we hate, we push far from us. What we love, we draw close to our hearts. It follows, therefore, that we cannot truly know if we cannot truly love. This is a lesson which, as we shall see, even the sage **Tiresias** has eventually to learn to his cost.

6

GAIA – THE WAY OF THE MOTHER

All women become like their mothers. That is their tragedy.
No man does. That's his.
Oscar Wilde: 'The Importance of Being Earnest'

GAIA is Mother Earth herself and every woman who embodies her. Round, maternal, ever-giving, she is also quick to take when taking is due. The goddess above all of motherhood, she is strongly present in all of us wherever the basics of existence and survival are at stake. Without the earth, we cannot survive: without Gaia, we are lost and orphaned.

Characteristics of goddess and host

For a man, the act of love tends to be a mere passing phenomenon. As far as the Greek myths are concerned, the successful father is typically one who sires his children, then moves on. At best he maintains a benevolent watching brief over his children, and then for the most part only at adolescence. Even **Zeus**, the Olympian father *par excellence*, prefers to stay aloof from family affairs.

In apparent reflection of this, his sanctuaries are often sited in remote caves or on far-flung mountain-tops, or are in other ways far removed from the centre of things, whether sacred or profane.

Embodiments of the Earth Mother

In the nature of things, history takes little account of mothers or mother-figures. Usually it is much more concerned with wielders of power in the world at large. Even in its best-known form – that of the Virgin Mary – the archetype has become strangely mutilated and corrupted. However, you have only to visit the local supermarket to see the archetype of the Earth Mother displayed in all its glory, in the form of the harassed mum doing her daily shopping. Politically incorrect though it may be to mention the typical 'fat lady' (hence the lack of publicity), it is by her that the archetype is best displayed in all her glory.

Whatever the validity or otherwise of the ancient Greek picture of things, once thing is certain. For a woman, things are very different. For her, the act of love is no mere rite of self-expression, but (consciously or otherwise) an act of commitment. Before it intervenes in her life, she is a unique, Artemisian being, an independent creature of spontaneous emotion and instinct, a wilful individual who places her own needs and whims before anything else. As soon as she takes the highly adventurous, even risky step of putting on the red mantle of **Aphrodite** and opening herself up fully to a man, however, motherhood is quite likely to ensue. And *mothering* has always meant something very different from *fathering*.

From that moment, in fact, everything is changed.

Suddenly she is two beings. On the one hand she is still a woman – one who retains all the atavistic needs and primal feminine impulses of the highly independent **Artemis**. On the other hand, she now has another role entirely – one in which she takes responsibility not only for her own being, but for another life, too.

That role is that of the mother. And the traditional archetype of motherhood is Gaia, the Earth Mother.

The symbolism of Gaia

Gaia is, quite simply, Mother Earth. And so, just as **Apollo** reflects the sun, **Artemis** the moon and **Aphrodite** the sea, Gaia in turn embodies Earth herself in all her aspects.

Earth is solid, reliable, generous and ever-welcoming. She is broad and rounded, too, and in constant relationship with sun and moon, air and sky and sea. She is self-evidently bi-polar, too. Narrow and specialised, consequently, she emphatically is not.

Ever clothed in blues and greens, to say nothing of browns and occasional whites, she rewards the farmer's care and toil with over-flowing abundance, and just as freely withholds her favours from those who neglect or abuse her. At times she is cold, at others infectiously – even unbearably – warm. She positively overflows with life. From birth to death she miraculously supports and feeds her human children. Indeed, it is through them that she constantly extends her livingness, for they are her eyes and ears, her hands and feet. They are her very organs of consciousness.

So it is, then, that Earth lives *through* her children. Far from merely living, as does Aphrodite, *in symbiosis with* the 'other', she actually puts her children first.

At the same time, however, Earth is fully aware that what her children want is not necessarily what they need. Putting her children first does not necessarily mean sacrificing herself to their every whim. If, out of sheer temporary expediency, they choose to poison her, she in turn will poison them, for she is their source of food. If they suffocate her, she will reciprocate, for she is the source of the air they breathe. Prepared though she is to put them first, she knows full well that, if they are to survive to full maturity, then *she* must initially survive too, and that their survival must therefore be a direct function of hers.

In short, she is totally attached to her children in the most literal sense. So much so that she is liable to be deeply possessive and jealous of them. She simply will not let them go. Given half a chance, she will keep them chained to her for life. Even if they insist on taking wing, she will continue to ensure that they always come back down to Earth again – with a considerable bump, if necessary. Even space-flight itself has not yet managed to change this basic situation.

And if they will not come back alive, then they must come back dead.

It may at first sight seem extraordinary that Earth is quite prepared to kill her own children. Yet the fact remains that, ultimately, she always does. Indeed, having killed them, she will go even further and *eat* them. However anxious they may be to live for ever, she is perfectly well aware that physical immortality would be neither in their best interest nor in hers. And so she duly commits them to the grave, taking them back into her own body in prospect of yet further human generations, yet further life to come.

The whole idea may seem barbaric and uncivilised, a relic from some remote, cannibalistic past. Yet the fact remains that that is the way the Earth Mother is and always has been – whence, possibly, that self-same cannibalistic past in the first place.

And so Earth is not merely a goddess of life, but of death, too. She has both her bright, daytime aspect and her dark, night-time aspect. Moreover, while these two aspects will normally alternate on a fairly regular and predictable basis, there is also a sense in which both operate simultaneously. In consequence, Earth's darker side is in some sense *always* present, and is therefore liable to strike the unwary at totally unpredictable and unexpected moments.

Thus, she is not merely a goddess of Earth's upper regions, but at heart a powerful underworld deity, too, always present and waiting beneath the surface. She harbours deep caverns containing fearful, unknown monsters of the night. And when she is ready to give birth to new dispensations of consciousness entirely, her violent spasms and contortions will cheerfully destroy the old ones in a trice and lay all their achievements in the dust.

Earth, then, is both a potential saviour and a lurking terror, a goddess and a demon, and on any given day nobody can be quite sure which it will be. In effect, she remains at heart an upredictable Artemisian creature of mood and deeply veiled instinct, much as we suggested earlier. (The point is an apt one, for the physical Earth, no less than the sea, experiences distinct lunar tides.) And however much we may wish it otherwise, she always wins in the end.

Gaia in myth

We need only to turn to the ancient myth of Gaia herself to verify this over-all picture. Inseminated by the sweet rain of Uranus (the sky), she first gives birth to the ancient Giants and Titans, to hell itself and to all that is unholy. Rebelling against the repressive tyranny of Uranus, she then incites her youngest son Cronus to castrate his heavenly father in the very act of re-inseminating her. Thereafter, with Cronus and, later, **Zeus** in control – and after siding with the Giants in their war against the latter sons of Heaven – she retires somewhat into the background, more or less restricting her activities to the uttering of dark threats and prophecies of things to come.

Clearly, then, she is not at all enamoured of male domination, especially when it is coloured by a heavenly, and thus other-worldly outlook. She is nothing if not down-to-Earth. Nor is this very surprising, for she is by definition *meter* (Greek: 'mother' – or, in Latin, *mater*), and to her it is therefore the here-and-now, the nitty-gritty of the *mater*-ial world which is the real, if not the only thing that *matters*.

And so she is characteristically crude and coarse – at least by Apollo's somewhat refined standards – as well as totally humble and genuine. At Olympia, the remarkably small *Metroön* (or temple of the Great Mother, whose cult was in ancient Greece more or less inseparable from the Earth Mother's) duly reflects these characteristics in its coarse stonework and generally unpretentious air. She is unashamedly materialistic, too, as well as acquisitive, immensely fat, quick-tempered and vengeful. At the same time she is the very embodiment of fertility, of healing, regeneration and protection. And in addition she is extremely instinctive, with a highly developed gift (as befits a mother) for anticipation and prediction on her children's behalf. Whence, of course, her former oracle at Delphi, where the duty-priestess regularly offered divinations for the children of men, allegedly under the influence of vapours issuing from deep within the Earth.

We should not assume, however, that the early fading of the Earth Mother from the mythical canon means that she ceases thereafter to be active in human affairs. She fades from the picture only because her myth is an extremely ancient one, and has in time been superseded by others that are equally maternal.

Prime among these is that of Demeter, whose name incorporates not only the word *Da* – a primitive name for Gaia herself – but the word *meter* ('mother'), too. Her myth, like Gaia's, is a very ancient one, and so comes down to us in a variety of guises. Yet what is clear from all of them is that, in Demeter, the primal Earth Mother who is Gaia still survives, retaining both her life-giving and her deathly aspects, though now identified primarily by her role as giver and withholder of the crops.

For Demeter is above all a corn-goddess. Indeed, she will later become the Romans' Ceres, who still gives her name to our *cereals* even today. And she has a triple identity and role.

Demeter's mysteries at the sacred sanctuary of Eleusis, just west of Athens, were consequently dedicated to celebrating her in all three roles. First, as Demeter the mature mother, the ripe ear of corn ready to give birth to a new generation; second, as Persephone (see under **Artemis**) or Kore ('maiden'), her nubile but as-yet innocent daughter, who is the new seed that must be lost and buried in the earth before it can rot and then sprout anew; and third, as Hecate, the grandmotherly crone and witch who presides over the whole process by virtue of the fact that she has seen – and been – it all before, and so knows all the secrets of the generative process from the inside. In her time, after all, she has been daughter, mother *and* grandmother, and so represents three generations rolled into one.

Yet Hecate, goddess of witches, is, as we saw earlier, merely the occult, underworld aspect of **Artemis** herself – a fact which confirms mythologically that Artemis, too, continues to lie hidden not far beneath the maternal surface, no less than within the maiden. It is the mother in Demeter, in other words, who must do the mothering, but the essential woman in her remains no less a woman than before.

The mysteries of Eleusis

The Eleusinian myth duly sums up the over-all process in the celebrated story of the rape of Persephone. While innocently gathering flowers (the flower being, of course, the natural precursor of the seed) she is snatched away – with the active connivance of the Earth Mother herself, and within earshot of Hecate, who does nothing whatever to save her – by Hades (see under **Zeus**), who is both Death and Underworld combined. The distraught Demeter searches high and low for her daughter, but cannot find her. After a period of panic and intense grief (including some time acting as an extraordinarily incompetent wet-nurse to the local palace) news comes to her that her daughter is in the underworld with Hades. The great Corn Goddess now withholds all crops from the earth until she manages, with Hecate's help, to force **Zeus** into ordering a compromise. In future Persephone will spend three months of each year in the underworld as the wife and queen of Hades (i.e. Death) – and thus as Queen of the Dead – and the rest of it in the surface world with Demeter. Honour having been duly satisfied, the crops are restored, and the skills of agriculture are promulgated to humanity.

The story is not difficult to decode. Demeter, as we noted earlier, is the ear of corn, and Persephone the new seed that falls to the ground. The latter's rape and subsequent spell with Hades in the underworld – in due course turned into an annual, three-month event – is the time spent by the seed buried in the earth (and thus, be it noted, *within Demeter herself in her Gaian role*). This is of course the regular winter which the very nature of Earth herself predicates, and during which the world is barren, just as Demeter herself is as it were 'without child'. Then comes spring, and the seed sprouts and grows anew in the rotting compost of the previous year's growth until it regenerates the original ear of corn – and thus produces not only an analogue of the original seed, but a whole host of others besides.

Thus, through her experience of motherhood, not only does Demeter discover 'out there' what was formerly lost to sight *and hidden within her*, but it actually turns out to be her own essence, her Self, her very life – a life, moreover, that she will henceforth live even more abundantly than before.

And so the world is restored to rights, and agricultural plenty returns.

As for Hecate, she in a sense embodies the whole magical process. She, after all, has a foot in both worlds and so, as the third aspect of Demeter, is in a position to regulate and oversee it. To this extent she may thus be regarded as the darker aspect of the Earth Mother herself – as, indeed, with Demeter, too, being merely the Earth Mother's *alter ego*, she inevitably has to be.

This, then, was the myth that was celebrated at Eleusis, and because of its obvious allegorical and mystical relevance to human life itself, it was in due course turned into a vehicle of revelation and initiation for the thousands of pilgrims who annually flocked there to witness and participate in its ritual.

After an initial procession from Athens along the still partially surviving Sacred Way, and various rites of ablution and purification on the nearby seashore, the so-called Greater Mysteries were celebrated in the initiation-hall, or Telesterion, a vast structure which (in its final rebuilding) had no windows apart from a central lantern in a roof supported by forty-two internal columns, and which could hold no less than three thousand participants.

Precisely what went on there amid the semi-darkness is unknown to this day, for it was kept secret upon pain of death. But what *is* known is that the central mystery revolved around the displaying of a single ear of corn and the enactment of the miraculous birth of a divine child known as *Brimos*. Moreover, the child was regarded as Demeter's own. In this infant, it seems, Demeter had not only re-discovered the child that she had lost, but also, in some strange, mystical sense, her own reborn self, too – for at this stage in the proceedings she herself was actually re-named *Brimo*. And the mysteries concluded with the ritual pouring of the revivifying waters of life to west and east, the symbolic directions of death and of rebirth.

The mysteries were not, however, a celebration of reincarnation, as is sometimes assumed, for this was a doctrine peculiar to the Orphics and Pythagoreans, and had no place at Eleusis. What the participants gained from the Eleusinian experience was a sense of belonging and continuity, of personal significance within the cosmic scheme of things, of self-identification with past and future, and thus of new and shining hope. Life was no longer just a single, brief expe-rience, a lone, bright candle amid the encircling night. It was a vital part of an over-all, never-ending process, with death merely the sym-bol and guarantee of yet further life to come. In the generations of the future all would have their guaranteed posterity. *In their children they themselves would live.* Each mother was the embodiment of her own mother before her, and her daughter would herself be her own mortal extension, and a mother in her turn. Womb within womb within womb. The process would go on for as long as seedtime and harvest remained.

But for this to happen, death was itself a vital precondition. The mature corn must die in order to form the compost for the next year's seed. Each generation in turn must learn to lose itself in order to find itself, each mother die to her children in order that, through her children, she might live. Only if each generation of children were 'given up for lost', and thus allowed to be itself, could that self which was essentially the parents' own Self finally come to fruition.

The mystery is not confined to mothers alone, nor even to the female sex. We each of us need to discover the 'mother' within ourselves, for we each of us have children of our own. They are our thoughts and deeds, the consequences of our acts, our contribution to the world we leave behind us. Though we die – indeed *because* we die – through them we live, by them we are *re-cognised* and have our being, in them we eventually find ourselves. Not just now, but forever.

The self-same mystery was in due course to reappear even within Christianity, so that Jesus of Nazareth could himself be recorded as saying, in the admittedly Greek-influenced Fourth Gospel, 'A grain of wheat remains but a single grain unless it falls into the earth and dies. But if it dies it bears abundant fruit.' And he then proceeded, if the accounts be believed, to live out the mystery in actual flesh and blood.

Death, then, is very much bound up with the universal theme of the mother, and especially with the myth of Demeter. Motherhood is birth, life and death rolled together in one. To ignore the death-aspect of motherhood is therefore to mutilate and do violence to it. Under the aegis of Hecate, the mother must be prepared to kill as well to give birth, symbolically to eat her children as well as to suckle them.

And then she herself must be prepared to die in order that they may have life and she, through them, her posterity.

And so to this day the grotto of Hades lours darkly over the Sacred Way leading to the Eleusinian sanctuary. Yet not forbiddingly. Death's little cave and shrine has an atmosphere not of horror or threat, but of reassurance, comfort and consolation. Indeed, it seems positively womb-like – which is, of course, precisely the point of the Eleusinian myth.

The gnosis of Gaia

The knowing that is characteristic of Gaia, the Earth Mother, is thus a complex and all-embracing form of knowing. Not only does it subsume all the emotional, intuitive, instinctive knowings of **Artemis** the archetypal woman. Not only is it essentially bi-polar, somehow always managing to present both sides of the coin of experience at once. It also goes on to embrace all the primal, vigorous, violent and often contradictory experiences that are inseparable from motherhood itself. Not merely knowledge of birth, but knowledge of death, too. Not merely the experience of maternal giving, feeding and nurturing, but also that of withholding, starving and neglecting. Not merely kindness and protectiveness, but cruelty and exposure. Not merely joy, love, confidence and security, but deep depression, hatred, insecurity and terror, too.

And always *through her children*, since it is ultimately through her children that Gaia does her knowing and learning. She is well aware, however unconsciously, that to the extent that her children are really herself, in them she has her immortality.

That is why she can be so self-sacrificial on their behalf. In her devotion to them she loses herself totally in order to find herself again.

And so it is that her children become both the instruments of her knowing and the beneficiaries of that knowledge. Through them her accumulated knowledge and experience, like the grain of wheat, go on to bear fruit even more abundantly.

Gaia's is therefore essentially a creative role, and her particular *scientia* is the knowledge of creativity in all its aspects. This involves not merely creation itself, but subsequent devotion to what is created and full acceptance of future responsibility for it.

That is why the *scientia* of Gaia is not confined merely to women – for men, too, have a deep feminine side to their nature. This fact was reflected in the Asiatic form of the cult of the Great Mother. Aspiring candidates for her priesthood would induce in themselves an intense, orgiastic frenzy at the height of which they would actually castrate themselves in order to depotentialise their inherent masculinity and adopt henceforward a purely feminine role – duly wearing women's clothes to match. Similar practices persist in parts of Hindu India to this day.

Modern Western men do not, of course, need to be either so brutal or so literal. Nevertheless they still have it within them to be just as 'feminine' as women, just as creative and 'maternal'. It is vital, therefore, that each man should learn, like Gaia, to create *responsibly* and to take a continuing interest in that creation – even, if necessary, to the point of destroying it again, or of sacrificing himself for it in the longer term. Only in this way can he hope eventually to find himself again in what he has created.

Gaia at large

The point is directly applicable today to humanity as a whole. For, on the broader scale, it is precisely the *lack* of such responsible creativity that has produced our current world environmental crisis – the sickness from which Gaia, the Earth, is now in danger of dying. Indeed, it is always with her most deathly aspect that she confronts us when we fail to discharge our responsibilities towards her. Having failed to accept full responsibility for the effects of our medical technology and its application, we are faced with a world population-explosion. Having failed to accept full responsibility for all the results of our commercial exploitation of the planet's resources, we are confronted with the death of the forests, with creeping desertification, with consequent mass-starvation. Having failed to accept full responsibility for all the end-products of our industrial production techniques, we are faced with massive environmental pollution and a global greenhouse-effect – a planetary fever which, like any fever, will finally break only when it has killed off or drastically modified the 'foreign' organisms that brought it about in the first place.

'Foreign' organisms which are, of course, our own alienated selves.

It is precisely because we have for too long ignored Gaia's way of knowing that she is now confronting us with it more starkly than ever before. More starkly – but not necessarily more strikingly. In December of 1968, for example, she contrived to display herself in the most dramatic way to humanity – solid, rounded and maternal as ever, and draped in luminous veils of blue and white – via the intermediary of circumlunar space-mission Apollo 8 and the eyes of astronauts Borman, Lovell and Anders.

Note specifically that it was to *Apollo* that the great revelation came – **Apollo** the head-orientated scientist, the cerebral astronomer, the ballistics expert forever in search of new worlds for his brilliant, vaulting intellect to conquer. As we saw earlier, the NASA scientists who christened the early American space-missions – with their dazzling electronic capsules named after the gods, and raised to high heaven on the massive shoulders of crude chemical rockets named after the ancient gods and Titans – evidently knew perfectly well what they were about, and their mythology was consequently immaculate.

Note, too, that that revelation came specifically at Christmas, the winter festival of the Nativity, of blue-and-white robed mother and newborn child.

The Three Wise Men of Apollo 8 duly got the message. Theirs, they clearly realised, was a solemn rite of passage, a major re-orientation for humanity. It was the Earth, not the moon, that all at once became the focus of attention – the Earth which you could cover with your thumb, and yet which was suddenly the most important thing in the universe, the ultimate jewel amid the cosmic night where the primeval Earth Mother had always had her preferred abode.

That memorable image has haunted the consciousness of humanity ever since.

The scriptures that the astronauts went on to read out to the listening millions on Earth reflected the feeling. This was a new beginning, a new creation. 'In the beginning,', crackled the message across the intervening void, 'God created the heaven and the earth.' Not *just* the heaven, not *just* the kingdom of Apollo, but Earth, or Gaia, too.

Back on Earth, the self-same realisation was already beginning to dawn. The relatively new science of ecology (Greek: 'study of the house', or 'domestic science') was already coming into vogue: the Green movement was starting to stir into action. So, for that matter, were new, more natural approaches to childbirth and a new respect for the maternal instincts of the mother-to-be.

Humanity was responding, as Gaia had clearly always intended that it should. But not sufficiently, and not quickly enough. Hence the subsequent crises and disasters. Somehow it still seemed to be assumed by humanity at large that ecology was merely for ecologists, the Green movement solely for the Greens. The environment was something 'out there', and doing something about it, equally, was therefore a matter of taking action purely on the external front.

But ecology is *not* just an external matter. It is something that affects all of us directly and personally both on a psychological and on a spiritual level. Just as too great an emphasis on Apollonianism can poison the outer environment, so it can poison the inner environment as well. Neither is any less deadly than the other. We each of us need an *inner* ecology, an *inner* Green movement to bring ourselves back into balance.

And this, above all, means *re-ac-knowledg-ing* and re-activating within us the myths of *all* the gods – and notably the wisdom of Gaia, the traditional knowingness of the mother, the true 'domestic science'.

Mothering, in short, is too important and too universal in its implications to be left to mothers alone. All of us are mothers in our own way. All of us have in the past conceived ideas and plans of action, spawned attitudes and routines, nursed loves and hatreds, nurtured habits and relationships, fostered opinions and pre-conceptions, adopted courses of action. Some of us have even given birth to whole life-ethics.

True, the initial spark of such initiatives pertains to a Uranic heaven – and specifically to Zeus – rather than to earthly Gaia. What traditionally strikes the ancient oak to engender the magic mistletoe is the bolt of lightning out of a formerly cloudless sky. Being thus neither truly of earth nor of heaven, but a new, living being in its own right, that mistletoe symbolises life itself – the independent life that all our initiatives, like our children, acquire once we have succeeded in bringing them into being.

Before it can finally be released into the world, in other words, every new idea or initiative needs to be first formulated, then expressed and finally promulgated, and all with a vigour and force that are truly *paternal*. The act of conception requires firm, positive, determined, even aggressive action that is essentially masculine in character. It is sudden, fiery, dazzling, electric. Coming within the celestial orbit of **Zeus** the Sky Father, such action is thus second nature to the most illustrious of his sons, the flaming **Apollo**, who has his preferred abode in that self-same heaven and from it derives his strength. But at the same time it is also second nature to the formidable goddess Athena in her flashing armour, who is not only Zeus' daughter, but quite literally his brainchild too (in the myth, after all, she is born fully armed directly from his head).

Both men and women, in other words, have within them the divine creative spark that is truly the gift of Zeus, if only they can also find within themselves the force, aggression and sheer *masculinity* with which to express it. What then needs to follow, however, is something much more feminine, for the spark now needs to be sensitively fanned and fed in the full spirit of Gaia, the Earth Mother, until it has become a flaming fire with a life and warmth of its own.

Yet even then our responsibility for it does not stop. If we wish to use that fire to cook on and keep ourselves warm, we must ceaselessly work to keep it burning through light and darkness, through rain and sunshine. Our very lives may depend upon it. So may those of our children. In a very real sense, then, we must actually be prepared to sacrifice ourselves to the fire, to commit ourselves to the flames – as, indeed, the ancient rite of cremation (albeit so recently re-introduced into Western Christendom) so vividly reminds us. At the same time we must take care to keep those flames within bounds, too. Indeed, if they threaten to spread to the point of burning down our whole house we must be fully prepared to take the ultimate action of extinguishing them altogether.

We need, in other words, to learn to take full responsibility for our own creations *in their totality* if we ourselves are not to risk death at their hands. Like the Jehovah of the biblical Old Testament, we must be prepared to conceive and to destroy them, to defend and to attack them, to give birth to them and to 'eat our words' again. And in devoting ourselves in this impartial and even-handed way to them, as well as in subsequently sacrificing ourselves on their behalf to the point of losing ourselves entirely (the Christian version of the Jehovah myth picks up on this aspect, too), we can eventually find ourselves again and so assure our own posterity, both individual and collective.

This latter is something that Jesus realised full well when he spoke of losing the soul in order to find it. Clearly he was well aware of his maternal role, too, when he spoke of gathering the children of Jerusalem to himself 'as a hen gathers her chicks under her wings'. Man though he was, he knew what is meant to be broody.

It is an experience that most of us – and the men among us especially – might do well to cultivate more assiduously, and one without which our knowledge of ourselves must forever remain incomplete. For the myth of Gaia, the knowledge of true motherhood, is a powerful, even essential tool in the quest for the total knower and thus, ultimately, for the Self.

VITAL ACTIONS

Ac-knowledg-ing our essential motherhood is something that we all need to do. But re-establishing contact with the inner Gaia is something that the men among us may well find a good deal more difficult than the women, many of whom are already engaged in actual, physical motherhood. Fortunately, however, the gods can be contacted not merely on the inner level, but on the outer one, too. Thus it is that, even for men, practical therapy becomes possible.

As usual, then, we each need to start by carefully assessing our personal situation.

1. Self-enquiry

Take time out to examine yourself, your attitudes and feelings from a Gaian point of view.

(a) Accepted aspects

Are you generally loving, generous and unselfish? Do you love children? Are you a parent? Do you enjoy sex either within marriage or within a similarly stable relationship? Do parenthood and/or responsibility for others' lives come naturally to you? Do you find it rewarding to take responsibility for those who are smaller or weaker than you? Do you find it fulfilling to calm the agitated, soothe the hurt and care for the distressed? Are you glad to help in the work of restoring strength to the weak and health to the sick? Are you sensitive to your own unconscious needs? Are you convinced that you are blessed with psychic powers such as telepathy and precognition? Are you alive to your protective instincts, intuitions and premonitions, and alert to any possible danger to those for whom you are responsible? Are you nevertheless able to release them and let them stand on their own feet when the time comes? Are you, in the long run, prepared to sacrifice your own interests to theirs?

If the answer to most or all of these is 'Yes', Gaia is truly alive within you.

However, Gaia has other, less welcome, aspects – and these, too, need to be considered. Do not be surprised, therefore, if you find the following list of questions increasingly disturbing. If you find yourself angry or affronted at what they seem to imply, that is actually a very healthy and promising reaction, as we shall go on to see.

(b) Rejected aspects

Are you inherently materialistic? Are you anti-intellectual – even anti-spiritual? Are you acquisitive? Are you overweight and liable to over-eat? Are you unpredictable? Are you forever at the mercy of your emotions? Are your unconscious urges virtually uncontrollable at times? Are you a terror-monger, especially within the family or the organisation for which you work? Are you subject to periodic angers and deep negativities? Are you vindictive, even destructive at such times? Do you resent being controlled by others? Are you prone to emasculate those who would bring order and logic to bear on what you are doing – or at least to undermine any pretensions to power that they may have? Are you always insisting on your rights? Do you sometimes deliberately appear unattractive in order to keep others in their place? Are you possessive and/or domineering? Do you easily get depressed when those for whom you are responsible insist on going their own way? Do you subsequently neglect your appearance, let your responsibilities slide and even absent yourself from work? Do you sometimes become homesick for your own mother? Do you suffer from manic and/or seasonal depressions? Are you drawn irresistibly to the esoteric and/or occult?

Once again, many of these 'rejected' aspects of the Gaian archetype are potentially fraught with emotion. It would be unusual if some of them at least did not arouse strong reactions within you. At the same time, though, the very strength of those reactions has an extremely helpful function. It suggests that the characteristics to which you are reacting are in fact *rejected aspects of yourself*. They pertain, in other words, to your own darker aspect, just as they pertain to the darker aspect of Gaia herself, and for that reason they are normally hidden from you – however obvious they may be to others. Indeed, much the same may even apply to the *positive* aspects listed under (a) above – in which case therapy is doubly urgent. (In practice, this probably means that you are so devoted to Apollo or some related god as to be unable for the moment to *ac-knowledge* the presence Gaia within yourself.)

What is important now, therefore, is to learn to *re-cognise* and accept not only the first list of characteristics, but the second list too (whether or not you actually put it into practice) – for if you are rejecting them you are by definition rejecting large parts of Gaia herself.

(c) Total non-recognition and projection

As ever, though, the most dangerous case is possibly where you have failed to identify with – or to react to – the listed characteristics at all. If this was so in your own case, go through the second list especially for a second time now and ask yourself whether you associate the qualities described mainly with *other people*. Do you despise people who are materialistic or acquisitive? Are you contemptuous of those who are fat or who over-eat? Do you get angry with people who are unpredictable and refuse to be tied down? Do you think that people who attach great importance to their own emotions and intuitions are egotistical and possibly deluded – not to say antisocial? Are you dismissive of people who keep standing on their rights? Do you go in virtual terror of people who are constantly negative and vindictive? Are you irked beyond measure by people who try to dominate you and seem to think that they know what is best for you? Do you have nothing but contempt for people who keep letting their depressions and other emotional states get in the way of their work and responsibilities? Are you incensed by people who think they are psychic? Are you disturbed by people who insist on taking refuge in the occult?

Once again, there are many who take such attitudes – often for reasons that they regard as perfectly logical and reasonable. The very strength of feeling with which they do so, however, reveals that the characteristics concerned *are actually part of their own Shadow*. Having rejected those qualities within themselves, they are now (naturally enough) unable to *re-cognise* them there, and so are forced to project them onto other people, where they can now safely go on rejecting and condemning them to their hearts' content.

This, as we saw earlier, is a recipe not for healing, but for continued division – whether in the inner or the outer world.

In such cases, then, therapy is especially urgent.

(d) Total acceptance

As ever, this is the ideal. We all need to be able to accept Gaia within ourselves not only in her more welcome aspects, but also in her darker manifestations. We need to be able to accept *all* the characteristics listed with easy-going equanimity, *re-cognising* that they are at very least potential or latent within ourselves – even if, as autonomous people, we choose not to express all of them in practice.

If you can already manage this degree of acceptance, in all probability little in the way of extra therapy is needed beyond what you naturally undertake as part of your normal life-routine. If you cannot do so, though, some kind of deliberate therapy is needed – and the ancient myths can as usual be relied on to suggest suitable measures to take.

2. Invocation

Start, then, in the usual way. Name the ancient Earth Mother as 'Gaia' and welcome her unconditionally into your life. Seek out pictures of her, especially in her geophysical form – in other words, those marvellous, shimmering, colour photographs of the Earth taken by astronauts on a whole succession of NASA space-missions. If possible use your holidays to visit her former sanctuary at Delphi, the temple of the Great Mother at Olympia, or that of Demeter and

Persephone at Eleusis (now known as 'Elefsis', just west of Athens: forty minutes by bus from Plateia Eleftherias). If you should find yourself on the isle of Paros, visit the Venetian *kastro*, built almost entirely out of blocks filched from Demeter's former temple there.

If you have the chance, buy a modern copy of one of those ancient, unashamedly corpulent figurines of the primitive Earth Mother dating from long ages before Greece was ever thought of. Consider setting it up in your bedroom and making a 'shrine' around it. Then meditate before it each morning and evening. Affirm your willingness to accept Gaia's basic characteristics in their entirety, both in yourself and in others, and express your refusal henceforth to feel either guilty or ashamed at what in fact are perfectly natural and normal aspects of the mother who is hidden within us all.

Meanwhile, invoking the gods also means deliberately giving yourself the chance to encounter their characteristics within yourself and to recognise them for what they are – and, as ever, thanks to our *penchant* for projection, this means (among other things) exposing yourself to outer circumstances that reflect them. In Gaia's case, these characteristics are mainly her gift for caring, her sense of total responsibility and her total earthiness.

Thus, if you are a parent, you already have a marvellous opportunity for making her acquaintance. Merely by relating fully to your children and catering for all their needs – physical and otherwise – you can scarcely avoid re-discovering Gaia's most basic characteristics within yourself. In this, your children will in fact become your teachers, just as we who are Gaia's children are her own organs of consciousness.

But Gaia does not express herself solely on the human level. She is present in the whole of the natural world around us, too. And so the more intensely you can engage yourself with it, the more you are likely to discover her within yourself. Especially is this the case where the growing and care of plants is concerned – for plants depend on the earth and are rooted in the earth. And so gardening has – like arable farming – to be an ideal way of re-contacting the Earth Mother. Gardening with your bare hands, getting intimately involved with the soil, compost-making, sieving, digging, weeding and hoeing all help to re-establish your natural connection with Gaia. To care for your plants from birth to death is to be her living agent. But be intuitive about it. Do not merely follow the gardening-books. Do not follow the directions on the seed-packet too slavishly. Consider carefully where each variety originally came from, attune to its needs, then use your own hunches about just where and when to sow. Try to understand just *why* one method works and another doesn't.

Resist especially the temptation to be too tidy. Avoid any tendency to turn the garden into a mere expression of Apollonian will. Your task is to accord with nature, not to force nature to conform with what you want. If you insist on removing absolutely all the natural vegetation (the so-called 'weeds') on which the slugs and snails normally feed, is it any surprise if they then concentrate exclusively on your vegetables? If you grow only one kind of plant, is it any wonder that its characteristic pests and diseases become all-pervasive? If you then eat it, is it any surprise that the soil becomes steadily more and more depleted of the very nutrients which that particular plant needs?

Meanwhile, if you remove all the brambles, you will get no blackberries. If you treat the hard verges with herbicides, you will get no wild strawberries. If you destroy the nettles, nearly all the butterflies except the cabbage whites will go elsewhere. If you leave no bushes, the birds that eat your so-called insect pests will likewise seek other homes. If you deluge the garden with general pesticides, you will kill far more helpful organisms than harmful ones. If you use enough poisons, you will even poison yourself.

As Gaia herself never tires of trying to teach us.

Take care, then, to respect nature just as she is. Observe her cycles, and *ac-knowledge* your own participation in them. Always return to the Earth what you have taken from her. Prepare and feed your compost heaps with love and care. And do not complain that you cannot get enough animal manure to put on them, when you yourself produce several hundredweight of it each year.

That is what completing the cycle means.

Ecology, in fact, is another ideal area in which to recall Gaia into your life. Consider, then, involving yourself with it. Actually join the Green movement in one form or another. Take up Green politics. Agitate for permaculture and organic farming. Plant trees. Investigate and promote alternative, non-polluting forms of energy – wind-power, water-power, wave-power, tidal power, geothermal power. And note all the time that the 'power' in question is not something that you are supposed to be exercising over nature, but something that Mother Nature gives you to operate on yourself, offering it freely of her own accord.

A third area in which you can effectively re-invoke Gaia is that of caving, pot-holing and mountaineering – as well of geology generally. In these contexts you are faced directly with Mother Earth in her most dramatic and awesome aspects. Especially is this so where her most 'sacred' caves or mountains are concerned. Thus, Mount Shasta in California, Mount Kailas in Tibet and Mount Fuji near Tokyo all qualify in this regard, as do caves such as that of the

Sibylline oracle at Cuma, near Naples. You may consider visiting some at least of them. But even in much more humdrum locations nearer to home, you can re-experience the ancient presence and force of Gaia in her every mountain cleft and cave. Even in old underground workings you can still sense her unbearable heaviness, her sheer solidity, the indescribably slow, yet unimaginably powerful movements of her continual, womb-like contractions that have given birth to the world in which we live and will, in the far distant future, produce yet other worlds that we shall never know.

Get out your climbing boots and/or caving gear, then. Join – or at least seek the advice of – your local climbing or caving club. You have a whole Earth to discover.

Pursuing the theme further, you can then go on to investigate Earth's even deeper mysteries – for Gaia, in her aspect as Hecate, is closely associated with every aspect of the hidden world, including the occult, witchcraft and what is generally known as geomancy, or Earth Magic. You could start by learning simple dowsing. Having found an experienced dowser to teach you, use the technique to attune to the spirit of place, to unlock Earth's unknown subterranean mysteries – and thus gradually to attune to yourself, too, and to unlock the deeper mysteries of your own unconscious. Then go on to investigate the vast network of ley-lines and power-points that reputedly litter the ancient landscape, enlisting the aid of any local groups that are active in this area. Join any expeditions they may mount to 're-activate' the ancient sites and sacred centres – thereby, perhaps, gradually learning to perform a similar magic upon yourself. You may even care to take up the ancient craft of *wicca* – the ritual worship of the Goddess at her equinoxes and solstices, her sabbats and festivals. You might be well advised to think very carefully, though, before going the whole hog and actually joining your local coven, with all its opportunities for delusions of communal and personal power – even if its popular connotations of dark doings and black mischief are possibly ill-deserved.

But then you do not in any case have to be anything like so unconventional. Lugging yourself out of bed on a Sunday morning, you need do no more than attend High Mass at your nearest ancient Roman Catholic church or cathedral to re-experience the full force of the ancient Earth Mother in her more spiritual aspect – for the magic of her cult has (fortunately for you) been faithfully preserved by the church for the last fifteen centuries or so under the unsuspecting aegis of none other than the similarly blue-robed Blessed Virgin Mary, very often on the self-same sacred sites where she was worshipped long ago.

Whatever your inclinations, then, you have ample opportunities to re-invoke Gaia and learn to *re-cognise* her presence within you. Indeed, in one way or another it is literally vital that you should. Otherwise you will be ignoring the archetypal mother who is hidden deep within you, and your knowledge of yourself will for ever be only partial.

3. Meditation

Merely by 'being fully with' the activities already mentioned you are, as ever, already participating in an appropriate form of meditation. The attunement that is inseparable from Earth Magic is an intensely meditative activity, while *wicca* – like the Roman Catholic Mass – actively pursues the meditative quest into the realms of ritual, worship and even trance. It therefore remains for you simply to contemplate Gaia's traditional symbols.

Can you, like the bee (and unlike Apollo), relate everything you do in the outside world to the everyday needs of the hive – i.e. of your own family? Is the call of home so clear to you that you can find your way unerringly back to it like the dove, and then immerse yourself totally in the bliss of domesticity? Can your focus become the simple hearth and everything that flows from it? Can you become like the mare, active and hard-working, yet also procreative and softly maternal when the need arises? Can you become like the corn, ready to drop your seed in its due time and then to die for its posterity? Can you become as productive as the fig-tree, as solid and resilient as the oak, as spreading and protective as the fern, as doggedly persistent – and as poisonous if need be – as the laurel? Can you relate yourself to the Earth as deeply as the serpent, actually wallow in its earthiness and seek sustenance from it like the sow, both for yourself and for those who are dependent on you? Above all, can you relate to the ancient image of virgin and child and, returning to the ancient Christmas cave, realise that it is not you, but the progeny to which you will give birth, that will go on to save the world?

Do not merely *think* about these matters. Allow yourself to *become* them, each in turn. Seek out their physical presence wherever you can. Use as many as possible of your senses on them. Then merge your identity with them. Immerse yourself fully in their reality.

Finish your meditation by asking yourself the following questions:

Am I fully acknowledging the feminine side of my nature?
Am I allowing myself sufficient experience of parenthood and contact with my 'children' – be they actual flesh-and-blood

children or merely the products of my life and work?

Am I making full use of my caring skills and protective instincts?

Am I allowing sufficient outlets for my generosity and sense of humour?

Do I have sufficient confidence in my intuition and premonitions?

Am I prepared to accept full responsibility for everything I create, even to the extent of destroying it if necessary – or, alternatively, of sacrificing myself for it?

Ponder on your answers, and consider whether this is the moment to adjust your way of life to reflect them.

4. Remedial activities

On the basis of the myths, there are a number of activities that seem designed positively to encourage you to develop your Gaian aspects. You may wish to consider adopting some of them, perhaps on a trial basis initially. Several of them pick up on themes that have been mentioned already. Add any favourite activities of your own that seem appropriate and natural to you. For convenience, the activities listed are, as usual, divided into two categories:

(a) Recreational and general

Depending on your mood, wear mainly green, brown or black. In your lighter, more inspired moments try more ethereal or 'spiritual' colours such as yellow or gold, blue or white. Should you become seriously involved in matters psychic or occult, though, choose mauve or violet for preference. Take up home-making. Light and tend fires. Bake bread. Learn cooking. Enjoy your food and refuse to feel guilty about putting on weight. Practise weaving and/or gardening. Enjoy sex within marriage or a similarly stable environment. Become a parent. Keep pets. Be creative generally. Participate in folk-music and dancing. Join the Green movement. Seek wilderness. Study ecology and cosmology. Go caving and/or climbing. Make a point of attending funerals and burials. Explore the arts and crafts. Read and/or write comic verse. Seek light or darkness as the mood dictates. Be prepared to drop everything and take time off work when depressed. Stick up for yourself and those for whom you are responsible – quite ruthlessly and ferociously if necessary. Avoid alcohol. Drink barley-water. As and when the interest dawns, embark on spiritual studies and/or self-transformation initiatives. Investigate geomancy and traditional magic. Attend High Mass at any ancient Roman Catholic church or cathedral.

(b) Professional
Particularly suitable areas for encouraging the development of Gaia within you are: full-time parenthood, gardening, farming, botany, work with wilderness-orientated organisations, ecology, exploration, archaeology, geology, geography, child-care, nursery-nursing, nursing generally, youth-work, handicrafts, catering, hotel-keeping, marriage-guidance and counselling, the law, and the writing of light novels or humorous verse.

SUB-PERSONALITIES OF GAIA

We have already broadly explored Gaia's most outstanding sub-personalities in the form of Demeter, Persephone and Hecate. Demeter's specific characteristics and therapies are outlined below, while you can explore her characteristics as Persephone and Hecate under **Artemis** (above). Thus, you may wish to consider the appropriateness of the following to your own case, especially if any of the above seems a less than perfect 'fit':

DEMETER

Possible symptoms

Nymphomania; resistance to marriage; withholding of favours when angry; unattractive 'mask' (as Medusa); tendency to scold; occasional temper; possessiveness; depression when children (especially a beloved daughter) die or leave home; resultant total lethargy and forsaking of home; neglect of appearance; loss of interest in clothes; deliberate disguise; refusal to eat, drink or wash; possible anorexia; absenteeism from work; absent-mindedness; lapses or parental attention; unintentional harming of others' children; winter depression

but also

Femininity; sexual love; fertility; goodness with children; gentleness; caring skills; healing presence; gratitude; generosity; underlying sense of humour; slowness to anger; love of peace; deep spiritual knowledge and insight.

Therapies

Name, imagine and welcome this generous, but sometimes deeply depressed Goddess of the crops and of fertility, at first radiant and golden-haired, then black-robed and veiled, and finally radiant and golden-haired again; agriculture; flower-gathering; bread-making;

growing and processing cereals (the word, as we saw, actually derives from her Roman name *Ceres);* corn-milling; wearing of rags, or self-disguise as old woman (long black dress and veil), when depressed by children's departure, and especially by daughter's marriage; deliberate neglect of appearance; time off work; conscious release of daughter; formal decision to come to terms with the new situation and share her with her new destiny; nursery-nursing; youth work; handicrafts instruction; offering marriage guidance; spiritual work of a pioneering character; self-transformation initiatives; mirror-oracles; light; perfumed clothes; light or comic verse; sex; avoidance of alcohol; barley-water flavoured with mint.

Symbols

Iris; ear of corn; fig tree; oak; dove; serpent; sow; porpoise; bee; mare; horse's head; beautiful corn-wreath; flaming torches; serpent-chariot.

Notes

A former earth Goddess, Demeter brings with her many ideal maternal qualities. Fulfilment and abundance follow her wherever she goes. But this positive side to her nature is bought at the price of some inner imbalance – an imbalance which tends to show at moments of stress. It is at such times particularly – and above all when her favourite daughter dies or leaves home to get married – that she needs all the spiritual support that she can get. In the latter case her prime source of healing may well lie in the time-honoured realisation that (to quote a well-worn cliché) she is not so much losing a daughter as gaining a son. Apart from this, her greatest consolation may well lie in contemplating the theme of ongoing death-

and-rebirth, or even of reincarnation – a theme which her suggested work with the growing and processing of cereals and other crops may well help to bring clearly to her attention. Her inherent sense of humour, too, may have a valuable role to play, especially in the latter stages. Whichever path she chooses, however, she is likely to find eventual peace and lasting reconciliation with her circumstances.

HESTIA = Vesta

Possible symptoms

Stay-at-home tendency; exaggerated self-effacement; over-concern with personal security; rigid sense of values; conservatism; willingness to buy domestic peace at almost any price; characterlessness; obsessive virginity; Olympian detachment from external affairs; inability to cope with the wildness and animalism of teenagers; tendency to leave home when under extreme pressure from this quarter

but also

Virginity or celibacy; love of home and hearth; hospitality; moral uprightness; transmission of received culture; enjoyment of personal security and happiness; stability; sense of order; centredness; psychological balance; sense of focus or direction; determination; sense of belonging; sense of place; perspicacity; self-effacing nature; unselfishness; emotional warmth.

Therapies

Name, imagine and invoke this least known of the Olympians, the colourless and rather straight-laced goddess to whom the Roman Vestal Virgins were dedicated; religious orders; giving of hospitality; open fires; home-making; house-construction; architecture; mead (WARNING: beware of alcohol-addiction).

Symbols

Hearth; fire; circle; *omphalos* or navel.

Notes

Hestia's myth seems to have been devalued since the time of her symbolic displacement from Olympus by the young **Dionysus**. What remains of it, however, suggests that Hestia is in many ways the archetypal maiden aunt, the 'shrinking lily', perfectly happy with her way of life and unwilling to put **it** at risk by introducing new variables into it. In her married form she expresses herself in the home-loving mother with no detectable sense of adventure and no wish other than to fulfil her chosen role. As such, she is the hub of the family, the hander-on of received values, the ever-watchful bringer of order and stability, the focus of the family's sense of security and belonging. Since she clearly brings happiness and fulfilment, there is no need to regard her as a problem unless and until she starts to get in the way of the continuing process of personal inner development, or threatens the continuing cohesiveness of the family when the children start to reach adolescence. In this latter eventuality, it may prove useful for her to leave home temporarily, at least until suitable therapy can be set in train.

RHEA

Possible symptoms

Possessiveness; incestuous relationship with, or rape by, own son;

over-protectiveness towards offspring; over-eagerness to promulgate divine mysteries; wifely frivolity; deflation; physical and mental illness; possible arthritis; danger of death

but also

Motherhood; knowledge of female mysteries; psychological integration; protection; restorative powers; healing; forgiveness; mediation; persuasiveness; canniness; worldly wisdom; down-to-earthness; promulgation of spiritual knowledge; shamanism; 'medicine woman'.

Therapies

Name, imagine and welcome the ancient Earth Mother and dark-robed sister of Cronus in her most possessive and yet most canny form — and notably as the grandmotherly guardian of much secret lore; motherhood; grandmotherhood; dark clothes; beekeeping; artificial respiration; first aid; water-divining; irrigation; metallurgy.

Symbols

Brazen drum; flute; cymbal; bull-roarer; dove; female snake; mountain lion; golden mastiff; oak; plane-leaf; the planet Saturn; non ferrous metals.

Notes

Rhea is the spirit of the woman who gives too much of herself and consequently smothers those around her with an excess of love. She has valuable spiritual gifts and a well-rounded wisdom, too, but is far too anxious to bestow them on others. Basically what she is looking for is love for herself, and the less she gets of it the more she gives. Outside her natural role as a mother, therefore – and even here her presence is a mixed blessing – she needs to discover that in fact love does not need to come from 'out there'. Charity, it has been said, begins at home. But this realisation is not easy to come by, especially as the problem generally has deep roots in infancy. The main role of the listed therapies seems to be to help take her 'out of herself' – a fact which might suggest painting as a further possible activity.

Rhea's association with her brother Cronus suggests that the symptoms are likely to become more accentuated with age, and especially once the children leave home, though they may well recede again once the grandchildren start to arrive. Astrologically, the link with Saturn suggests that any problems are likely to be severest around midwinter.

SUMMARY

By learning to *re-cognise* Gaia within yourself you start to *ac-knowledge* that you have an inherent creative, caring side that is capable of taking on and discharging long-term responsibilities. Those responsibilities may involve you both in positive and in negative actions. You may be called upon both to create and to destroy. But the true Gaia within you knows perfectly well that the one is merely the reverse side of the other's coin. You cannot destroy without creating, nor create without destroying.

Knowing yourself inevitably has to mean knowing *all* of yourself. It therefore has to mean knowing this too.

7

ZEUS – THE WAY OF THE FATHER

I'll meet the raging of the skies,
But not an angry father.
Thomas Campbell: 'Lord Ullin's Daughter'

ZEUS is the great sky-father, king of all the gods. But he also has two brothers, each responsible for a different element. Poseidon rules the sea and the depths of the earth, Hades the underworld. Moreover, through his brainchild Athena, he constantly manipulates and attempts to control the everyday world of men and women, too. Wherever power and rulership are at stake, we are just as prone to encounter this mighty family of gods within ourselves as we are in the world 'out there'. Lest we let power go to our heads, it is therefore vital that we learn to come to terms with this troublesome and quarrelsome clan.

The myth of the Sky Father

Sun and moon, earth and sea, the world of animals and plants as represented by the humble goat and vine – in all of these basics of human experience we see ourselves reflected through the mirror of their respective gods and goddesses (above). It is they that have ultimately helped to make us humans what we are. All of them, consequently, offer us direct routes to rediscovering our Selves. Yet overtopping all of them – so, at least, our eyes assure us – is the very sky itself.

And the sky is Zeus.

In the tongue of the ancient Indo-Europeans from whom his myth has come down to us, the very root of his name *means* 'sky' (or 'brightness'). And so Zeus is essentially *yang*. He is to be sought in earth's highest places. Just as Yahweh, the Hebrews' own 'father in heaven', reveals himself to Moses on Mount Horeb (the very word seems to derive from Egyptian *hor'ib*: heart of Horus – i.e. heart of the sky), so Zeus, too, dwells on the mountain-tops, veils himself in clouds, even makes them his chariot. And out of them, when his anger rises, he sends the thunder and lightning that are the instruments of his almighty power.

Almighty because, as the sky, he is manifestly the earth's 'top god'. How could he be other, then, than authority personified?

Thus it is virtually inevitable that Zeus, like Yahweh, should come to be cast in paternal mould. As the celestial opposite and counterpole of Earth, the Great Mother **Gaia**, he is the Great Father. His lightning-bolt is the very phallus with which he inseminates the earth. The life-giving rain is his semen, just as it was that of heavenly Uranus before him. The thunder is his mighty voice. And it must be obeyed.

So it is, then, that Zeus in due course becomes the Romans' Jupiter ('sky-father'), having long since come to lord it over all the other gods.

It was not always so. In ancient Egypt the sky was feminine. It was identified with the goddess Nut. She it was who over-arched Geb, the masculine earth. The life-giving sperm passed not from heaven to earth, but vice versa. The tradition represented the earlier, basically matriarchal way of thinking that is known to have survived even into dynastic times. Just as in those remote, former ages the feminine was always dominant, so it was through the queen that the royal bloodline was held to descend. If, therefore, a pharaoh was to be succeeded by his son, then *that son must first marry his sister.*

Even in subsequent, patriarchal times, in other words, the ancient matriarchal paradigm was still preserved as a kind of cultural insurance policy. And not merely in ancient Egypt. In Greece, too, the original paradigm had been matriarchal. Even the myth of paternal Zeus himself reflects the fact. Not only is his mother (as the ancient cult of the Titans actually required) his father's sister. Zeus, too, goes on to marry *his own sister* for the sake of the posterity of the race.

Yet such mythological 'belt-and-braces' strategies should not be allowed to obscure the historical fact that the arrival of Zeus and his cult marked the introduction into Greece of an entirely different social order. It was one that had been long in the making. When the migrating Indo-European tribes swept in out of central Eurasia during the second and third millennia BC, it was a new, exclusively patriarchal system that was imposed on the old, settled, matriarchal, agricultural societies. To the former nomads to whom the Indians were later to refer as the *Arya,* or Noble Ones – and whom Max Müller, Helena Blavatsky and Adolf Hitler were in due course to transmogrify into the noble 'Aryans' of 'Master Race' fame – male supremacy was a *sine qua non.*

The culture of the horse

There was a certain, inevitable logic about it. It was, after all, the men alone who were mobile enough to ride the range, to herd the semi-wild flocks, to hunt the game across far-flung plains.

Horseback-riding was not for pregnant women or mothers with young children. Any woman young enough not to be either was still a child herself; any woman too old for either was too old for hunting and herding, too.

It was the horse, in other words, that was the primary catalyst for change.

In reflection of this, the horse was the Indo-Europeans' sacred animal *par excellence*. Among such of the tribes as remained nomadic, the tradition persisted well into historical times. Even as late as the Saxon era, the leaders of the Angles, Saxons and Jutes who invaded post-Roman Britain in the year AD 449 were allegedly called *Hengist* and *Horsa*. Since the two words mean, respectively, 'stallion' and 'mare' (the second of which seems a distinctly odd name for a presumably male chieftain), it seems more than likely that the reported twin names (perhaps picked up by the later chroniclers from hearsay) referred not to human beings, but to the still-remembered Indo-European horse-cult and the hallowed tradition whereby the tribes were routinely led to their new pastures by a horse that had simply been released to follow its nose.

And not just a horse, but a pure white stallion.

It is no surprise to find, then, that the same tradition seems to have been brought by the ancient Indo-Europeans into Greece as well, so that both of Zeus' lordly brothers, Poseidon and Hades, were themselves said to be closely connected with horses. With Poseidon revered as the god of the sea, his horses were naturally white ones (even today we still use the term 'white horses' for its foaming whitecaps), while the chariot of Hades, god of death and the underworld, was inevitably drawn (as were funeral hearses until quite recent times) by black ones. This naturally begs the question of whether Zeus, too, might not originally have had an equine connection – and specifically one with the former Indo-Europeans' white stallion. In which case it would have been only later, as the incoming nomads put down roots and began to tackle the serious business of ploughing and farming, that the association would have started to slip – as it appears to have done with Poseidon too – in favour of a new one with the former subject races' chief draught animal, the ox or bull. And certainly it is with the bull – the *white* bull, inevitably – that Zeus has been associated ever since.

Both animals, of course, were the very embodiments of creative masculinity, of male domination, of patriarchy and thus of the whole social order that the Indo-Europeans were eventually to impose not only on Greece, but on Persia, Europe and India too. In Crete, the original prototype of the Minoan bull-cult seems significantly to have shaped the myth of Zeus himself. The Mithraic bull-cult of Persia was to spread out during classical times all across the Roman Empire. And to this day the cult of the sacrificial bull continues to be almost ritually celebrated all across Spain and Latin America.

Even in modern Europe and America, in other words, the cult of Zeus and/or Poseidon is alive and kicking yet.

All of which naturally has nothing whatever to say about the relative merits of patriarchy and matriarchy. Any society in which one sex routinely devalues and oppresses the other would seem, *a priori*, to fall a good way short of perfection – and neither sex has any exclusive claim to virtue in this regard, as the respective myths of **Apollo** and **Artemis** both make clear.

Nevertheless, the myth of Zeus has a specific function. It exposes to view the true nature of fatherhood and the inherently masculine qualities that go with it. As ever, those qualities are not restricted to men alone. All of us have within us a strong potential for creativity and for positive, even violent action of a truly 'masculine' type – and women particularly can therefore benefit enormously from learning to *re-cognise* it. For it, too, is a natural part of themselves, and as such it demands, as ever, to be *ac-knowledged*.

The kingdom of heaven

For all his animal connections, Zeus was and is (as we saw above) primarily a personification of the sky. Taking over the former celestial role of his grandfather Uranus, he is thus self-evidently both durable and permanent. Indeed, he is utterly indestructible. To this extent, then, he is reliable. Even his somewhat distant presence proves somehow reassuring.

Yet his very durability necessarily means that he has what it takes to survive. In practice, this presupposes a native adaptability. And indeed, the sky constantly demonstrates the fact. Ever-changing, it is totally impossible to pin down. It can be as generous with its life-giving rain at one moment as it can be miserly the next. Its brilliant, lighter aspect alternates with its darker aspect on a more or less regular basis. The same, then, applies to Zeus, and in this way he contrives to combine and support both the intolerable brilliance of the solar **Apollo** and the more sombre countenance of lunar **Artemis**. And not merely in alternation, for in Zeus each tends to be infused with aspects of the other. Even his sunniest moods can be overshadowed by dark clouds, even his blackest looks relieved by a starry twinkle in the eye.

Yet the fact remains that he always remains firmly 'up there'. He tends to come across as remote, even inaccessible. He has to be addressed, if at all, from afar – and preferably from some eminence well nigh as lofty as himself. His authority is all but unassailable. Nor can his job be taken over by anybody else. He is alone in his field. Inevitably, therefore, he turns out to be something of an autocrat, and jealous with it.

As with a whole range of sky- and storm-gods, then – from the Babylonian Anum, through the Syrian Baal and the Semitic Adad or Hadad, to the biblical Yahweh or Jehovah – power is his speciality: power in the service not only of his own ego, but of the creation, preservation and protection of family and social order too. He positively enjoys wielding it, almost for its own sake. Yet when he does so, his normally bright countenance often clouds over: he tends, in other words, to mask both his intentions and his own true nature. Truth and openness are subordinated to practical eventualities, to the demands of the moment.

And then he strikes with lightning speed, almost at random.

Neither his timing nor his targets can reliably be predicted. His impact is devastating. And all the more so for the fact that, through the medium of his thunderbolt, he tends to strike first and talk only afterwards. Yet even this fact is somehow reassuring – for it means that his anger has not yet reached its peak. The true climax comes only when he thunders and strikes at one and the same instant.

And then it is time to beware.

At such moments, in fact, it is unwise to be out in the open at all. The best that can be done is to seek shelter deep underground in the womb of Mother Earth, in the hope that she will divert his anger. For **Gaia** is always happy to protect her children against his rages, while at the same time she herself welcomes the life-giving rain that almost always accompanies them. It is almost as though the one were in some sense the flip-side, or shadow, of the other – the sex and the insemination of the anger, the anger of the sex and the insemination. With Zeus – as with Poseidon and Hades too – the two aspects are not always easily distinguishable. Not only can the one be replaced with astonishing speed by the other, but the two can all too easily become intermingled. At which point sex can turn into rape, while aggression itself acquires a distinct sexual edge about it that tends to breed yet more of the same.

The story of Zeus in myth

The myth of Zeus hints at a possible explanation for this. He is born, after all, as the youngest son of the titaness Rhea (see under **Gaia**), wife and sister of Cronus. And since Cronus, paranoid and fearful of rivals and palace coups, has already swallowed all his previous children at birth – Hestia, Demeter, Hera, Hades and Poseidon all in their turn – Rhea takes care to give birth to Zeus himself at dead of night. She then hands him over to Mother Earth, who smuggles him to the safety of the now-celebrated cave on Mount Dikte in Crete. There (or in another, equivalent cave on Mount Ida) he is suckled and brought up with the young Pan himself by an assortment of ash-tree nymphs, bees and doves, along with the goat-nymph Amaltheia, who will eventually go on to be immortalised as the constellation Capricorn. Immortalised she will need to be, for Zeus, on attaining adulthood, goes on to slay her and take her goat-skin upon himself, additionally wearing on his back the protective *aegis* – the severed head (or mask) of the dreaded Gorgon Medusa whose looks, even in death, can turn the beholder to stone.

It is a strange and fanciful story, yet out of it certain deeper elements do start to emerge. Zeus, it is clear, starts life as an outcast. Resented and rejected by his father, he is deprived, exiled, virtually orphaned. Weak and powerless, the runt of the litter, all that he can rely on is his own native wit, his instinctive, animal cunning, his essentially **Pan**-like aspect. He is driven, in other words, primarily by fear, motivated by nothing more than *pan-ic*. He is essentially a child of nature, of the birds and the bees. And so, when he seeks to make his way in the world, he has nothing to wrap himself in but the self-same animal nature. Yet he still feels vulnerable, and so he learns to project a sternness of mien, a petrifying demeanour that belies the soft, surprisingly sensitive being that still cowers all unsuspected underneath.

Zeus' lust for power and dominion, then, is perfectly understandable. It is a natural compensation for the feelings of infant vulnerability and insecurity that still persist within him, as within a good many of us. It is a classic case, in other words, of Freud's so-called inferiority complex. And its results in terms of dominant husbands and fathers, of aggressive business executives and brutal, totalitarian dictatorships are all too familiar to all of us. To say nothing, on the female side, of domineering wives and mothers too.

The already-mentioned links between Zeus, the lordly 'Aryans' and Hitler's fascistic instincts, in other words, are far from accidental.

Such things were all too familiar to the primitive Greeks and Cretans too. And so when Zeus, in the traditionally approved manner, marries his own sister Hera, the marriage is a disaster. Stormy, dispute-ridden, a constant tale of tempers, tantrums, quarrels and shouting-matches, it throws up crisis after crisis. There are revolts, repressions, would-be palace-coups and domestic walkouts, to say nothing of wifely depressions and alienated and traumatised children – all of whom bear within themselves the barely-concealed seeds of their father's own ingrained aggression. And, inevitably perhaps, there are a whole rash of extramarital affairs too.

Not that Zeus is by any means all bad news. Child of nature that he is, his aggression is ultimately no more than a form of self-defence. And so, by extension, he is quite capable of using it, too, to protect both his family and the group or society within which he lives. He will perform prodigies on their behalf. He is prepared to invest all the power and strength that he has in creating new world-orders in his own image, and in bringing stability and security to the world around him. No adversary is too great, no rival too powerful to be confronted.

In all this he relies on two main weapons. The first is his thunder-bolt – his sheer, naked, masculine power, essentially creative in function and largely sexual in origin, through which his inbuilt aggression tends to channel itself. This manifests itself as dramatically in the world of social and professional affairs as it does in that of sex.

The second weapon is his inbuilt cunning, his talent to dissemble, to mask his intentions, to conceal his true nature. This weapon, too, he is prepared to use just as readily in the contexts of business and politics as in those of personal relationships and amorous affairs – where he has an amazing ability to become all things to all women (to say nothing of all youths and young men as well). A cuckoo, a snake, a swan, a bull, an eagle – no role is beyond his ability to play it when it serves his purpose.

Flawed though he undoubtedly is, then, Zeus tends to be an extraordinary, larger-than-life character whose impact on those around him can be immense. A terror to his subordinates, a threat to his competitors, a well-nigh impossible challenge to his partner, a tyrant to his children – there is nobody who does not feel the power of his presence. Resent him though we sometimes may, respect him we nevertheless must. He gets things done. He changes the world. To a large extent he sets its agenda. About him our lives tend to revolve: beside him other people seem mere ants. He is truly great in every way, his faults every bit as great as his virtues.

Poseidon and Hades

Yet in the king of heaven and of Olympus, threatening though he sometimes seems, we see only the healthier, more open side of the human father archetype. For Zeus is but one of three brothers. Just as the Great Mother (see **Gaia**) tends to reveal herself in triple guise – as Demeter, Persephone and Hecate – so the Great Father, too, comes to us in triplicate.

And so the myths recount how responsibility for world-affairs was not assigned to one ruler alone, but divided among the brothers Zeus, Poseidon and Hades. To Zeus was assigned the sky and the earth beneath it, to the rebellious and cantankerous Poseidon the sea and everything in it, and to the gloomy and reclusive Hades the underworld. All three were co-equal. Indeed, Poseidon was originally given a thunderbolt just like that of Zeus. To this day, consequently, it remains next to impossible to identify ancient statues of them in isolation, unless the weapon itself happens to survive in their right hands. For in Poseidon's case the thunderbolt was eventually to be changed into a three-pronged fish-spear, as being more suited to his maritime nature, and so the trident duly became his prime symbolic marker.

No such marker pertains to Hades, however. He is characterised merely by his grotesque, back-to-front head and his so-called

Helmet of Invisibility. His coming, in other words, is forever hidden, his face eternally unseen, and nobody knows when or where he will appear in order to snatch the unwary into his chariot of death with its four black horses, and to drag them off forever into the darkness of the underworld.

In the maritime Poseidon and the subterranean Hades, then, we see Zeus himself in two alternative guises. Poseidon, god of sea, gales, tidal waves, subterranean streams and earthquakes, represents a more repressed incarnation of Zeus – one who is unpredictable, unreliable, restless, shifty, moody and often positively stormy. At such times truly terrifying destructive forces are liable to emerge from the deepest wells of the unconscious to devastate the world around us. So great are those forces that they simply cannot be contained – possibly not even survived. And so there is nothing for it but to flee him, avoid him and generally keep out of his way.

Far from being essentially creative like Zeus, in short, Poseidon presents the reverse side of the coin. He is quintessentially destructive. He is a threat to all around him. Politically he is a rebel, socially a misfit, sexually an out-and-out rapist of indeterminate sexual orientation. Indeed, it is in the sexual sphere that – as his identification with the sea makes almost inevitable – his instinctive aggression tends to surface most readily.

With Hades things are different again. This time Zeus' constitutional aggression has mellowed with age. Hades is neither truly creative nor truly destructive: instead, he is simply *conservative*. True, there are still flashes of the old, sexually motivated aggression – as, equally, of the old, aggressive sex. In whatever context, he is still quite capable of rape. He is fiercely miserly, too, and jealous of his rights. But now that he feels more secure in his kingdom and less moved to prove himself at every turn, he begins to be less active and outgoing, more pensive and reclusive. Stripped now of all the colour and vigour of youth, he increasingly becomes a gloomy shadow of his former self, a grey ruler over a grey kingdom.

Even so, thanks to his new-found material security, a slow change starts to come over him. In place of his characteristic miserliness, he begins to show once again something of the other side of the Jovian coin – the generosity of Zeus at his best. To the aged, consequently, his ministrations can start to seem positively reassuring and comforting. Inspired by him, they start to give away their most prized possessions, to bequeath their goods to their descendants. Often they are moved to give up even life itself with an astonishingly good grace. Hades sees death, after all, not as the end, but as some kind of return to the maternal womb, and so – as embodied in his elderly acolytes – he eventually learns to welcome it with open arms.

As well he might – for it is, of course, none other than himself.

Zeus in woman: his brainchild Athena

Thus far, then, Zeus, along with his brothers Poseidon and Hades – each of whom is in some respect his *alter ego*. In them we see the typically masculine Father Archetype in triple aspect. Zeus, despite all his faults, is its brightest, most creative and beneficent manifestation; Poseidon its comparatively repressed and thus more surly, troublesome, even destructive persona; Hades that darker, less conscious facet of it that tends eventually to emerge in old age and represents the slow and painful mutual reassimilation of life's opposites.

Yet there is a further twist to the story. For the Father Archetype is not limited to men alone. Women, too, are perfectly capable of discovering it within their souls. And it is to this fact that the myth of Zeus' daughter Athena goes on to bear due witness.

Born fully-armed from the head of her father, Athena quite naturally turns out to be *his brainchild*. Determined and courageous, domineering and confrontational, instinctively political and militant (not to say militaristic) she reflects his nature in everything except her sexuality – which, in the natural tradition of girlish **Artemis**, is much more demure and restrained. By the same token, though, she is even more capable than he is of diverting her creative instincts into constructive channels capable of benefiting humanity as a whole. Indeed, she tends to become a veritable pillar of society, a valued leader, an activist for reform, a champion of just causes, a promoter of civilised values, a source of positive initiatives in the fields of law, politics, civics, diplomacy, education, health, medicine and the arts and crafts. Distinctly Britannia-like in aspect and even appearance – though replacing Britannia's unashamedly Poseidonian trident with a simple spear – she is skilled, too, in the arts of war, yet moved to apply them only so far as is necessary to preserve the established order and the survival of civilisation as she knows and understands it.

The sacred sites

Athena's most celebrated temple is, of course, the Parthenon ('temple of the virgin') of Athens – the Greek metropolis that is actually named after her. And, true to form, this huge edifice reflects her nature with great force and vividness. There is absolutely nothing dainty or feminine about it. From its lofty rock-citadel it projects an aura of almost brutal masculinity, of sheer weight and power, of political supremacy and confident international confrontation. At the same time the enormous pile is pervaded by a sense of order, regularity and perfectly-judged proportion that is equally characteristic of the goddess herself.

But this is by no means Athena's only sanctuary. At her secluded site just to the east of Delphi's Castalian spring, for example, she reveals her much more humble, dutiful, religious side. At Sparta, she seems to preside merely in a more or less nominal, civic way, as though knowing perfectly well that the city really belongs in spirit to her half-sister **Artemis**. Her once-resplendent temple at Syracuse in Sicily, now incorporated bodily into the structure of the city's Roman Catholic cathedral, is (understandably perhaps) deeply maternal in atmosphere, while her near-perfectly preserved sanctuary at Agrigento – likewise once used as a church, and better known today as the 'Temple of Concord' following the discovery of a Roman inscription bearing the word – seems to speak primarily of her virtues of reliability and protection. (The later Christians were particularly drawn to converting Athena's temples into churches, since every one of them was by definition a *parthenon*, and thus dedicated specifically to 'the Virgin' – indeed, to the 'Virgin Mother' at that.)

Some of these typically Athenian qualities also pervade the temple that Athena shares with the local goddess Aphaia on the island of Aegina. In particular, a simple sense of propriety pervades the site. Erected after the great Athenian naval victory over the Persians at Salamis, this sanctuary additionally reflects the general mood of thanksgiving at the time, as well as radiating a certain aura of communal assurance.

Elsewhere, too, Athena is perfectly happy to share her

sanctuaries with other gods. On the Athenian *agora*, for example, she shares a temple with the lame smith-god Hephaestus, at the same time revealing a certain primness and decorum proper to a goddess charged with presiding over the city's artisans and with keeping the armourers and metal-workers under strict, civilised control.

But her most frequent partner is (as might perhaps be expected) her father Zeus himself. On the isle of Delos, for example, she shares a small mountain-sanctuary with him on the summit of Mount Kynthos, duly surveying the scattered islands of the Cyclades with a sense of ordered power and serene self-satisfaction.

True, the site seems rather remote for Athena who, as on the Athenian Acropolis, loves to be at the centre of things. But Zeus, as befits his nature, prefers to be far out under the sky, and as near to it as possible. Most of his sanctuaries are therefore to be found on mountain-tops. Alternatively, he is to be found in one of his numerous 'birth caves' high on remote mountainsides, and not too far from the all-important summit. In such cases, though, it is his infant humility and vulnerability that are most easily sensed.

Only at major cult-centres such as Athens and Olympia does Zeus usually deign to descend to the plain. At Olympia he completely dominates the site, apparently paranoid lest his resentful and apparently rather snooty wife Hera (who, it has to be said, was there and in control well before him) should take over power in his stead. At Athens, however, he is content to retire grandly to a safe distance, understandably confident – for all his evident megalomania – in his daughter Athena's ability to rule over the ancient acropolis on his behalf.

His eldest brother Hades, by contrast, dwells mainly in dark, womb-like subterranean grottoes whose atmosphere turns out to be remarkably soothing and consoling, as befits his increasingly calm acceptance of old age and death. As for Poseidon, the middle brother, his kingdom is over the sea rather than the dry land. And so his sanctuaries tend to be perched on craggy headlands such as that at Cape Sounion, not far east of Athens. Curiously, though, his celebrated and immensely photogenic temple there radiates little of his surly, troubled, destructive nature. Instead there is a sense of almost calm responsibility and reassurance – almost as though what is being reflected is the local mariners' concern to protect themselves *against* Poseidon and his stormy temper, rather than to reflect his own nature. That, indeed, was the original reason for building it there. To this extent, though, the project has turned out to be an abject failure. Even in fairly calm weather, the cape is still subject, even today, to violent squalls and sudden flurries that can flatten the unwary sailing-ship. The fact contains a salutary warning to us. Placating the Poseidon within us is not an easy job, still less a once-and-for-all one, however dramatic and resplendent the would-be exorcistic initiative.

The gnosis of Zeus and his family

What, then, is Zeus' typical way of knowing, whether reflected in himself, in his brothers Poseidon and Hades or in his daughter Athena? Clearly, creative power and dominance lie at the root of it – which has to mean that he learns about himself primarily through his interactions with those who are subordinate to him. As in the case of Gaia and her children, they are, in a sense, his eyes and ears, his arms and legs – and having such a multitude of them at his disposal, he is in a position to spread his knowing over a very wide field indeed. Whether in male or in female guise, in other words, Zeus learns to know himself – as does his daughter and female counterpart Athena – through the families that he creates, through the groups that he heads, through the societies that he increasingly comes to dominate.

In Poseidon's case, the position is reversed. Unlike Zeus, he tends to learn as it were by default. He knows himself not so much through the authority that he exerts as through the authority that he opposes. And so, through his family, his group, his society, he actually learns to know the rejected aspects of himself, and to know them the hard way.

In the elderly Hades, finally, the process nears its completion and consummation. Now the father-figure in us at last learns to *re-cognise* the dark aspects of himself as constantly present and valid in their own right. In particular, he learns to *ac-knowledge* the death-aspect of himself that is merely the reverse side of the vigorous life-aspect that, as Zeus, he has so obsessively projected all along. As a result, he finally becomes more complete, more whole, more bipolar like the Earth Mother herself, and consequently is at last able to retire once more into the bowels of the earth, the primal womb that originally gave him birth.

Like the Hindu *trimurti* of Brahma the creator, Shiva the destroyer and Vishnu the preserver, then, the sacred trinity of Zeus, Poseidon and Hades expresses the archetype of masculine endeavour and self-assertion in all its most primal, vigorous aspects, at the same time encapsulating within its triple nature all our anger, aggression, resentment, confrontationalism and propensity to sexual violence in vivid, almost tangible form. As a result, learning to cope with this male-orientated triplicity teaches us to cope, too, with these most difficult aspects of ourselves, and so ultimately helps us to know the whole being that we truly are.

Zeus and family at large

With the relationship so strong between Zeus, Poseidon, Hades and Athena on the one hand and sheer power and authority on the other, it is inevitable that history is full of their representatives. The fingerprints of Zeus can be found as easily in the pharaoh Ramses II, in the Emperor Augustus, in Charlemagne, Henry VIII of England and Peter the Great of Russia as in more recent avatars such as Nicolae Ceausescu and Saddam Hussein. Equally, as the troublesome, unruly Poseidon, traces of the archetype can be found in Beethoven, Marl Marx, Lenin, Stalin, Hitler, Mao Tse Tung and Fidel Castro. Hades, too, has left his mark in most of these as they have grown older, desperately clinging on to power for all they are worth. And, as Athene, the archetype appears to have left its resplendent legacy in powerful female figures such as the pharaoh Hatshepsut, her remote successor Cleopatra, the mature Elizabeth I of England, Catherine the Great, Golda Meir, Indira Gandhi and the modern Margaret Thatcher.

All of us, in fact, have it within ourselves to be lords and fathers in our own particular ways. But at the same time we also need to learn to cope with the many side-issues that dominance and fatherhood necessarily raise – issues such as violence to others, negative emotions and antagonistic attitudes, as well as its more positive aspects such as creativity, protection and sheer leadership.

In all developed societies such issues (like Zeus himself who embodies them) are bound to be well to the fore. And so it is vital for us not to sweep them under the carpet as we are often wont to do (thus committing them willy-nilly to the malicious schemings of the threatening Poseidon) still less to expunge them from our consciousness altogether (thus condemning them to rot and ferment in the gloomy realm of Hades, from whence they will eventually emerge to haunt us and demand our full attention in old age). Instead we need to address them in all openness and seriousness, valuing each for what it has to contribute to our ultimate survival, whether personal or collective.

VITAL ACTIONS

It is above all, then, in our most creative, self-assertive and manipulative aspects that we experience the presence of Zeus (or his daughter Athena) in our lives. Whenever we exercise power – or whenever power exercises us – he is close at hand. As creators and protectors of our families, as pioneers and leaders in our own particular social, political and cultural fields, we are his direct agents and representatives. As victims of our own anger and resentment, of our aggression and confrontation, even of our tendency to sexual violence, it is of him that we are really victims – though in this case more in his persona as the surly Poseidon. More especially is this so when we feel ourselves to be on the receiving end of them from others, and duly react in kind. But only in our declining years, when we start consciously to re-cognise and accept not only the brighter, more positive aspects of the power-drive within us but its darker, more threatening aspects too, can it be truly said that the Father within us has finally come into his own and that, with Hades, we are truly ready to re-enter the ancient womb of the Earth Mother from which we originally sprang.

This in turn suggests that much time and patience may be

necessary before we can learn to accept the influence on us of the Father Archetype *in full*. Learning to cope with it can be a life-long task. Prone as we are to reject our tendency to reject, to confront our instinct to confront, to react violently to our drive to violence, we too easily jump to the immediate conclusion that whole aspects of him have 'nothing to do with us'. Whereupon rejection, confrontation, violence and aggression become 'problems' instead of natural instincts, and long-term therapy becomes essential.

Nevertheless, the extent of the need for therapy needs first of all to be carefully assessed in the usual way.

1. Self-enquiry

Take time out, then, to examine yourself, your attitudes and feelings from the point of view of Zeus and Athena, Poseidon and Hades.

(a) Accepted aspects

Are you at heart a creator and taker of new initiatives? Do you have a healthy and active sex-drive, whether or not you choose to exercise it? Are you by instinct fatherly and paternal? Are you a model of domestic authority, a source of reassurance and protection to your whole family? Are you a pillar of society, a tower of strength to your community or social group? Do you positively exude reliability, power and authority? Do you have flashes of intuitive insight regarding the best answers to particular problems, and are you then prepared to act on them? Are you resolute and decisive? Can you make up your mind quickly? Are you prepared to stick to your own decisions, once made, through thick and thin, regardless of what others say, think or feel? Do you have a powerful personality that tends to make you the centre of attention? Do the groups and organisations to which you belong tend in the end to revolve about you and your ideas? Do others seek your opinion and cultivate your support? Do they often ask you to advise them, even – on occasions – to make up their minds for them?

Are you generous, good-humoured, magnanimous and compassionate? Are you canny and tactful, politically astute and always adaptable to circumstances? Do you have a large ration of worldly wisdom culled from direct personal experience? Are you a good negotiator, manager and organiser?

If the answer to most or all of these is 'Yes', either Zeus or his daughter Athena is likely to be healthily alive and kicking within you.

However, the Sky Father has other, less welcome, aspects – and these, too, need to be considered. Do not be surprised, therefore, if you find the following list of questions increasingly disturbing. If you find yourself angry or affronted at what they seem to imply, that is actually a very healthy and promising reaction, as we shall go on to see.

(b) Rejected aspects

Are you domineering and dictatorial, whether within the family, socially or at work? Are you prone to disregard the views and wishes of others? Are you aggressive, ruthless and sometimes violent? Are you sometimes petulant, even vindictive, in your efforts to get your own way? Do you often quarrel with those about you and even lose your temper with them? Do you sometimes get into well-nigh murderous rages? Are you prone to resort to bluster when your bluff is called? Are you quite prepared to resort to pretence and dissimulation if necessary? Are you a victim of your own pride, prone to take on bigger and bigger challenges that you know you would be better off avoiding? Are you so wedded to the world of the mind and the intellect as to be totally floored by any brush with the deeper aspects of your own being – as revealed, for example, by drink, drugs, illness, midlife or personal or family tragedy? Are you prone to cramps, paralysis or back-problems?

Do you, in the process, find it difficult to relate to your own children? Are you still suffering from the influence of an over-possessive mother, and so inclined to put women down or even abuse them? Are you at heart, in other words, something of a chauvinist? Are you over-sexed? Do you have a tendency to sexual violence? Are you inherently promiscuous, and driven to seek all kinds of sexual thrills outside marriage? Are you tempted to commit rape, whether within marriage or outside it?

To turn to the more Poseidonian elements of the archetype, are you additionally prone to all kinds of destructive urges? Are you sometimes savagely violent in your aggression? Are you frequently irrational, surly, rebellious or plain bloody-minded? Are you a self-centred power-maniac, an out-and-out empire-builder? Are you jealous of others' power, possessions and achievements and acutely possessive of your own? Are you sexually a positive threat to others, with a strong tendency to commit heterosexual, homosexual or even pederastic rape? Are you also prone to all kinds of tremors and shakes, to hypertension and/or to heart-problems?

Finally, do others find that, with age, you are becoming increasingly like Hades – ever more miserly and reclusive, as well as obstinate, stiff and inflexible? Do they accuse you of being drily puritanical and addicted to routine? Do you yourself find that you are more and more gloomy, and prone to nostalgia and retrospection

– yet at the same time still plagued by occasional violent sexual urges? Are you also starting to suffer from sight-problems or even actual blindness?

Once again, many of these 'rejected' aspects of the Father Archetype are potentially fraught with emotion. It would be unusual if some of them at least did not arouse strong reactions within you. At the same time, though, the very strength of those reactions has an extremely helpful function. It suggests that the characteristics to which you are reacting are in fact *rejected aspects of yourself*. They pertain, in other words, to your own darker aspect, just as they pertain to the darker aspect of the Archetypal Father himself, and for that reason they are normally hidden from you (however obvious they may be to others). Indeed, much the same may even apply to the *positive* aspects listed under (a) above – in which case therapy is doubly urgent. (In practice, this probably means that you are so devoted to some other god – possibly a female one – as to be unable for the moment to *ac-knowledge* the presence of any other archetype within yourself, least of all the inner Father.)

What is important now, therefore, is to learn to *re-cognise* and accept not only the first list of characteristics above, but the second list too (whether or not you actually put them all into practice) – for if you are rejecting them you are by definition rejecting large parts of your inner Father too.

(c) Total non-recognition and projection

As ever, though, the most dangerous case is possibly where you have failed to identify with – or to react to – the listed characteristics at all. If this was so in your own case, go through the second list especially for a second time now and ask yourself whether you associate the qualities described mainly with *other people*. Are you irked by people who are forceful and decisive, and resentful of their apparent determination to organise and control others? Are you appalled by people who throw their weight about? Are you dismissive of leaders and administrators (and parents, too, perhaps) who revel in making grand gestures and decisions, yet seem unwilling to involve themselves in the nitty-gritty of down-to-earth details? Do you hate their scarcely-concealed aggression, feel contempt for their innate ruthlessness? Do you find them patronising and overbearing? Are you disturbed by their general chauvinism, self-centredness and lack of consideration for anybody else's wishes or feelings? Do you find them childish in their determination always to have their own way, as well as in their moodiness and vindictiveness when thwarted? Do you despise their petulance and their quickness to shovel off all responsibility onto others when things go wrong? Are you contemptuous of their proneness to take on more than they can chew? Do you scorn them for their inability to cope with their own lives and families, especially in the emotional and sexual sense?

On the more Poseidonian level, do megalomaniacs and empire-builders frankly sicken you? Do their predatory sexual instincts disgust you and make you wish that they could be locked up for good? Are you disturbed by people in authority (or elderly parents) who are aggressive to the point of being surly, con-frontational, bloody-minded, violent and even downright destructive? Are you inclined to have them shut away in institutions or homes for the elderly?

At the level of Hades, finally, are you incensed by older parents, leaders and/or administrators who are determined to hang on to power at all costs, clinging on with iron fingers to the old ways of doing things and refusing to allow anybody else a look-in? Are you angry at their rigidity, frustrated at their refusal to change, contemptuous of their apparent meanness of spirit? Would you have them dismissed, disempowered and even banned by law from holding responsibility of any kind?

Once again, there are many who take such attitudes – often for reasons that they regard as perfectly logical, natural and moral. The very strength of feeling with which they do so, however, reveals that the characteristics concerned *are actually part of their own Shadow.* Having rejected those qualities within themselves, they are now (naturally enough) unable to *re-cognise* them there, and so are forced to project them onto other people, where they can now safely go on rejecting and condemning them to their hearts' content.

This, as we saw earlier, is a recipe not for healing, but for continued division – whether in the inner or the outer world.

In such cases, then, therapy is especially urgent.

(d) Total acceptance

As ever, this is the ideal. We all need to be able to accept the archetypal Father within ourselves not only in his more welcome aspects, but also in his darker manifestations. We need to be able to accept all the characteristics listed with easy-going equanimity, *re-cognising* that they are at very least potential or latent within ourselves – even if, as autonomous people, we choose not to express all of them in practice.

If you can already manage this degree of acceptance, in all probability little in the way of extra therapy is needed beyond what you naturally undertake as part of your normal life-routine. If you cannot do so, though, some kind of deliberate therapy is needed – and the ancient myths can as usual be relied on to suggest suitable measures to take.

2. Invocation

Start, then, in the usual way. Name the great creator-god of the sky and/or his illustrious daughter. Alternatively, if the circumstances warrant it, name the masculine gods of sea or underworld. Welcome them unconditionally into your life, *re-cognising* that you yourself have a strong, creative, even over-riding spiritual aspect, as well as harbouring within yourself a deep ocean of destructive unconscious drives and instincts and a whole underworld of unexpressed hopes and mortal fears. Seek out pictures of Zeus, Poseidon or Hades (or, failing that, watch plenty of movies starring Jack Hawkins, John Wayne, Richard Burton or Laurence Olivier in their grandest, most commanding roles – whether on the side of the law or against it – as well as those featuring dark, sinister, manipulative enemies of progress such as the aptly-named Godfather or the black-helmeted Darth Vader). If possible, use your holidays to visit their temples –

- those of Zeus at Olympia and Athens in mainland Greece, as well as at Agrigento and Selinunte in southern Sicily, plus the small sanctuary which he shares with Athena on the summit of Delos's Mount Kynthos (not forgetting, either, his secluded oracle at Dodona in north-western Greece and his reputed 'birth-caves' on Mounts Dikte and Ida on Crete);
- the temples of Athena at Delphi, Sparta and Athens (the Parthenon and Hephaestion), at Syracuse (the cathedral) and Agrigento (the Temple of Concord) in Sicily, and at Priene in

Turkey, plus the temples which she shares with Zeus on Delos
and with the goddess Aphaia on Aegina;

• the celebrated temple of Poseidon that looks out from Cape
Sounion to the east of Athens (a spectacular bus-ride from the
city along the Greek 'riviera');

• the small grotto and sanctuary of Hades at Eleusis just to the
west of the city (40 minutes by bus from Plateia Eleftherias), and
the forbidding Necromanteion of Ephyra, the reputed 'entrance to
the underworld' near the villages of Kastri and Mesopotamo in
north-western Greece.

If you have the chance, buy a small statuette of whichever god is
appropriate. When you get home, consider setting it up in your
bedroom and making a 'shrine' around it. Alternatively, substitute a
small bust or statuette – or even just a picture – of any outstanding
'father-figure' (or possibly 'godfather-figure') from history or
fiction. Then meditate before it each morning and evening. Affirm
your willingness to accept the basic characteristics of the Father
Archetype in their entirety, both in yourself and in others, and
express your refusal henceforth to feel either guilty or ashamed at
expressing what in fact are perfectly natural and normal aspects of
the vigorous, decisive, powerful inner father who is latent within
us all.

Meanwhile, invoking the gods also means deliberately giving
yourself the chance to encounter their characteristics within yourself
and to recognise them for what they are – and, as ever, thanks to our
penchant for projection, this means (among other things) exposing
yourself to outer circumstances that reflect them. And so your next
task has to be deliberately to expose yourself to circumstances that

draw forth your innate powers of initiative and creativity (as well, of course, as your destructiveness), that involve you in making decisions and taking responsibility for them, that encourage you to make your voice heard in debate, that force you to assert your will and that place you in positions of power over others.

These are, of course, all qualities which traditional courses in leadership are specifically designed to encourage and develop. And so your first task is deliberately to seek out experiences of this kind. You could do this by volunteering for officer-training in the armed forces, or equally by undergoing intensive management-training in the context of commerce or industry. Since, however, both types of course are likely to involve you in a considerable degree of personal commitment over a number of years, you may prefer to seek similar training in more amateur, part-time contexts. If you are young enough, for example, there may still be time to gain experience as a school prefect, or as a senior army, navy or air force cadet. If you are slightly older, helping out with the local cubs, scouts or guides – or a whole range of other youth-organisations – can provide you with similar experience (whatever it may do for those you are in charge of!). Pursuing the theme, taking up teaching of any kind places you willy-nilly in positions of trust and responsibility in which you will be forced to impose your will on others and take the rap for your own decisions. Inevitably you will be called upon to be creative and destructive by turns as the occasion requires, to make your voice heard among a whole host of competing demands, and even to defend your own way of doing things against those in authority who for largely political or theoretical reasons would ride roughshod over your personal inclinations and decisions with little or no regard to your own views on the matter.

But there are other activities, too – activities that can combine leadership-training with experiences that are symbolically a good deal more apt to the Jovian initiative than teaching (which, as we shall see, is more the province of **Orpheus**). Courses and group-expeditions of the Outward Bound type, in particular, can combine training in leadership and personal initiative with such highly appropriate activities as caving, hill-walking and mountaineering. Almost any wilderness-activity that involves the taking of decisions on behalf of others in difficult circumstances is meat and drink to the archetypal Father within us. And if it additionally involves handling or controlling large animals such as bulls or horses, so much the better.

Where Poseidon is in evidence, indeed – and especially among young offenders or people with severe problems of social adjustment – this last-mentioned form of therapy can prove particularly valuable. Moreover, the very nature of Poseidon also suggests a whole range of maritime activities such as sail-training, coastguard or lifeboat-work and the organisation of group scuba-diving. At the same time courses in public speaking and voice-projection are also grist to the archetypal paternal mill. These could then lead on naturally to an involvement in politics – whether (with Zeus) of the right or (with Poseidon) of the revolutionary left. And so you may well wish to consider becoming an active member of your local political party or trade union, subsequently working to achieve a position of prominence and power within it.

Meanwhile, there is a further decision to be taken. You will need to decide whether you can successfully combine all this with marrying and starting a family or whether, with Athena, you feel that you should become a dedicated career-man or career-woman pure and simple, channelling all your creative instincts into matters political, commercial, social, legal, scientific, medical and/or cultural.

If, however, you have already succeeded in reaching the second half of life, the time may have come for you to consider adopting the typical activities of Hades – or rather the relative lack of them. In this case refuse to feel guilty about hanging on to power and control for as long as you feel able to in the teeth of opposition from people who are younger than you are. Unashamedly use your wealth to invest and play the market. Then, when you feel that the time is right, *give it all up*. Simply rest on your laurels, retire on the amassed proceeds and refuse to move with the times. Be perfectly prepared to insist on your rights, to be thought old-fashioned and a fuddy-duddy, to become set in your ways, to withdraw into yourself, to become nostalgic, to give yourself over to introspection, even to become a relative recluse. Remember that, under the traditional Hindu dispensation, such things are regarded not only as the prerogatives, but actually as the *duties* of old age. Only when the mood takes you should you start to open up, to give in gracefully, to hand over responsibility to others, and eventually to pass on your accumulated wealth little by little to the next generation.

In the role of Hades, then, meditative activities naturally start to enter the picture. But even before that, a range of more purely contemplative activities can help to offset and enrich the Jovian and Poseidonian penchant for vigorous action.

3. Meditation

Merely by 'being fully with' the above activities you are, of course, already participating in a kind of meditation. But pure thought and cogitation are also germane to the nature of Zeus, even if they tend to replaced in the case of Poseidon by more subliminal and even unconscious thought-processes – and are nearly always, in either case, designed to lead specifically to subsequent action.

Zeus, like all the other gods, has his typical symbols, too, and these can duly serve as objects for your contemplation. Ask yourself, then, whether you have the courage to allow yourself to thunder with rage, or your temper to flash like the lightning. Can you admit to all your continually-changing moods like the sky, being unashamedly sunny and darkly cloudy by turns? Can you accept both sides of your nature – the humble powerlessness and vulnerability of the dark birth-cave and the resplendent light and glory of the mountain-top? Can you succeed in connecting the two, *re-cognising* that the one is in reality merely the flip-side of the other? Can you be at one and the same time as sturdy and resilient as the oak and as light and airy as the white poplar, as humble and simple as the crocus and as resplendently leafy as the laurel or the bay tree? Can you, in short, be just as two-sided – and, if necessary, two-faced – as the ancient double-axe itself, fully accepting that your innate vigour and initiative are apt to 'cut both ways'?

Turning to Zeus's animal-symbols, are you prepared to be as creative, and as extravagantly and aggressively masculine, as the white bull or wild stallion? Equally, can you be as hierarchical, aggressive and (if need be) violently destructive as the wolf, as predatory and individualistic as the eagle, as self-willed and self-regarding as the swan, as resilient, ingenious and constructive as the beaver? Do you have it within you to be as generously life-giving as the she-goat or sow, as mobile and wide-ranging as the dove or quail, as deceptive and dissimulating as the cuckoo?

As Athena, are you inherently as fit as a horse, as robust and terrible as a lion? Are you fully prepared to be as self-willed as a goat, as wily and insinuating as a serpent? Can you be as wise as the proverbial owl, calmly waiting amidst the night for the right moment to strike with silent and terrible fury? By day, too, are you ready to descend on your victims out of a cloudless sky like the eagle, the gannet or even the vulture? Can you be as sublimely confident in your freedom to act as are the shearwater, the swallow, the dove or the lark, while remaining no more cramped by your highly-developed intellect than the irrepressible dolphin? Are you strong enough to be a shield and helmet in the defence of those whom you lead, as well as their spear in times when aggression becomes necessary? Are you prepared to invoke the double-edged magic of the ancient swastika, symbol of the sacred lightning-flash (in German, *Blitz*)? Are you prepared to turn a terrible, petrifying countenance on all who oppose you, after the model of the Gorgon Medusa? At the same time, do you have it within you to spread about you the peace of the willow and the olive branch, to promote those independent, new, creative initiatives that are symbolised by the magic mistletoe, to encourage music and the plastic arts as symbolised by the flute and the clay bowl?

Turning to Poseidon's symbols, are you prepared to be as vigorous and slippery as the fish, as intelligently independent as the dolphin? Are you prepared to express your aggressive instincts with all the force and energy, not merely of the ram or white bull, but of a whole herd of stampeding white horses? Are you prepared, like the ash-tree, to seek your energy from levels of yourself that lie far below the surface of the conscious world? And are you ready to express your anger and resentment not merely in the form of a well-directed lightning-flash directed at a single target, but at all and sundry via the triple prongs of the traditional trident or fish-spear?

Finally, as Hades, are you quite prepared to be regarded as the black sheep of your family or society? Are you content to wear the dark helmet of invisibility – retiring from the limelight to do your own thing in your own way, and without any regard for the approval or disapproval of others? Are you ready to give up the trappings of power and avert your gaze from the everyday world, in the process becoming so inscrutable that people frankly don't know whether you are coming or going? And are you prepared to drive your own dark chariot and its four black horses through the deepest night of your own inner kingdom, snatching what you need and desire wherever and whenever you find it?

Do not attempt to answer these questions. Merely pose them and then allow yourself to sink into meditation, so that the answers have a chance to emerge of their own accord. Wherever possible, make actual, physical contact with the objects, plants and creatures involved. Then finish by asking yourself the following questions, this time attempting to answer them, too:

Am I feeling guilty about my vigorous, assertive 'masculine' instincts?

If so, can I overcome that guilt by learning to realise that they are not only perfectly natural to myself but, have a perfectly valid place in the human scheme of things?

Am I finding legitimate contexts for expressing those instincts by deliberately seeking positions of power, leadership and responsibility?

Am I prepared to take big decisions and, having taken them, to stick by them?

Am I succeeding in expressing my anger and resentment, even to the extent of losing my temper and resorting to violence from time to time?

Am I prepared to let go of self-doubt and take full responsibility for myself, for my family and ultimately for all those in my charge?

Am I taking myself too seriously – and if so can I make more space in my life for my natural sense of humour to emerge, to say nothing of my natural magnanimity and generosity?

Ponder on your answers, and consider whether this is the moment to adjust your way of life to reflect them.

4. Remedial activities

On the basis of the myths, there are a number of activities that seem designed positively to encourage you to develop your paternal aspects. You may wish to consider adopting some of them, perhaps on a trial basis initially. Several of them pick up on themes that have been mentioned already. Add any favourite activities of your own that seem appropriate and natural to you. For convenience, the activities listed are as usual divided here into two categories:

(a) Recreational and general

As Zeus, dress well. Show off with expensive, dazzling watches or jewellery. Wear a whole range of colours – but especially light blue and dark grey – and change them frequently according to the season, the weather and the time of day. Get married and start a family.

Alternatively accept the fact that in future your life is going to be your work, and your work your life. Involve yourself in cultural and artistic activities of every kind. Go horse-riding. Attend and/or participate in race-meetings, show-jumping and eventing. Whether in the French Camargue, in the Australian outback or elsewhere, get as close to wild horses as possible. Eat beef and other red meats (you are, after all, no chicken!). Enjoy good wine.

Listen to majestic, grandiose music such as that of Liszt, Wagner, Bruckner, Mahler, Elgar or Walton. Go walking in the rain or in stormy weather. Go hill-walking and mountaineering, if possible sleeping in a cave or under an overhang the night before setting out for the summit. Once there, drink in the full feeling of exuberance and exaltation that the distant view of the world below brings with it. Attend leadership courses – or, in the 'alternative' context, courses in 'mastery' such as those run by the Findhorn Foundation. Seek voice-training – perhaps in the context of acting or drama-school – and take up public speaking. Involve yourself in local or national politics (right-wing in the case of Zeus, far left-wing in the case of Poseidon). Buy a big a house and a big car – possibly with personalised number-plates. Engage servants. Create an organisation around yourself. Unashamedly seek pre-eminence and renown in whatever you do.

If you identify more with Athena, make sure that you dress tastefully, but also in such a way as to impress, concentrating on bright colours such as yellow or gold, and not forgetting the odd flash of golden jewellery. Concentrate on this much more than on beautifying your face, bearing in mind that you will need to use your features much more to impress and subdue others than to appear soft and attractive to them. Devote your energies wholeheartedly to all kinds of civilised arts, crafts and sciences. Become a spare-time spinner, weaver, potter, sculptor or metalworker. At the same time, though, consider taking up various of the traditional martial arts.

In the case of Poseidon, wear mainly deep blues, greens and purples, perhaps with a touch of white somewhere. Learn to know the sea in all its moods. Go sailing, cruising, swimming, surfing or scuba-diving. Gain plenty of experience of typhoons, hurricanes and storms at sea. Visit sea-caves and grottoes. Observe fish and dolphins from close quarters in the wild. Eat fish and seafoods. Seek plenty of opportunities to be physically violent. Knock down old sheds and buildings. Find plenty of opportunities to use pick-axes or sledge hammers. Where necessary, get involved in tree-felling. Possibly take up wrestling, boxing or weight-lifting. Help look after large animals such as bulls or horses. Attend bullfights and bull-running events in Spain or Latin America – carefully examining any initial aversion you may have to the idea in the light of the possibility that what you are objecting to may really be not so much the cruelty to animals involved, but being forced to face the violent, aggressive, bullish aspects of yourself. Join your local trade union. Become a social or political agitator. Be an unashamed revolutionary. Listen to disturbing or turbulent music such as that of Beethoven, Berlioz, Liszt, Stravinsky or Bartók, as well as parts of Holst (e.g. 'Mars the Bringer of War' from the *Planets Suite*).

In the case of Hades, dress mainly in black or dark grey. Keep yourself to yourself. Be as reclusive as you like. If you have a cellar, convert it into a private den. Explore underground workings and cave-systems. Stay mainly indoors in the daytime. Go out mainly at dead of night – and then wear a hat pulled down well over your eyes. Remain incognito. Practise introspection, contemplation and meditation. Recall and record your dreams. Eat red meat (preferably still runny in the middle) and blood-based products such as black pudding, and ensure that your diet has a high iron content. Listen to calming, hypnotic music such as that of Debussy, Satie, Ravel, Fauré, Delius, Vaughan Williams or other parts of Holst (e.g. 'Saturn' and 'Uranus' from his *Planets Suite*), or 'grey' music such as that of Hindemith or Schönberg.

(b) Professional

As Zeus, seek any post of responsibility and leadership in industry, commerce, politics or the professions. Go into law, administration, planning, insurance, the rescue services, large-scale charity work or even general trouble-shooting. Always think big and aim for the top. Best of all, start your own business – thus (like a well-digger!) actually *starting* from the top. Also consider work (part-time or otherwise) with large animals or in the field of meteorology and weather-forecasting.

As Athena, take up any or all of the arts and sciences. Go into mathematics, medicine (especially obstetrics) and healing generally. Campaign for personal and public hygiene. Take up law, civics, politics, diplomacy, mediation, marriage-guidance, and/or teaching. Become a militant campaigner for just causes of every kind.

In the case of Poseidon, take up any marine profession. Join the merchant navy and work your way up to sea-captain. Go into marine biology. Join the submarine service. Become a hydrographer. Take up marine surveying or engineering. Seek work as a seismologist, and take a special interest in submarine earthquakes and *tsunamis* (tidal waves). Gain plenty of experience of heavy-weather sailing in the worst possible conditions. On land, take up water-divining.

Become a water- or river-engineer. Go into competitive commerce, and be fully prepared to destroy the opposition. If the idea grabs you, go into the demolition industry. Seek work with large and difficult animals – especially bulls and horses.

Finally, as Hades, use your acquired riches to move into geology, mining, drilling and mineral prospecting. Speculate in oil, minerals and precious stones. Then, once you have made your pile, retire and enjoy it all. Do not be tempted to make a come-back. Sit back and relax. You have earned it.

SUB-PERSONALITIES OF ZEUS AND HIS FAMILY

ARES (for Poseidon)

Possible symptoms
Conflict for its own sake; combativeness; belligerence; revenge; jealousy; possessiveness; irrationality; unconscious rage; impetuousity; insensitivity; violence; contempt for process of law; mistreatment or betrayal of mother; tendency to scream when hurt; drunkenness

but also
Fertility; competitiveness, growth; expansion; tallness; fleetness of foot; masculinity; strict control.

Therapies
Name, imagine and welcome this fearsome and brutal martial god, who is both armoured and armed to the teeth; love; self-sacrifice in some idealistic cause; approved military activities; martial arts;

military administration; team challenges; justice; civilised arts and sciences; peaccmaking and mediation; dancing; female company.

Symbols

Spear and shield; horse; wild boar; blackthorn; violet; and, latterly, the sword, bugle, rifle and rocket-missile.

Notes

Ares (who has a sister and female analogue called Eris) is the Greeks' young, straight-limbed, impetuous God of War – and for that very reason not the easiest of customers to deal with. His difficult nature seems to spring mainly from the absence of a father in his early years, together with the malign influence of desperately violent young companions. Female company may help, but by and large the safest course appears to be simply to give him suitable outlets for his aggression, appropriate situations for him to control, and safe areas in which to indulge his passion for trouble-making – at least until the youthful, martial impulse starts to mellow with age. The use of 'team challenges' as therapy seems not to be without its dangers; the story of the Argonauts' theft of the Golden Fleece from Ares' temple at Colchis suggests that it could merely serve to stir up subterranean passions which only drugs (in the form of Medea – see under **Artemis**) can then hope to calm. Astrologically, as the Roman Mars, Ares seems most likely to make his presence felt in spring and late autumn.

ATLAS (for Poseidon)

Possible symptoms

Rebelliousness; sedition; implacable fury; aggression; tendency to 'bear the world on his shoulders'; proneness to accept over-heavy responsibilities; hunched shoulders; possible hypertension; back or heart problems; possible hernia; gullibility; simplistic outlook; dangerous intuitive wisdom; inhospitality

but also

Marine knowledge; strength; rock-like resolve; solid presence; leadership.

Therapies

Name, imagine and welcome the mighty leader of the Titans and elder brother of **Prometheus**, condemned forever to hold up the sky; diving; submarine activities; revolutionary activities; government; large-scale administration; positions of responsibility; leadership; especially in war; gardening; sunset.

Symbols

Moon, oak.

Notes

Atlas is a tower of strength. Terrible when thwarted, and an insufferable subordinate, he flourishes when given responsibility, and turns out to be a magnificent leader, especially in times of crisis. He has broad shoulders, a massive, solid presence and an earthy, simplistic nature that sometimes translates itself into a lack of insight and finesse. His main problem is that other people tend too readily to saddle him with theirs: indeed, once he has taken up a given burden, they will not allow him to put it down again. Management and administration therefore beckon, but for his own health he would do well to delegate, and to surround himself with good advisers. Perhaps his major task is to make up his mind just when is the best moment for him to resign and finally call a halt. By and large, the answer is likely to be sooner rather than later.

CRONUS (for Hades)

Possible symptoms

Ageing; dying; impotence; constriction; repressive attitude to own children; obduracy; rigidity; dogmatism; coldness; child-cruelty; infanticide; self-destruction through own misdeeds; continued resentment of parents; regret; nostalgia; introversion; melancholy; depression; insomnia; destructive attitude to new initiatives; fear of change; fear of the new and of the future; mania for order; obsessive counting; self-justification; rebellious sons; perjury; left-handedness; clumsiness; possible stroke, with paralysis of right side

but also

Precocious mental powers in childhood; intellectuality; administrative and organisational ability; good powers of self-healing and regeneration; oracular gifts; inspiration; eventual serenity based on happy memories.

Therapies

Name, imagine and welcome the gloomy, materialistic old Titan, the murderer of his own father Uranus and usurper of his kingdom, but now threatened in his turn by his own children; literature; writing (e.g. memoirs); reflection; reminiscing; self-immersion in present interests; administration; planning; forecasting; harvesting; ponies; horsemeat; fire; sunset; autumnal oracles; spring festivities; high mountains.

Symbols

Crow; vulture; golden-crested wren; ass; horse; barley; cornel cherry; golden falchion (sickle-shaped short sword); the planet Saturn.

Notes

Cronus is Old Father Time. He comes with his sickle to reap the harvest of life and make way for next year's seed. Provided that the task is acknowledged and co-operated with, his function is entirely healthy. His negative side, however, is nostalgia and chronic negativity – 'Old is good; new is bad' – the result of failure to co-operate with **Hermes** at midlife and to realise that death is the ultimate goal, and not the antithesis, of life. The result is a particularly repressive and heavy-handed old man, clinging on for all he is worth to former ways of thinking and acting, and living out the motto 'If it grows, cut it; if it moves, kill it.' This attitude in turn is liable, if persisted with, to provoke violent opposition from his children, leading to the forcible limitation of his power and freedom.

Astrologically, as the Roman Saturn, Cronus is most likely to make his presence felt at midwinter – whence his universal presence as the Spirit of Christmas Past. Untreated, he tends eventually to take on the character of **Hades**.

EPIMETHEUS (for Hades)
Brother of PROMETHEUS

Possible symptoms
Retrospection; regret; guilt; resentment, especially of hard work and ageing; incompetence; ineffectualness; profligacy; lack of planning-ability and foresight; heedlessness; unsatisfied passion; false hope; marriage as an attempt to escape inner problems; severe marital difficulties; psychosomatic illness; general health problems; vice; insanity; suicidal tendencies; morbidity

but also
See Prometheus (below).

Therapies
Name, imagine and invoke this powerful, yet backward looking and incompetent Titan; see Prometheus.

Symbols
See Prometheus.

Notes Epimetheus (whose name means 'afterthought') suffers from much the same problems as his more illustrious brother, except in reverse. Instead of always looking to the future, he indulges in the even more futile activity of living in the past. His most characteristic saying is 'If only…' Nevertheless, his basic problem is the same: avoidance of the present, and refusal to live *now*. Any suitable Promethean activity which helps to correct this attitude may thus prove useful.

HERA (for Athena)

Possible symptoms

Fatal softness; gullibility; dependence; ill-treatment by husband and sons; shame; embarrassment; bickering; scheming; meddling; intrigue; lying; insane jealousy; use of sex as a weapon; 'unnatural' passions for animals; anger; ruthlessness; vengefulness; repeated desertion of husband; retreat into isolation; hatred of own children, adopted children, servants or agents; long periods of depression; temporary paralysis; rheumatism or back-problems; risk of death

but also

Beauty; femininity; fidelity; motherhood, tenderness; emotional warmth; pity; love of virginity; conventionality; insistence on monogamy; physical modesty; eventual reconciliation with children or adopted children.

Therapies

Name, imagine and welcome the jealous and rather shrewish wife and twin of Zeus, the cow-eyed leader of the female faction on Olympus and Goddess of Death and Resurrection; monogamous marriage; childbearing; midwifery; fostering, adoption; separation; divorce; backstairs politics; all-concealing clothing; female athletics and gymnastics; back-stretching exercises (seek qualified advice); gardening; attention to calendar and the phases of the moon; swimming and bathing, especially in clear spring-water; wearing of bangles, bracelets and anklets.

Symbols

Cow; cuckoo; apple tree; pomegranate; mayflower or white-thorn; double axe.

Notes

Hera is a complicated character. Endowed with all the positive characteristics of a good wife and mother, she is at the same time so prone to feelings of jealousy that she is prepared to sacrifice and destroy everything she believes in – even her own life, if need be – in an attempt to re-establish what she believes to be her rights. Consequently her married life tends to be dogged by ever-growing crisis. In this she tends to be motivated more by her image of men than by the way her man actually is, and so tends to come into fatal collision with his parallel tendency to see only his image of woman, rather than the actual human being beside him. The victim of early paternal conditioning, she may thus do well to seek an alternative destiny outside marriage, and particularly in close proximity to nature.

PELOPS (for Zeus)

Possible symptoms

Early paternal cruelty or psychic damage; seething resentment; fevers; childhood wasting disease or disfigurement; seduced by older member of same sex; difficult courtship thanks to opposition of intended's father; competitiveness; dirty tricks to achieve ends; ruthlessness; reneging on agreements; pride

but also

Goodwill; idealism; sense of propriety; magnanimity; canniness; fame; respect; power; wealth; wisdom; courage; fertility.

Therapies

Name, imagine and invoke the misused son of Tantalus who by hook or by crook manages to make good; administration; government; public works and services; speedboats; hovercraft; sea-bathing; mountaineering; philanthropy; rope-dances.

Symbols

Ivory human shoulder-blade; spear-sceptre; horse.

Notes

Pelops – for whom the Peloponnese is named – is a classic case of compensation for early ill-treatment and disadvantage. In childhood he is 'eaten up' by those around him, all of whom tend to want a piece of him for themselves. Although, as an adult, he may have problems in achieving his aims, his sheer drive and ruthlessness tend to ensure that he eventually achieves power and status more than sufficient to offset anything that has gone before. All that is necessary in the way of treatment is sufficient outlets for his constant excess of energy. Mountaineering could well appeal particularly.

PROMETHEUS (for Poseidon)

Possible symptoms

Worry; anxiety; mental and spiritual torments; 'pierced to the quick'; possible hypertension or heart-problems; devious or dishonest reasoning; head-orientated living; headstrong behaviour; craftiness; wariness; two-facedness; sedition; rebelliousness; belief in rights and principles; militancy; chip on the shoulder; support of revolutionary causes; chafing at physical limitations; frustration; temper; rage; belief in progress; undervaluing of the feminine; contempt for unconscious; chronic digestive disorders or hepatitis; possible back-problems, arthritis, or paralysis from the neck down.

but also

Thought; reason; logic; anticipation; planning ability; wisdom; compassion; philanthropy; support of the underdog; craftsmanship; good recuperative powers; tolerance of cold; toughness; earthiness; eventual accommodation to spirituality; overcoming of health-problems through Herculean efforts.

Therapies

Name, imagine and welcome the vigorous, wilful and cunningly subversive herald of the Titans who steals fire (i.e. the light of reason) from heaven for mankind and is condemned to be impaled on a stake (or chained to a rock) for his pains, while his liver is pecked out daily by a vulture (or eagle); crafts (especially those involving metal and clay); civilised arts and sciences (including architecture, astronomy, mathematics, navigation, medicine and metallurgy); backstairs politics; heroic endeavours on behalf of others; philanthropy; work for the underprivileged and underdog; blood-sacrifices; investigation of spirituality; sleep; probing of physical limits; the open air; mountains and hills; solitude; naked exposure to cold, e.g. snow baths (these and other associated activities such as cold showers or baths and year-round open-air swimming should be approached, if at all, gently and by easy stages; if other than young and fit, seek medical advice; desist at once if adverse side-effects arise).

Symbols

Fire; fire-drill; jewelled iron ring; crocus; willow; wreath of subjection; the constellation Sagitta.

Notes

Prometheus, the Titan whose name means 'forethought' (or possibly 'swastika'), is the mythical creator of mankind, i.e. the entity responsible, along with Athene, for making human consciousness what it is. But there is a price to pay. His act incurs the wrath of Zeus on behalf of the whole archetypal pantheon. It represents a kind of unilateral declaration of conscious independence, a split within the psyche — and this is a state of affairs which cannot be sustained for long, and which the unconscious will do its Olympian utmost to avenge, however long it takes. The inner state of civil war is duly reflected in the form of physical symptoms, which in turn serve as pointers to appropriate remedial action if illness is to be avoided. There seem to be hints that the subject may need to be literally shocked out of his state of inner tension. Indeed, the myth of Cheiron, king of the Centaurs (see **Dionysus**), suggests that there is some prospect of success, provided only that Prometheus's characteristic militancy can be quietly allowed to die.

Prometheus is not merely one of the most familiar daemons of modern Western males; he is the masculine guiding spirit of the whole of traditional Western civilisation. Consequently his myth has important lessons for all of us.

TYPHON (for Poseidon)

Possible symptoms

Repressed unconscious urges generally; bad dreams; horrors; delusions; irrationality; pyromania; hot temper; blazing eyes; fiery words; muddled, incomprehensible utterances; fevers; murderous inclinations; temptation to rape; sabotaging of heroic impulse; direct opposition to spirituality; skin problems; possible hypertension and/or heart-problems; possible paralysis

but also

Great strength, at least while angry; healing dreams.

Therapies

Name, imagine and invoke the violent, red-eyed demon of nightmare and spirit of the sirocco; permitted violence; wrestling and other forms of combat; storms; earthquakes; volcanic eruptions; activities involving fire.

Symbols

Ass; snake; volcano; fire.

Notes

Typhon personifies the eruptive surfacing of repressed unconscious urges — the Freudian 'subconscious' red in tooth and claw. His special trademark is violence. The product of repressive parenting – possibly violent in its turn – he may appear only at times of crisis (perhaps in association with **Dionysus**), or be constantly in attendance. In the former case he is more liable to long-term illness:

in the latter case he may be inherently healthier, but more dangerous to those around him. In both cases, therefore, he needs to be allowed suitable escape valves if he is not to 'blow his top'. And in general this involves providing safe contexts in which he can express his inner violence with minimal restraints. Provided that he can be kept in balance for long enough, it is possible that he will eventually become, if not extinct, at least dormant. But it is likely to be a highly demanding task, as, in the myth, even the mighty Zeus finds to his cost.

SUMMARY

All of us – men and women – have it within us to be paternal in our own way. We are all in some sense 'God the Father'. Whether we are prepared to admit it or not, we have within us a vigorous, aggressive, 'masculine' drive to power and domination that can be either creative or destructive in its effects. Both are perfectly valid. By seeking suitable outlets for both kinds of energy we can learn to *re-cognise* the extent to which those energies are truly native to ourselves.

Self-re-cognition thus demands that we give full rein to this currently somewhat undervalued aspect of ourselves. The experience may not be comfortable. Zeus rarely is – indeed, Poseidon *never* is – while Hades can be distinctly unnerving. Being a shrinking violet is all very well, but we need to assert ourselves too.

Assert yourself, then. Dare to be vigorous, outspoken, domineering, even bloody. Lead from the front. The sky is the limit where you are concerned. You can be just as great as you care to be.

You are quite capable of leaving your mark on your family, your group, even your society. Even if you try to avoid that responsibility you will still be forced to leave your imprint in the end. Poseidon will take care of that. So choose your mark carefully, and then go all out to make it. Only when you have succeeded in doing so will it be time to retire. Remember that it is missing the mark – Greek *hamartanein* – that is the sole ancient theological definition of sin.

In asserting yourself you will have helped to fulfil yourself. And in fulfilling yourself you will ultimately have helped to fulfil – and to discover – your Self.

8

HERMES – THE WAY OF THE TRAVELLER

And what should they know of England who only England know?
Rudyard Kipling: 'The English Flag'

HERMES is the cosmic joker, the universal travel agent, the speaker with forked tongue, the lateral thinker, the underminer of all our best plans, yet at the same time the spirit of true change, of new initiatives, of every major turning point in our lives. His is the true 'wisdom of the idiots' that can always be relied upon to guide us, but only if we are astute enough to delve into what it really means, and to realise that, taken literally, it isn't really reliable at all. In the course of our lives – at birth, at adolescence, at midlife, at death – we repeatedly encounter him, and so if we are successfully to make each of these transitions we need to make him our constant friend and counsellor.

Hermes at large

Unlike most of the other gods whom we have encountered so far, Hermes has few, if any, temples dedicated specifically to him. For Hermes is essentially the god of travellers. He is ever on the move. And so, except for certain wayside caverns and grottoes, he feels uneasy and restless in any settled sanctuary.

In antiquity Hermes was the god of borders and crossroads. His original symbol was no more than a cairn, or heap of stones. Later on, the symbol developed. It became a square, sculpted pillar. It grew a human head and face – or, quite frequently, *two* faces pointing in opposite directions. And finally it grew, of all things, an erect phallus below each face.

The result was the so-called *herm*. Its presence became both familiar and ubiquitous. It appeared wherever there was human commerce and intercourse, wherever there was constant coming-and-going, toing-and-froing. It presided over crossroads and market-places. It even took up residence outside people's front doors.

And, as is ever the case with the gods' major symbols, the *herm* said it all.

In Hermes, in other words, we are confronted with a god who takes us out of ourselves, who leads us out beyond the sacred precincts of the more homely, familiar deities that have been our concern thus far, and who exposes us to the hurly-burly of the world 'out there'.

As man and woman, as child and adolescent, as lover and parent, as mirrored in the various gods whom we have considered so far, we have, so to speak, *made our selves at home*, but now we need to go further. Having found our feet on home ground, we now need to use them to get well away from it.

For until we have gone far enough to look back at where we have come from and know it *as a whole* there is little prospect that we shall learn to know where we are going, either.

Distance may lend enchantment, but it also lends perspective.

The god of crossroads

And so we *come to the crossroads*. The very expression generates within us overtones of crisis (Greek: 'judgement'), of indecision, insecurity and risk. It also suggests that, the decision once taken, our world will never be quite the same again. Somehow we are passing from one dispensation to another, from a former way of life to a new existence entirely in which we shall hardly recognise ourselves.

Which way, then, to turn? The *herm* suggests that there are always at least two possibilities, each of which necessarily excludes the other. Yet each is likely to be just as valid and worthwhile as the other, too. This, perhaps, is one of Hermes' major lessons for us – for logical, Apollonian thinking too easily assumes that there is only one possible 'right answer', that there is no alternative.

Hermes knows better. There is *always* an alternative. And so he actually revels in the uncertainty that this situation creates. He lives on a continual knife-edge, feeds on the risks involved, knows that insecurity, like variety, is the very spice of life. He spurns security, abhors safety. 'Safe for what?' he is inclined to ask.

Thus, Hermes is in no hurry to commit himself or to arrive at firm conclusions. He is in no hurry to arrive at all. He actually derives energy from the constant play of opposites. He is fully aware that, merely by staying where he is for a while and watching what is going on around him without committing himself to either direction, he is quite likely to stumble across some unexpected *third* way that renders the first two obsolete.

Hermes, then, is the god of spontaneity, of serendipity, of the main chance, of lateral thinking. As the *herm*'s phallic symbolism itself suggests, he uses the play of opposites as a creative force for change, for discovering the new, for unlocking the hidden powers of the unconscious. And so the human being who embodies him comes across as something of a magician, a constant source of amazement to others. By the same token, he or she can be something of a healer, too – though always the Hermetic approach is original and unexpected, and is therefore likely to be regarded as vaguely disreputable by those of a more Apollonian cast of thought.

Symbols of the cosmic magician

Nevertheless, the mythical Hermes does wield **Apollo**'s golden staff (gained, in the myth, in exchange for the lyre which he has devised out of a tortoise-shell). Entwined first with the white ribbons of the messenger, and later with the twin serpents that reflect the *herm*'s twin phalluses, it duly becomes the celebrated *caduceus*, long famed as a potent token of healing. But the change of shape reflects a change of function, too. No longer is its healing role merely cleansing and antiseptic, as it might tend to be in the hands of Apollo. Nor does it imply Apollo's passion for surgical intervention. In Hermes' hands it embodies the creativity of the opposites, the power of paradox. Its healing comes neither from this nor from that, but from somewhere in between – from that unsuspected space, or void, within the psyche which is the true source of all dreams, all insights, all healing.

So it is that the hermetic staff becomes the proverbial cleft stick, and Hermes himself the *angelos*, the true messenger of the gods.

The role of the crossroads is thus clear. It represents the moment of indecision, of conscious – even deliberate – *not-knowing*, at which the god can strike deep within us. As the god of all transitions, Hermes is that god. His is the pregnant moment before the dice land on the table. His is the sudden silence that descends upon an animated conversation. His is the stillness out of which all true change comes, the calm before the storm.

And so he is essentially elusive. Like the wind, he cannot be grasped or controlled. Like the wind, he passes in a moment, and we either pass with him or let him pass us by.

The choice, the opportunity is ours. But it depends on a certain relaxed passivity, on abandoning our previous expectations and preconceptions, on allowing ourselves to live in the moment. Otherwise we shall not be aware of that magic instant when it comes. And the outcome can never be guaranteed.

All that a crossroads is likely to lead us to, after all, is another set of crossroads.

And so there is always an inherent unreliability, even deviousness, about Hermes. As the *herm* makes perfectly clear, he is essentially *two-faced*. By the same token, he is two-sexed – i.e. bisexual – too. In other words, he is no more firm or settled about matters of sexual orientation than are most of the gods that we have considered so far, and especially the childhood ones. In conjunction with love, or **Aphrodite**, he merely produces the *hermaphrodite*.

Possibly there is something of significance here. Possibly Hermes' constitutional ambivalence, his spontaneity and ability to live in the moment, are basically infantile characteristics which now find a new value in adulthood. This would tie in with his extraordinary infant prodigies – his invention of the lyre, his crafty theft of Apollo's cattle, his invention of fire and burnt-offerings *on the very day of his birth* – almost as though, in Hermes, childhood and adulthood were forever inextricably one. It would tie in, too, with his almost juvenile humour and crude sense of fun.

Possibly, in other words, Hermes has either preserved or

rediscovered **Pan** within himself – and, by that very token, has contrived to release all the primal energy of childhood which too easily becomes bottled up and inhibited by the process of upbringing and education.

Which would make sense – for Pan is none other than Hermes' son.

In Hermes, consequently, there is renewed hope for the world, as for the individual too. He is an expression of what Jung dubbed the 'child archetype'. He represents the possibility – but also the *chance* – of new birth, of new beginnings, of fresh initiatives, of unexpected insights and magical transformations. He is the Joker in the pack, the wise fool, the holy idiot.

But at the same time this makes him a perpetual outsider, even an outlaw. He is never reputable. He has about him something of the vagabond. He comes, if at all, like a thief in the night.

And what he steals is *souls*.

The thief of souls

The idea may at first seem astonishing. Yet not only does his symbolic *phallus* have a surprisingly close etymological connection with the idea of 'soul' (Greek *phallaina* = 'moth': yet at the same time 'butterfly' = *psyche* = 'mind', 'soul'). Hermes is traditionally known as the *psychopompos*, the Guide of Souls. His function is specifically to escort the dead to (and from) the underworld.

As in death, so in life. Whenever the soul needs guidance, it is Hermes who typically supplies it. He may speak to us with the voice of inner wisdom or, equally, through the mouth of another from 'out there'. Whether at birth, at adolescence, at midlife or at death, he it is who stands at the crossroads and points the way with his phallic finger.

But at this point, as we have seen, he proceeds to speak with forked tongue. What he says is inherently ambiguous. His truths are always half-truths. He means both more and less than he actually seems to say. There are dangers in taking him too literally, in assuming that the obvious meaning is the real one. Especially are there dangers in climbing up the signpost instead of following the road.

Yet, inherently untrustworthy though he is to this extent, there is nothing for it but to let go and trust him. He alone, it seems, knows the way through the encircling night. He will lead us along mysterious paths illuminated, if at all, only by the light of will-o'-the wisps and strange, deceptive shadows. Yet eventually he will bring us to the dawn.

And so, on the outer level, Hermes (who may also appear in female guise as Hecate the witch – see under **Artemis**) comes to us as the archetypal guru-figure – yet by the same token always as something of a charlatan as well. What he says cannot be trusted. What he knows can only be guessed at. Yet it is the best we have, and so there is nothing for it but to make the best use of it that we can.

Hermes the traveller

Meanwhile one thing is certain. Hermes' insights are no mere speculations. When they come, they are the fruit of long experience. And that experience may well have come from an immense amount of travelling. The travelling may have taken an outer form, involving many months and even years spent in foreign lands in a quasi-Dionysian search for wisdom and truth, drinking in life's

Avatars of Hermes

History knows many a Hermes-figure. Typically, he is the guru who is also a charlatan – as in fact every true guru probably is. Thus, we find him in the Sufi Nazruddin, in the rascally Russian mage George Gurdjieff, in the former Californian cult-figure Alan Watts (who perceptively described himself as a 'genuine fake') and in the notorious Indian guru Bhagwan Sri Rajneesh, or 'Osho'. In his role as traveller and hero we similarly find him in King Richard the Lionheart, in Francis Drake, in the explorer and writer Richard Burton, in the explorers Scott and Shackleton and in many a modern round-the-world solo sailor.

experiences both directly and through others' eyes and ears, and as translated into other thoughts and languages. Such 'meetings with remarkable men' are, after all, likely to produce a much broader perspective, a more rounded view of life in its entirety, and a familiarity with a whole range of wisdoms, philosophies and therapeutic techniques.

'Travel,' as we say, 'broadens the mind.'

Equally, that travelling may have occurred purely on the inner level. There may have been a long, spiritual journey leading through the darkest night (St John of the Cross's 'dark night of the soul') and back out again into the light of day – but a light now modulated by the filters of newly-gained inner experience.

More likely, however, both will have happened. The outer journey will merely have been the reflection of the inner one, and the inner of the outer one. The returned traveller will consequently be outwardly the same person, but inwardly totally transformed.

He will, as we say, be truly 'knowing'.

And so Hermes re-appears 'out there' as the sandal-maker poet, the tentmaker-prophet, the grocer-guru, the storyteller-sage, the beggar-seer. Perhaps, indeed, as Jesus himself. Spurned and despised by polite society, passed by unnoticed by the man or woman in the street, his apparent inconsequentialities and infantile babblings are pregnant with deeper meaning. They are the knowledge of the Sufis, the wisdom of the idiots.

And we ignore it at our peril.

True, following his advice is itself a gamble. Games of chance were always Hermes' speciality. Yet once again, as the saying has it, 'Nothing venture, nothing gain'. And, curiously, the choice, where Hermes is concerned, tends to be between winning and winning, rather than between winning and losing.

Certainly it is never clear whether he really believes what he says. Perhaps he does; perhaps he does not. Often it may seem unenlightened, at other times purely superstitious. Almost always it will seem foolish in somebody's eyes, the very opposite of common sense. If it did not, it would not be the wisdom of Hermes. It is precisely his function to propound and encourage a very *un*common sense. And, for that, few are likely to thank him.

But Hermes does not care. He is what he is. And so he will continue to sit, or wander, or tell stories, or offer divinations and predictions, or dispense herbal remedies, or throw dice, or generally play the fool as the fancy takes him, and always without the slightest trace of self-consciousness. Indeed, quite literally so. For, whatever the nature of his wisdom, it is almost always expressed in simple, outward terms, rather than as abstruse 'inner' verities. Self-consciousness is simply not an issue with him – or, at least, not in so many words. He is concerned above all with people, with stories, with therapies, with techniques. Often he gives the impression that these are all that really matter, that truth is to be discovered 'out there', and for this reason he will be despised by spiritual purists who insist that truth lies exclusively 'in here'.

Hermes knows, of course, that there is no such opposition. He is fully aware that the 'out there' and the 'in here' are ultimately one and the same – i.e. reality pure and simple and thus, by the same token, the self-same reality that he himself is. Possibly that is why he appears to us externally just as readily as internally. Possibly, too, it is why he appears to concentrate so much on those outer, physical techniques and therapies to which most people relate more easily. Or possibly it is not.

With Hermes, you can never be sure.

But then that is the nature of Hermes' salvation. Being sure is a certain recipe for failing to find out. Thinking you know the answer is a sure-fire guarantee that you will fail to ask the question.

Hermes, then, is essentially the spirit of uncertainty, and as such his advent, whether 'out there' or 'in here', offers us life at its most living, opportunity at its most limitless.

The inner Hermes

The moment for discovering Hermes in our lives is any moment of transition. It is a moment, consequently, that actually comes at each successive instant of our lives, for we are *always* in transition. But birth, adolescence, midlife and death are clearly marked out for us as our most critical Hermetic moments – and the most obvious and significant of these may well be seen as midlife.

Midlife, after all, is truly the crossroads of our existence. It is the moment when the growing powers of youth begin to give way to the waning powers of age. It is the moment when the gods that have happily accompanied us thus far along our way start to turn into their opposites, or to appear in their most negative guises; the juncture, in other words, at which our former travelling companions suddenly turn into bandits. It is typically a time of crisis, of *angst*, of insecurity, of depression, even of temporary madness. In men it brings resignations, abandoned careers, marriage-breakdowns, love-affairs with seductive juveniles, elopements, disappearances and a whole catalogue of further crises. In women it is associated additionally with the menopause and the 'change of life', and often is signalled by a particularly curious quirk of behaviour that brings the thieving Hermes suddenly and unexpectedly out into the open – namely involuntary kleptomania.

The women who experience this strange compulsion are often totally shocked by what they have done, and at a complete loss to explain it. Filching knick-knacks from supermarket shelves, after all, goes against everything they believe in. It flies in the face not only of their whole upbringing and code of morality, but even of logic itself, for they do not even *want* the items they have stolen.

And so the self-contradictory, virtually incomprehensible nature of Hermes once again comes out into the open.

Midlife, then, is possibly the prime time for getting to know the deceitful god of transitions. With Hermes all about us, disturbing us both inwardly and outwardly, there can be no better moment for discovering what he has to say to us.

Which is not to say that he cannot be encountered at other times, too.

How, then, to discover the knowledge of Hermes? Once again,

we need to return to his symbol, the *herm*. Clearly, it is a token both of decision and of indecision, of certainty and of uncertainty, of setting out and of staying put. As a mere, static signpost, it contemplates both possible paths, yet commits itself to neither of them. What is above all necessary when the crisis strikes, in other words, is to *make space in our lives* – to stand back both from ourselves and from what we are currently doing, and to allow the opportunity for something unexpected, something 'other', to come in, quite possibly from 'out there'. We need to take time out, to withdraw from the fray for a while, to give ourselves a chance to chew things over. We need to permit our routines to crumble, our certainties to collapse, our inhibitions to drop.

Travel, clearly, is an ideal way of making all this possible – travel to faraway lands, among strange people, among unfamiliar customs and ideas, perhaps even to the sacred sites of the ancient world. And preferably travel of a totally unplanned and unprepared kind, too – for Hermes abhors plans and timetables, reservations and insurances, and prefers to rely on chance, on synchronicity and serendipity. If, after all, everything is foreseen, nothing can be learnt.

It is above all the unforeseen which makes our journeys memorable.

Hermes' pilgrimage, then, is a rather more mature version of the evasion that, earlier in life, is typical of **Dionysus**. The main difference is that Dionysus quite often thinks that he knows where he is coming from or going to, whereas Hermes freely admits that he has no idea. Dionysus starts from here, Hermes from nowhere. Dionysus' head is full of departures and arrivals, Hermes' merely of doubt.

What the Hermetic journey amounts to is a kind of pilgrimage to an unknown goal – even though the goal of all pilgrimages is actually very 'known' indeed. For all pilgrimages end up where they began, and so they really constitute a journey to the centre of the Self.

And that of Hermes, did he but know it, is no exception.

As on the personal level, so on the collective level too. Now that Western civilisation itself is arguably entering its own 'mid-life crisis', current events are increasingly demonstrating to us this archetypal paradigm of pilgrimage – this self-revelatory process of departure and return – in the most literal of ways. With the recent universal advent in our lives of the archetype of Gaia, the Earth Mother – itself largely the result, as we have seen, of our recent technological pilgrimage into outer space – the world is rapidly becoming less a collection of separate nation-states than a single, interconnected planet. In consequence, our former pigeons of projection are coming home to roost, our rejected shadows coming insistently to light again. The formerly despised 'savages' whom our ancestors sought first to contact and then to enslave 'out there', the nations on whom we once so arrogantly imposed our own form of civilisation as if there were no other, are actually coming to live among us in ever greater numbers. Within a remarkably short time they are actually becoming 'ourselves' – incorporated into our communities, assimilated into our local or national identities. Their exotic customs are becoming home-customs, their ethnic music home-grown music, their foreign cuisine home-cooking, their far-flung wisdoms home-truths. Moreover, dare one say it, their feelings of rejection and injustice resulting from our own past treatment of them are also coming home to roost. The colonialist pilgrimage, in other words, is ending up where it began. And in the process we ourselves are transformed.

That is always the point of the Hermetic journey, the archetypal pilgrimage. The point of running away from ourselves is ultimately to be confronted by ourselves.

It is a point, however, that can too easily be forgotten. Travel and adventure can become ends in themselves, even a form of drug. The pilgrim can become so absorbed in the pilgrimage as to forget to come home.

The archetypal pilgrimage

In a young person this tendency is excusable, even normal. Setting out on essentially Dionysian voyages of exploration, pitting oneself against the elements, gambling one's very survival against apparently insuperable odds – all this is the very stuff of youth, of growing up. It provides the raw resistance that is needed for muscles of every kind to develop, be they physical, moral, psychological or spiritual. It lays the very foundations of the youthful ego. And so the mighty Heracles must set out to transform the world, embarking on a whole series of larger-than-life labours in order that, through them, he may develop into the full, autonomous being that he inherently is.

Yet even for Heracles the process can prove all too addictive. From a mere tool for developing himself the process too easily turns into a means of proving himself, of asserting his superiority, of acquiring prestige. He has to excel at all costs. He can never give up. Reinforcing the ego becomes an end in itself. Yet, as the very manner of his death seems to indicate, it can all amount to a way of flaying himself alive. Atop his self-organised funeral pyre, his skin seared by unbearable pain, he finishes up literally a burnt-out case.

Such were ever the rewards of the unmitigated egotism that fuels every hero.

But if the risks of getting lost are great for young people, they are even greater for those who are enmeshed in their midlife crisis. For them the temptation never to come home again can prove almost irresistible. Again and again, consequently, the ageing Odysseus, the wandering and allegedly 'homecoming' hero of the Trojan war, pits himself against the sea, even though he knows full well that, unless he finally gets it out of his blood, it will get him in the end. And even though he does eventually return to his native island of Ithaca, he leaves his homecoming far too late, and the forces of the sea – in the form of the spine of a sting-ray wielded by his own son – finally catch up with him just when he least expects it.

Self-destruction, in fact, is immemorially the fate of almost every mythical hero. Far from being (as a good many would-be psychomythologists would have us believe) the supreme, overlighting archetype of mature adulthood or, at very least, a long-term model for our over-all inner development – let alone some kind of ultimate ideal – the hero is usually portrayed in myth as something of a brutish oddball, a superannuated child, a case of arrested development, an almost pathological deviation from healthy normality, a deluded soul engaged in a futile attempt to outdo the very gods themselves. As well he might be. For all that the obsessive hero and monster-slayer reveals is in fact his own immaturity. In the footsteps of both Perseus and St George, he is still symbolically engaged in confronting the enemy that is really his father and slaying the dragon that is ultimately his mother, in order that, with his final achievement of independent adulthood, the archetypal maiden may at last be released to him. There is, of course, a proper time for all this. But if he has continually to repeat the exercise throughout adulthood, this can only mean that his efforts to date have been fruitless. The enemy still refuses to accept defeat. The dragon within him will not lie down. All that he succeeds in releasing, consequently – far from the hoped-for damsel, the ideal bride and helpmate – is a whole series of further dragons, each of them still his mother in disguise.

And so he never manages to make a real go of setting up home and finally settling down – let alone of living happily ever after – for the simple reason that he has never really succeeded in growing up.

Society may well be grateful for the hero's flamboyant efforts on its behalf. But, as the myths constantly make clear, they do him personally no good at all. He is consumed by his own fire. His very heroics in far-flung climes are signals not of achievement, but of failure. And ultimately they will be the death of him.

The ancient Greek sagas, consequently, return to the theme again and again. The obsessive hero is basically a human being with delusions of grandeur, a man who would be a god. Forsaking the cautious moderation always enjoined by **Apollo**, he has fallen prey to the ultimate crime of *hubris*, or overweening ambition and pride. And to fall prey to *hubris* is to condemn oneself to inevitable destruction at the hands, not of one god only, but of the whole of an outraged Olympus.

The vital point, consequently, needs to be borne constantly in mind: the object of the Hermetic pilgrimage – be it heroic or otherwise – is not the journey itself. The adventure is merely a means to an end. And that end is not to conquer Olympus, let alone Zion, but merely to rediscover the hearth of home.

It was ever so with pilgrimages. A pilgrimage that does not

end up where it began has simply not finished. Indeed, it is no pilgrimage at all, but merely an evasion, an escape. Enjoyable and stimulating it may be, but ultimately it misses the point. And 'missing the point' (Greek: *hamartanein*) is the original theological definition of 'sin'. It is a crime against nature, whether human or divine.

The hunting is a waste of time unless the hunter brings his booty back home again. The returning bridegroom must bring home his bride and, forsaking his parents, enter the bridal chamber. The fruits of the journey are laid out to view only when the traveller has come inside and finally locked the door.

The journey within

Which brings us directly to the other aspect of the Hermetic exercise. For the alternative (or rather, complementary) response to the advent of Hermes in our lives is to use the opportunity provided by midlife to undertake an *inner* journey – a direct journey to the centre of the soul. This might involve a deliberate and thorough course in relaxation, meditation and contemplation. It might entail joining all manner of cult-groups and esoteric organisations which offer training in the associated skills and techniques. It might lead to the experience of various Hermetic therapies. It will almost certainly involve intense study and reading.

Even here, though, addictive nomadism can once again take over. The inner journey can too easily become an end in itself. Alternatively, the traveller may become so firmly hooked on one particular experience along the way (as we shall see in our next chapter) as to come to regard it as the ultimate truth, thus forgetting to complete the journey at all. Once again, therefore, the point needs to be borne in mind that the journey is not over until the traveller has returned home. The only certainty along the way is that there are no certainties; the only fixed point of reference is the fact that nothing is fixed. And therefore the purpose of the Hermetic journey is not to discover 'fixed verities' or ultimate certainties, but rather the opposite – to learn to live with that *appropriate uncertainty* that is the ultimate hallmark of Hermes.

Such is the uncertainty that is above all the hallmark of midlife, and learning to live with that uncertainty is therefore a prime precondition for learning to cope with the associated 'change of life'. It is towards uncertainty, after all, that life thereafter tends. Towards the dropping of what has hitherto been acquired, towards the losing of what has hitherto been gained. Death is the only ultimate certainty, yet even it ends only in uncertainty.

And Hermes, as ever, is its presiding genius.

So it is, then, that the knowing that is Hermes' is essential to us if our lives are to be truly fulfilled and to move towards their completion. It is not sufficient for us to be man and woman, child and adolescent, lover and parent. We need to leave home, to become travellers, to make good our 'right to be a pilgrim'. We need to seek out the unknown that is beyond us in order to understand what is within us. We need to let go of ourselves in order to get a firmer hold on ourselves. We need to drop what we think we know in order to learn what we *really* know.

In the words of the *Tao Te Ching*, 'In the quest for learning, every day something is gained: in the quest for Truth, every day something is dropped.'

VITAL ACTIONS

Truly to learn to know the Hermes within is to make the acquaintance of all the uncertainty and spontaneity, the instant creativity and lateral thinking which have been latent within us ever since childhood – and which Apollo in particular is so keen either to deny or to bring under firm and sensible adult control. Inevitably, then, any successful Hermetic therapy is likely to increase our energy-levels very considerably.

As usual, though, the process needs to start with careful self-assessment and diagnosis.

1. Self-enquiry

Take time out, then, to examine yourself, your attitudes and feelings from the Hermetic point of view.

(a) Accepted aspects

Are you intelligent – even precocious? Do you have a youthful outlook? Do you have a taste for the new? Are you always open to change? Are you flexible and adaptable? Are you naturally spontaneous and original? Are you quick-witted, and able to adjust to new situations in a flash? Are you a fast learner? Are you sharp-eyed? Are you keenly aware of everything that is happening around you? Do you have the skill and cunning of the natural survivor? Do you have a strong sense of adventure? Are you a true opportunist? Do you think of yourself as lucky? Are you confident, open-minded and easy-going? Are you sexually uninhibited? Are you friendly, kind and gentle? Do you have a lively sense of fun? Are you naturally athletic? Are you musical? Are you good with your hands? Are you something of a craftsman? Are you clever with words? Do you have a flair for languages? Are you good with animals and young children? Do you have healing gifts? Do people turn to you for ideas and solutions when they are in trouble?

If the answer to most or all of these is 'Yes', Hermes is truly alive within you.

However, Hermes has other, less welcome, aspects – and these, too, need to be considered. Do not be surprised, therefore, if you find the following list of questions increasingly disturbing. If you find yourself angry or affronted at what they seem to imply, that is actually a very healthy and promising reaction, as we shall go on to see.

(b) Rejected aspects

Are you constitutionally incapable of settling down to anything for more than two minutes together? Are you restless? Are you impossible to pin down? Do you unsettle other people and make them feel insecure? Are you addicted to change for its own sake? Are you altogether too clever for your own good? Are you elusive, even shifty? Are you inconsistent and unreliable? Are you sometimes deceitful, dissimulating and/or secretive? Are you willing to perpetrate all kinds of trickery on others? Are you prepared to perjure yourself if necessary? Are you a habitual liar, fraud or cheat? Are you shameless and insolent? Are you light-fingered, even positively kleptomaniac at times? Are you naturally a bit of a nudist? Are you tempted to expose yourself to others? Are you often quite obviously randy? Are you inherently bisexual? Are you quite prepared to seduce others?

Once again, most of these 'rejected' aspects of the Hermetic archetype are potentially fraught with emotion. It would be unusual if some of them at least did not arouse strong reactions within you. At the same time, though, the very strength of those reactions has an extremely helpful function. It suggests that the characteristics to which you are reacting are in fact *rejected aspects of yourself.* They pertain, in other words, to your own darker aspect, just as they pertain to the darker aspect of Hermes himself, and for that reason they are normally hidden from you – however obvious they may be to others. Indeed, much the same may even apply to the *positive* aspects listed under (a) above – in which case therapy is doubly urgent. (In practice, this probably means that you are so devoted to Apollo or some related god as to be unable for the moment to *ac-knowledge* the presence of any other archetype within yourself, least of all Hermes.)

What is important now, therefore, is to learn to *re-cognise* and accept not only the first list of characteristics, but the second list too (whether or not you actually put them into practice) – for if you are rejecting them you are by definition rejecting large parts of Hermes himself.

(c) Total non-recognition and projection

As ever, though, the most dangerous case is possibly where you have failed to identify with – or to react to – the listed character-istics at all. If this was so in your own case, go through the second list especially for a second time now and ask yourself whether you associate the qualities described mainly with *other people.* Do you deplore inconsistency in others? Do you regard people who are shifty and unreliable as beneath contempt? Are you angered by liars, frauds and cheats? Are you incensed by others' dishonesty, and by people who are quite prepared to help themselves to others' property? Are you disturbed by inveterate nudists, offended by bisexuals, outraged by people who are quite open and shameless about their sexual urges? Are you disgusted at so-called 'flashers', and almost beside yourself with anger at people who are obvious rakes and seducers? Would you like to see some or all of these last few groups banished from society, imprisoned, castrated, sterilised or even exterminated?

Once again, there are many who take such attitudes – often for reasons which they regard as perfectly logical, natural and moral. The very strength of feeling with which they do so, however, reveals that the characteristics concerned *are actually part of their own Shadow*. Having rejected those qualities within themselves, they are now (naturally enough) unable to *recognise* them there, and so are forced to project them onto other people, where they can now safely go on rejecting and condemning them to their hearts' content.

This, as we saw out earlier, is a recipe not for healing, but for continued division – whether in the inner or the outer world.

In such cases, then, therapy is especially urgent.

(d) Total acceptance

As ever, this is the ideal. We all need to be able to accept Hermes within ourselves not only in his more welcome aspects, but also in his darker manifestations. We need to be able to accept all the characteristics listed with easy-going equanimity, *re-cognising* that they are at very least potential or latent within ourselves – even if, as autonomous adults, we choose not to express all of them in practice.

If you can already manage this degree of acceptance, in all probability little in the way of extra therapy is needed beyond what you naturally undertake as part of your normal life-routine. If you cannot do so, though, some kind of deliberate therapy is needed – and the ancient myths can as usual be relied on to suggest suitable measures to take.

2. Invocation

Start, then, in the usual way. Name and imagine the young, bearded god of crossroads and transitions, with his broad-brimmed hat and his pilgrim's staff or snake-entwined *caduceus*, and welcome him unconditionally into your life.

But do not restrict yourself merely to this. Invoking the gods also means deliberately giving yourself the chance to encounter their characteristics within yourself and to recognise them for what they are – and, as ever, thanks to our *penchant* for projection, this means (among other things) exposing yourself to outer circumstances that reflect them. In Hermes' case, these characteristics are mainly his unpredictability, his spontaneity, his openness to change, his uninhibitedness and his inherent adventurousness, together with his gift for healing.

Perhaps the main key to the therapy of Hermes, though, is his addiction to travel and commerce of all kinds. You may care, then, to take the hint. Simply set out on a journey. Anywhere – it doesn't matter. Just set out in your car or on your bike, *but taking care to leave all your maps behind*. Alternatively, buy yourself a railway rover ticket. Jump on the first bus or coach. Take the first stand-by airline ticket available. When you get there – wherever 'there' happens to be – set out on foot (still without map or compass) and just see where your feet take you. When you get to a crossroads, simply sit down and open yourself to the various possibilities. Then just follow your nose. Be prepared for surprises. Do not fear them, though. They may involve you in some hurried, even emergency measures. Yet most of your surprises are quite likely to turn out, in the event, to be unexpectedly pleasant and profitable ones.

You would be well advised, of course, not to set out on foot entirely without map or compass in uninhabited regions such as the desert, moors or mountains – though you can always choose not to consult them. That apart, though, you are likely to find that you do not need half as much paraphernalia and organised social support to survive as you may have thought you did. Somehow, the universe seems to provide. It is not, after all, the hostile place that you have possibly been taught to think of it as being. Instead, you will find yourself making all sorts of unexpected personal contacts, learning things about yourself and the world about you that you never imagined, taking an interest in a whole range of things that previously were a closed book to you.

In short, you will find yourself changing – perhaps quite rapidly. Moreover, when you finally come home, you will find that home has unaccountably changed, too, perhaps almost beyond recognition. Somehow you will have started to see things in an entirely new light.

If such journeys are not 'on' for you at present, consider the alternative of encountering the 'other' in your own home-environment. Visit your local market-place. Observe the farmers, the stallholders, the visitors, the customers. Sense the energies that are being drawn into your own home-town from far around by the mere sale of goods and/or animals. Then involve yourself in the process. Make contact. Try bidding or haggling. Once you have gained enough confidence, consider applying to set up your own stall on a regular basis. Be ready to respond to new initiatives. Play everything by ear. Stay alert to every business opportunity. Be prepared to strike whatever instant bargains suit you – even if some choose to see it as daylight robbery.

With your ill-gotten gains, you may then feel ready to set out on a different kind of Hermetic pilgrimage. Arrange to go on a tour of the ancient sites of the classical world. Visit Greece in particular, and seek out the sanctuaries and temples of the gods. Try to absorb the energy and atmosphere that is characteristic of each. In particular, look out for any sites sacred to Hermes. If it turns out that you do not find any, consider the implications. Perhaps you have really been contacting Hermes all along? Perhaps his nature does not reside in any settled sanctuary, but in the very journeying that, in the event, serves to link them all?

During your visit, meanwhile, take care to seek out pictures and/or statuettes of Hermes. Consider setting one of them up in your bedroom and making a 'shrine' around it. Then meditate before it each morning and evening. Affirm your willingness to accept Hermes' basic characteristics in their entirety, both in yourself and in others, and express your refusal henceforth to feel either guilty or ashamed at what in fact are perfectly natural and normal aspects of the magical and unpredictable child-adult who is hidden within us all.

At which point you may feel ready to embark on any one of a number of *inner* pilgrimages in search of Hermes. You may feel moved to join an esoteric or occult group or community, to take up with the New Age movement in general, to experiment with a whole variety of transformative therapies ranging from Sufism and

Gurdjieffianism, through Neurolinguistic Programming to Zen. You may care to start reading vaguely esoteric books – as, indeed, you have already started to do merely by tackling this one. You may seek out arcane healers and gurus, or embark on a variety of therapies and techniques of your own devising. And note how the right books suddenly seem to jump off the shelves at you almost of their own accord, how the right people turn up at the most extraordinarily propitious moments, how the right opportunities present themselves unbidden, and the necessary funds manifest themselves without any apparent effort on your part. All these, in fact, are infallible signs that Hermes is coming to life within you.

In these and similar ways you can successfully re-invoke Hermes and learn to *re-cognise* his inner presence. Indeed, it is literally vital that you should. Otherwise you will be ignoring the natural trickster, the magical child and transformer who is hidden deep within you, and your knowledge of yourself will for ever be only partial.

3. Meditation

Merely by 'being fully with' the activities already mentioned you are, of course, already participating in an appropriate form of meditation. Many of the forms of 'inner' pilgrimage just mentioned, in particular, will already bring with them their own particular meditative practices. Zen meditation in particular – in its *Rinzai* form essentially the contemplation of paradox – is overwhelmingly apt to the Hermetic quest. Who else but Hermes, after all, could possibly ask such impossible riddles, or *koans*, as 'What is the sound of one hand clapping?' or 'How long is a piece of string?'

It will then remain for you merely to contemplate Hermes' characteristic symbols.

Are you prepared to set out with the crane and the wild goose on the long, migratory journey that will take you to far countries of experience that you have never heard of – only to bring you back home again as a totally transformed creature? Are you prepared either to run with the hare or to plod with the tortoise, knowing full well that it is not the speed that is important, nor even the getting there, but simply the travelling itself? Are you prepared to be as cunning and intelligent as the dog, and every bit as natural a survivor? Are you willing to drop your inhibitions and express your natural creative instincts like the ram?

Are you ready to put on the archetypal Traveller's cloak, to disguise yourself under his broad-brimmed hat, to wield his magic wand with its twin serpents that represent the uniting of the outer and inner wisdoms, the Above and the Below, the conscious and the unconscious, the left brain and the right brain, the sacred and profane, the esoteric and the exoteric, the dark and the light, the Yin and the Yang, the masculine and the feminine? Are you willing to put on the Wanderer's winged sandals and, approaching the critical crossroads of life, to set out with the wind in whatever direction it blows? Are you ready to cross all frontiers, to break down all barriers, to ignore all restrictions, to jettison all plans, to ignore all considerations of supposed personal 'safety' in order eventually to discover the sacred spring of life that will transform your whole existence?

Do not merely *think* about these matters. Actually seek out the creatures and accoutrements mentioned and use as many as possible of your senses on them. Then allow yourself to *become* them, each in turn. Merge your identity with them. Allow yourself to become the very questions themselves. Immerse yourself in their very open-endedness.

Then finish your meditation by asking yourself the following:

Am I giving free enough reign to my intuition and intelligence?

Am I putting my skills in learning and adaptation to full use?

Am I exploiting not only my linguistic skills, but also my ability as an interpreter in a more general sense?

Am I allowing others to cramp my open-mindedness and originality, my lack of sexual inhibitions or natural opportunism?

Am I prepared to trust to luck, to take risks, to gamble with my future?

Am I prepared to 'let go and let (the) god', without necessarily knowing where I am going?

Am I placing sufficient trust in my skills with animals and young children, my natural athleticism, my sense of humour, my healing and musical gifts, my inventiveness and my sense of the mystical and magical?

Actually think about your answers this time, then ponder on them and consider whether this is the moment to adjust your way of life to reflect them.

4. Remedial activities

On the basis of the myths, there are a number of activities that seem designed positively to encourage you to develop your Hermetic aspects. You may wish to consider adopting some of them, perhaps on a trial basis initially. Several of them pick up on themes that have been mentioned already. Add any favourite activities of your own that seem appropriate and natural to you. For convenience, the activities listed are as usual divided here into two categories:

(a) Recreational and general

Wear old, ragged clothes. Equip yourself with a stick and go hiking, wearing anything you like, but especially a broad-brimmed hat. Learn to sail, glide or fly. Take up athletics, gymnastics and/or boxing. Learn to improvise on any musical instrument, but especially wind and string instruments such as the flute, organ, guitar or piano. Take up musical conducting. Acquaint yourself with primitive or exotic forms of music, and especially those traditionally used to induce trance-states. Pay attention to your dreams, apparent omens and coincidences. Seek out the hidden meanings of all three. Be prepared to take gambles – perhaps even to indulge in actual gambling. Go into buying and selling, and learn to haggle. Investigate magic and alchemy. Join any esoteric groups or movements that appeal to you, especially ones with New Age, Sufi or Gurdjieffian connections. Alternatively, go into Zen. If expert guidance is available, try fire-walking. Go walking at night. Take up secret naturism. Insist on regular (or irregular!) siestas. Remain incognito. Deliberately change your appearance and experiment with disguises. Subject to the laws of your society and considerations of medical safety, express yourself sexually in any way that you feel comfortable with. If prone to over-excitement or over-stressed, be prepared to use prescribed sedatives if necessary. Use alcohol only in moderation. Meditate at any crossroads or in any market-place.

(b) Professional

Particularly suitable areas for encouraging the development of Hermes within you are: athletics, work as a doorkeeper or watchman or in any post involving responsibility, domestic service or its commercial equivalent (e.g. nursing, portering, waiting, airline stewarding), work with animals or as a travel-guide or courier, teaching, work with young children, public relations, travel, commerce, diplomacy, translation, interpreting, musical performance or criticism, musical conducting, administration, forecasting, planning, academia generally, the arts, philosophy, rhetoric, the law, work as a detective, counselling, herbalism and other forms of healing, psychotherapy, hypnotism, dream-interpretation, work with the dying, and the priesthood – or other professions involving initiating others into new and unfamiliar knowledge.

SUB-PERSONALITIES OF HERMES

HERACLES = Hercules

Possible symptoms

Machismo; male chauvinism; antagonising of women; confronta-tionalism; combativeness; bloody-mindedness; providence-tempt-ing; flouting of civilised conventions; wounding of mother; sexual excesses; promiscuity; unfaithfulness; enslavement to female sexuality; possible domination by wife; brief homosexual escapades; transvestite interludes; restlessness; evil dreams; bitterness; vengefulness; inability to settle down; temporary depression or madness; skin-problems; possible shingles or herpes; hyper-sensitivity

but also

Physical strength; youthful prodigies; heroism; sense of challenge;

originality; all-round ability; urge to push back limits; persistence; opposition to cruelty; sympathy for living things; admiration of father; courtesy; aggression only when provoked; mournfulness; humour; sense of the ridiculous; sensitivity to omens; eventual recognition of own dispensability.

Therapies

Name, imagine and welcome the archetypal hero and strong-man, always game for a challenge; competitive sport, especially athletics; women; hunting and shooting; animal-taming; physical challenges; hard manual labour; rescue work; military activities; expeditions; portering; austerities; feats of endurance; opening up new fields of endeavour; civilising missions; entrepreneurial activities; civil engineering; city-founding; little food at midday; isolation and darkness when depressed; auguries based on vultures; wild marjoram, cow parsnip (heracleum), henbane or aconite (WARNING: HENBANE IS POISONOUS, AND ACONITE INTENSELY SO: consult a reputable herbalist).

Symbols

Ox; club; lionskin cape; wild olive tree; poplar; aspen; upturned thumb; the Zodiac.

Notes

Heracles is the archetypal hero (the two words are actually connected), and mythical founder of the Olympic games. He is the guiding spirit of male adolescence, most prominent from puberty until the early twenties. He glories mainly in physical strength and achievement, and may have little time for intellectual pursuits, let alone for spiritual matters. He loves the company of women, but his attitude to them is abysmal. In his proper time he represents a major developmental archetype whose promptings need to be acknowledged. He becomes a major problem only if not released when his work is done – and especially if he is persisted with after midlife, and in the face of the growing weakness of old age.

ODYSSEUS = Ulysses

Possible symptoms

Irascibility; anger; red hair; childhood trauma or sexual mal-treatment; lameness; short legs; deviousness; craftiness; roguery; scheming; treachery in self-interest; boasting; pride; insistence on own rights; neglect of wife; take-it-or-leave-it attitude; restlessness; inability to settle down; obsessive nomadism; addiction to insecurity; courting of danger; tendency to dress in rags; secret worry; tinnitus (ringing in ears); possible asthma at times of deep disturbance; emotional vulnerability; masochism; feigned madness at times of own choosing; plotting; terrorism; violence; ruthlessness; victim of *grandfather's* hatreds; destruction by own success – or successor

but also

Respect for ancestral wisdom; puritanical streak; inconspicuousness; sense of honour; strong will; strong survival instinct; single-mindedness; leadership; planning; initiative; resourcefulness; versatility; originality; lateral thinking; adventurousness; inquisitiveness; caution; cunning; anticipation; prophetic wisdom.

Therapies

Name, imagine and welcome the resourceful, determined and somewhat masochistic hero of the *Odyssey;* exploration; expeditions; the sea; navigation (both in company and single-handed); feats of endurance; low-profile military work; special operations; espionage; sabotage; ambushes; disguise; old, ragged clothes; life as a beggar or tramp; diplomatic work; negotiation; athletics; martial arts; retirement abode well away from the sea.

Symbols

Cockerel; the seaman's oar and the wooden horse of Troy might also be appropriate.

Notes

While Odysseus is not himself a god, nor even an immortal, the myth of Ulysses that he expresses does seem to have a much older and more primal pedigree. And since every human being is perpetually engaged in some sort of symbolic odyssey, whether inner or outer, the myth of Odysseus is capable of speaking to all of us. At basis he is the determined, competitive, self-made man who relies on his wits, backed up by sheer brute force. Often insecure inwardly, and somewhat masochistic by disposition, outwardly he is the Man of Action, the Archetypal Hero, the Triumph of Will personified. His motto is 'Don't just sit there: *do* something.' In short, he is the very model of the modern, go-ahead, dominant Western male. As in all heroic myths, however, there is (quite literally) a sting in the tail. Odysseus is destroyed by his own achievements – in this case, his own son wielding the tail of a sting-ray. (The sea, it seems, is a particular source of ultimate danger to him.) The moral seems to be that the hero-role, however personally and socially valid in its day, should not be identified with too closely or for too long. At the proper time it needs to be quietly allowed to drop. In particular, he needs to work the sea out of his bloodstream as early as possible, along with any associated domineering, ambitious tendencies and/or delusions of grandeur. In the words of the *Tao Te Ching,* 'Retire when the work is done.'

In the meantime, high altitude (e.g. mountaineering, flying) may prove helpful in easing any asthmatic symptoms, while any tendency to tinnitus may reduce in time of its own accord, especially if the inner ringing is *consciously listened to,* or if the ear is deliberately flooded with noise of a similar type.

PERSEUS

Possible symptoms
Victim of grandfather's fears; infant hardship, possibly as outcast or refugee; youthful banishment; obsession with self-exposure to danger; confrontationalism; ill-considered, though short-lived opposition to **Dionysus**, whether in self or in others; ruthlessness; deviousness; dissimulation; dependence on second-hand skills and ideas; destructiveness; over-willingness to use catastrophic weapons in self-defence; antagonism to unattractive or dominant women; tendency to be at loggerheads with grandfather and/or his age-group – eventually, perhaps, with unintended tragic effects on them

but also
Possessiveness towards mother; taste for challenges; dragon-

slaying; adventurous spirit; sense of honour; courage; doggedness; thoroughness; physical strength; sporting or athletic prowess; survival skills; persuasiveness; pragmatism; willingness to make use of other's skills and ideas; fleetness of foot; soaring self-confidence; popularity; attraction to, and success with, beautiful women, despite their families' doubts; good luck and prosperity, both financial and political.

Therapies

Name, imagine and invoke this restless and determined son of **Zeus** with a taste for power, as he flies eastwards and homewards over the sea, triumphantly bearing the head of Medusa; challenges of all kinds; sports and athletics (especially discus); confrontations; enterprises involving self-exposure to danger; expeditions; sea and air travel; exploration; exile; marriage; politics; administration; government.

Symbols

Winged sandals; magic wallet; adamantine sickle of Hermes; bright shield of Athene (see under **Zeus**); mirror; Hades' helmet of invisibility (see under **Zeus**); head of Medusa.

Notes

Perhaps in response to infant hardship and/or rejection, Perseus' story is one of constant high-risk endeavour and a literal living-out of the truism that 'nothing breeds success like success'. Never stopping to consider what danger he may be exposing himself to, he rushes headlong from adventure to challenge, from challenge to adventure. His youthful physical prowess even attracts the admiration and support of solid, middle-aged women of the stamp of Athene, as well as of the normally somewhat equivocal Hermes, i.e. the sceptics and turncoats. So infectious is his enthusiasm, indeed, that he is able to call on the very armoury of the aged Hades, and cunning enough to use it. And this despite the fact that his relationships with the elderly are not always of the best, and that he is particularly prone to make enemies of unattractive and/or forceful women. His transcendence particularly of this latter problem may turn out in practice to be a major source of strength for him, provided only that he can bring it off. But then, given his natural eye for the main chance, this is always quite likely.

At times, meanwhile, his sheer bravado, and the foolhardiness of his risk-taking, is enough to petrify even Atlas (see under **Zeus**). Yet, given time to mature, he will eventually find it possible to settle down into responsible domesticity, while channelling his still considerable energies into the high-profile social and political activities characterised by Athene (see under **Zeus**). Here, by dint of borrowing ideas indiscriminately from right or left as circumstances demand, he is likely to remain as successful as ever, continually attended by the luck of the gods, and reconciled at last to the more formidable aspects of mature womankind.

THESEUS

Possible symptoms

Selfish and self-seeking attitudes and behaviour; egotism; urgent need for feminine help; thoughtlessness for others; overdoing of heroism; brute force; unnecessary self-exposure to danger; engendering of suspicion and even rejection on the part of others;

male chauvinism; cavalier treatment of opposite sex; subjugation of women; desertion of wife when the going gets rough; provocation of female opposition; a late 'season in hell'; eventual disillusion, defeat or destruction

but also

Manliness; courage, heroic impulse; daring; taste for challenges; intuitive capacity to solve intricate problems; supportive friends.

Therapies

Name, imagine and invoke the swashbuckling, over-ambitious hero who slays the Cretan Minotaur with the aid of Ariadne; athletics; expeditions; physical challenges; feats of daring and endurance; wrestling; bullfighting; diving and underwater swimming; marine salvage; rescue work; trouble-shooting; problem-solving; intricate mixed dancing; mazes and labyrinths; guidance by a trusted woman.

Symbols

Club; bull-sacrifice.

Notes

Another version of the hero archetype – this time with early affinities to the young King Arthur – Theseus pushes his heroics rather too far. He is prepared to use anybody to serve his ends, and is not over-careful about whom he hurts in the process. Women in particular suffer from his bull-like behaviour, and consequently any activity which can constructively engage both his gifts and women at the same time can serve as a useful corrective, His competence at solving labyrinthine problems suggests that any area of intricate planning which can also involve women may serve him well in this respect. In the modern context, computer programming seems one obvious possible application. Such less blatantly physical activities also have the positive merit that they are less likely to be immediately ruled out of account at midlife, when the heroics are going to have to be quietly dropped if mental health is to be maintained. It is possible that one woman in particular may eventually be able to help him make this change towards a better balanced psyche, but he should not necessarily expect the encounter to mature into a close, long-term relationship.

SUMMARY

Fully to know Hermes is to have in your pocket the key to self-transformation. With it you are able to unlock the door that leads to the rest of your life. Without it you merely condemn yourself to stasis and eventual death.

Ac-knowledge, then, the presence of Hermes within you, and you will have life more abundantly.

9

ORPHEUS – THE WAY OF THE MYSTIC

I love to lose myself in a mystery; to pursue
my reason to an O altitudo!
Sir Thomas Browne: 'Religio Medici'

ORPHEUS is the natural mystic, the religious zealot who thinks that there is only one way and that he has found it. Many of us encounter him in the course of our lives, and in order to break his spell we need to make ourselves fully aware of his presence within ourselves.

Orpheus in myth

The myth of Orpheus is well-known. The story tells how this gifted poet and priest of Apollo, renowned for his skill on the lyre and for his enchanting singing-voice, uses both of them to cast an almost magical spell over those around him. From Egypt to Greece, and even on the Argonauts' expedition in quest of the Golden Fleece, this semi-divine being is capable of charming the very birds off the trees. And so when his wife Eurydice dies from snakebite, he descends (like the mother-lorn **Dionysus** before him) into the underworld – i.e. into hell – in an attempt to charm its overlords into letting him bring her back to life again. He nearly succeeds. Forbidden by Hades, God of the Dead, to look back at her until he has success- fully led her back out into the light of day, he gives in to temptation only at the last moment, and so loses her forever.

Worse follows. His persistent preaching and teaching on behalf exclusively of **Apollo** angers the latter's rival, Dionysus, who sets his raging Maenads onto him. The hapless Orpheus is torn limb from limb. His head is thrown into the river Hebrus. Yet – miracle of miracles! – it simply goes on singing all the way down to the sea where, together with his lyre, it is eventually washed up on the isle of Lesbos. Here, suitably honoured, it continues to preach and prophesy until finally silenced by Apollo himself. The lyre, for its part, is transformed into the constellation Lyra, which remains aloft the firmament to this day.

As it happens, we are already familiar with most of the story's elements, and so its symbolism is not hard to decode. Orpheus's inherent Apollonianism is self-evident from the outset. His lyre, too, is the characteristic gift of Apollo. As such, it is the instrument not only of joy and of sleep, but of love. Yet not, in this case, of *sexual* love. For Apollo's love is primarily of an ideal, other-worldly kind.

Orpheus in history

The history of world religion has been marked by numerous Orpheus figures, from Pythagoras, through Jesus of Nazareth himself, to Origen, St Augustine, St Benedict and the Persian poet Jalal'uddin Rumi right up to the 19th-century missionary Dr David Livingstone and the more recent organist, doctor and missionary Albert Schweitzer. Today the archetype is perhaps most clearly expressed by the whole rash of strident American television evangelists from Billy Graham onwards.

It is spiritual love as opposed to physical lust, *agape* as opposed to *eros*.

Orpheus the 'sweet singer', then, is essentially a Minnesinger, a Troubadour, even a Sufi of the stamp of Jalal'uddin Rumi. He *seems* to sing of romantic love, but in reality his love is Apollo's – the love of some unattainable ideal, some transcendent reality that has no physical counterpart on earth. His characteristic knowledge, in other words, is the knowledge of higher truth.

He thus becomes the prototype of all spiritual pioneers and idealists, with all their weaknesses as well as all their virtues.

And so, inevitably, he *gets himself into deep water*.

For Orpheus's central theme, as befits a priest of Apollo, is nothing less than rejection of the body and its natural instincts and emotions. The wife whose death through snakebite consigns her to the underworld is his 'other half', his feminine side, the dark, rejected aspect of his own being. (It seems inherently unlikely that she is actually his physical wife since, as a priest of Apollo, Orpheus, like the historical Plato, is by definition homosexual, as the myth itself specifically confirms.) And although he imagines that he can somehow redeem that rejected aspect through sheer spiritual merit, he finds in practice that this is impossible. For his Apollonian eye merely to contemplate it in the solar light of day is to consign it once more to the shadows of hell, the world of the occult (= 'hidden'). His whole *out-look* condemns it, rejects it, separates him from it.

Inevitably, therefore, the body exacts its revenge. The instincts will out, the emotions will have their say. Orpheus is attacked by their symbolic instruments, the Maenads – the specifically female representatives of Dionysus. It is primarily the sex-instinct, in other words – and the feminine aspect of it in particular – that tears

Orpheus apart. And the eventual outcome reveals the situation for what it really is: cast into the river, his head continues to sing away as if nothing had happened. It is totally divorced from his body, totally cut off from reality, totally unable and unwilling to understand what is happening to the rest of him. Even on Lesbos it continues to prattle away, now mouthing dire prophecies of things to come, until it outdoes even Apollo's own oracles to the point where the god himself is forced to put a stop to it.

Only the lyre attains the immortality that Orpheus craves. For all eternity it hangs as a heavenly constellation above our heads, its strings silent and forever frozen into immobility.

The lessons of Orpheus

The story contains its own lessons, and they deserve to be looked at carefully. Perhaps the first point to notice is that Orpheus (who may, indeed, have been an actual, historical person) is initially something of a pilgrim after the stamp of **Dionysus** or **Hermes**. Even his lyre is originally Hermes' invention. In search of wisdom and truth, he first visits Egypt, then joins the Argonauts on their perilous voyage to Colchis in search of the Golden Fleece. By the same token, then, we may assume that he has been engaged on an inner pilgrimage, too.

At some point during that inner journey, however, Orpheus 'forgets to come home'. He discovers in the cult of Apollo what he takes to be the absolute truth, a transcendent ideal to which he resolves to commit his whole life to the exclusion of all else. His pilgrimage, consequently, is abandoned.

His subsequent life duly reflects the fact. He settles down as a priest of Apollo. He preaches that Apollo is supreme among the gods. In harmony with the nature of Apollo, he advocates homosexuality. And we may safely assume that he sees the life of the head – be it intellectual or spiritual – not only as 'sacred', but as somehow threatened by the human instincts and emotions, to say nothing of that posed by the body itself and the messy, untidy, everyday world in which it has its being.

Whence, it seems, his evangelical 'missionary syndrome' – an ultimately fear-based phenomenon which so often characterises followers of idealistic, head-orientated, Apollonian cults and religions, and which traditional Christianity in particular amply demonstrates in its own way. The true faith, the approved, word-based dogma must at all costs be shielded from unruly, brute reality, from actual human experience, from the dire threat of competing beliefs and ideologies. Lest reality force the theory to change, there-fore, the theory itself must undertake the gigantic task of changing reality. By hook or by crook the world must be 'straightened out', 'put right', 'converted', 'evangelised', made to conform to the idealistic picture of it that the committed devotee holds in his head. Every 'dark continent' must be flooded with the familiar, kindly light that is really the light of Apollo. Heaven must be brought down to earth, matter be made to accord with spirit. And for this the cultic scriptures are held to provide the sacred, unchanging blueprint.

But Orpheus does not restrict himself to the mere spoken or written word. He enlists the lyre, the human voice, the magic of singing and dancing in the service of his missionary ideal. And not merely as a ritual adjunct, as Apollo himself might have done, but as a magical tool, a drug, an instrument of ecstasy.

Now to this extent, it is quite evident, Orpheus is trespassing – and apparently not for the first time – upon the territory of Dionysus.

He is, in a sense, co-opting Dionysus to fight Dionysus. He is gratefully using Dionysian ecstasy to transcend the familiar world of everyday reality, only to replace it with Apollo's rarefied, *anti*-Dionysian world of purely head-based spiritual ideals.

No wonder, then, that Dionysus is so enraged. To ignore the emotions and instincts is one thing: actually to misuse them in the service of the head is quite another.

The result is all but inevitable. The instincts and emotions strike back – and in the most catastrophic way, at that. Much as happened in Nazi Germany when Adolf Hitler attempted a similar sleight of hand, the forces of the unconscious exact a terrible revenge. They totally lay waste Orpheus's world of light and logic and sweet reasonableness, of order and discipline, of idealism and civilisation. He is torn apart, his body consigned to the grave, his head to the waters of the river and the sea.

But the sea is the element of **Aphrodite**, and Aphrodite is sex. Despite all Orpheus's efforts, in other words, sex still has the last word. And even Apollo, the very embodiment of the light of reason, eventually comes to see the folly of the enterprise.

As, indeed, he always does, given half a chance. Pursued to its ultimate end, logic always undermines logic, reason sees through reason, thought destroys thought. In relativity, quantum mechanics and cosmology, similarly, science eventually tears science apart.

Or rather, one form of *scientia* realises that it has to make way for another.

Orpheus within

If there is one thing that the story of Orpheus makes clear, then, it is that there is no future in unmitigated idealism, nor any salvation even in salvationist religion. No future, because unmitigated idealism freezes the world into conceptual immobility; no salvation, because religion places the world in thrall to an unchanging set of beliefs that are the exclusive copyright of the head and that have no necessary counterpart in reality.

The Apollonian Plato admittedly thought that the world of ideals was the Real world, and propounded his famous allegory of the cave to illustrate the point. To prisoners chained for life in a cave with their backs to the light, the shadows projected onto the back of the cave must inevitably appear to be reality itself, while the real world outside, being invisible to them, must remain totally unbelievable. Yet, for all its unbelievability, that real world *is* the real world, while the shadows are only a two-dimensional image of it.

Plato may or may not have been right in the conclusions that he drew from his analogy. But what he did *not* suggest was that the world outside the cave necessarily corresponds to any particular image of it that the prisoners may care to dream up. A Real world there may indeed be, in other words, but if there is, then we can never know it until we finally turn around and face it – and even then we are quite likely, as Plato himself pointed out, to find it totally incomprehensible.

Orpheus, however, is *not* facing reality. As we saw earlier, he is by definition turning his back on it. He is joining the prisoners in the cave. He is engaged in a Dionysian evasion, losing himself in rapture, *beside himself* with ecstasy.

True, that exercise can be an immensely valuable one in itself. Losing oneself, as even Dionysus eventually discovers, is an essential precondition for finding oneself again. But Orpheus is not interested in finding himself. He wants to stay lost. He is determined not to come back home again. 'This', he feels, 'is It.'

Immersed in his gratifying world of self-generated illusion, his eyes firmly closed, he luxuriates in his religious ecstasy, does his utmost to ensure that it continues for ever. Shamelessly using music and dancing to maintain his spiritual 'high' (the word is, of course, totally appropriate to the dispensation of Apollo), he tries to arrest time, to freeze his own development, to stop life dead in its tracks.

And, indeed, he succeeds. His life *does* stop dead, and he with it.

For he has failed to realise that there can be no highs without lows, no mountains without valleys. The road of life never runs true. Our very development depends on the uphill tasks as well as the downhill runs, the challenges as well as the rewards. Even within ourselves, we have not only our elevated side, but our baser side too, our light aspect and our dark aspect, our head and our heart, our masculine and our feminine natures, our Yang and our Yin, our day and our night – and to ignore these facts is to stop the very sun in its tracks.

Which no doubt is why even the solar Apollo eventually has to intervene in protest.

Orpheus, then, is something of a false prophet, a pedlar of illusion, a Pied Piper. He may temporarily get rid of the rats, but he is all too prone to take the children too, and much more permanently. The price of his salvation, in other words, can all too easily be the sacrifice of our future development, the loss of our true posterity. The point was not lost even on the ancient Greeks, who looked somewhat askance at Orpheus's powerful influence on his young male devotees – for his constitutional asceticism, together with his homosexual proclivities and propaganda must inevitably, if universally applied, threaten the future of the race.

Fortunately, however, the threat is more imagined than real. Orpheus's lyre is not the only constellation in the firmament, nor Apollo the only star. It is in paying *all* the gods their due that our true posterity lies. And not merely our posterity, but the Self-knowledge that is its ultimate aim.

As we have seen, however, knowing our Self means first learning to know *our selves*, and this is a task which needs to be pursued sequentially – even though the particular sequence we choose is not itself predetermined. Rather like music, life cannot be tackled all at once. At any one moment, Beethoven's Fifth Symphony does not exist – whatever may be said about the black marks on paper that stand for it or the discs and tapes that can be used to reconstitute it. A book, similarly, needs to be absorbed a few words at a time.

Much the same applies to our journey through life towards full and ultimate Self-knowledge. Not only does it, like any journey, need to start with the first step. Thereafter, too, it has to be pursued step by step. And each of those steps, inevitably, is unique and unrepeatable. Even when we choose – as most of us do from time to time – to *retrace our steps*, we generally discover that each step has subtly changed in the interim. Neither the assumptions we bring to it nor the lessons we learn from it are the same as they were before.

The Orphic initiative, clearly, is one such step. As such, it can prove of inestimable value to us. As part of our Hermetic pilgrimage – indeed, possibly as part of its more juvenile, Dionysian equivalent, too – we positively need to immerse ourselves in traditional systems of belief, to commit ourselves to at least one fixed cult or religion, to lose ourselves in the particular form of ecstasy offered by at least one of the major psychospiritual technologies. Having done so, we need to use it as a tool of experience, as a catalyst for self-development and self-discovery. We owe ourselves no less.

But then we need to move on. The next step needs to follow. Otherwise we merely remain standing on one leg, off-balance and liable to topple at any moment.

As the myth of Orpheus itself demonstrates only too clearly.

Whatever our preferred system of belief may be, then, it is never the end of the road. 'This' (our current turn-me-on) is *never* 'It' (our ultimate goal). At best, it is 'Here' – the place where we happen to be at this moment. True, it is vital to be here, and to be *aware* of being here, too. But all the while we are still in mid-pilgrimage – and until our ultimate transformation we are *always* in mid-pilgrimage – that 'here' can only serve as a stepping-stone to 'there', so that it, too, may duly turn into a 'here' and become the next stepping-stone on our journey.

'Life is a bridge,' declared the Mogul emperor Akbar the Great, allegedly quoting Jesus of Nazareth. 'Cross it, but build no house on it.'

The cult of Orpheus

Curiously enough, for all his inherent fixity, the legendary Orpheus and the teachings attributed to him were to give rise to a movement which actually *enshrined* this concept of moving on. What is now known as Orphism posited the fundamental idea of metempsychosis, or the transmigration of souls – better known today as reincarnation. Where the idea originally came from is anybody's guess. Possibly it came from Egypt, possibly from further afield, perhaps even India. Certainly the doctrine as preached by Orphism was not a native Greek one, while its resemblances to Hindu and Buddhist teachings were striking.

The Orphic scriptures taught that the *psyche* (Greek: 'soul') transmigrated, at death, from body to body, from human to animal and back again. Only a life of great purity, assisted by a strict moral code and the performance of the appropriate Orphic rites, could free it from what was called (as in India) 'the wheel of rebirth' and ensure its eventual reunion with its divine source. Until then it was to all intents and purposes 'dead' – and *only* then would it finally attain its inheritance of eternal life. Or, to quote a favourite Orphic slogan, *Soma, sema* ('Body equals tomb').

This last idea, clearly, is one that is familiar to all of us. That it is so familiar is largely due to the influence that it was subsequently to have on Pythagoras, and later on Socrates and Plato, whose ideas were in turn to figure largely (if for the most part unacknowledged) in early Christianity.

But what is particularly interesting about the Orphic scheme of things is its very insistence on life's continuity. We are indeed in mid-pilgrimage, and until we attain our ultimate goal we shall remain so. In this respect Orphism actually seems to contradict the obsessive fixity of Orpheus himself, and this fact, among others, casts some doubt on whether the Orphic movement really had its source in Orpheus at all.

Orpheus, after all, was and is a quintessentially Greek character. In many ways he is Apollo personified, albeit with a dash or two of Dionysus thrown in. Historical Orphism, on the other hand, was extraordinarily *un*-Greek in a whole number of ways. For a start it was run by a highly dogmatic clique of priestly ideologues who took it as their task regularly to initiate small groups of young male devotees into their beliefs, while producing a whole body of official scriptures to back up such doctrines. And the theme which ran through all of them was sheer other-worldliness. Human nature was part Dionysian (i.e., in this case, spiritual) and part Titanic (i.e. earthly). The task of every human being was to purge away the earthly element in order to purify and so release the immortal soul. The body was thus to be despised, heterosexual intercourse shunned. A whole range of ascetic practices must be performed on a daily basis, and this general regime must be backed up by regular participation in the cultic Mysteries.

The whole scheme, it is quite evident, is much closer to later Christian thought than it ever was to the ancient Greek way of life (and this very largely as a result of Orphism's influence on Christianity via the philosophers already mentioned). Unlike the Eleusinian ethos, it is personal rather than collective. It concentrates on the fate of the soul after death rather than of the *psyche* before it. It lacks all the cautious moderation which the cult of Apollo had always enjoined. It places religion on a pedestal far above the messy concerns of daily life, and so tends to divorce the two. And it is sufficiently suffused with *hubris* to offend the whole of Olympus; for it encourages men to forget their mortality and to place themselves on a par with the gods – whereas the heroic sagas of native Greek mythology are, as we saw earlier, replete with warnings against doing any such thing.

No doubt it was for such reasons that the movement never really caught on in Greece. Until Orphism finally died out under the Roman empire (significantly enough, at about the same time as Christianity itself was coming into vogue) it remained a secretive and very much minority cult whose importance lay not so much in its numbers or popularity as in the influence that it was to exert on the major Greek philosophers. Pythagoras in particular was to develop and promulgate a doctrine of the soul very much along Orphic lines. And the Pythagorean Mysteries that the members of his sect went on to perform were very much in line with Orphic practice.

The sacred rites

As is ever the case where the ancient Mysteries are concerned, remarkably little is known of the precise content of the rites of Orpheus. What *is* known, however, is that they were apparently a version of the earlier, Dionysian Mysteries, whose ritual served to dramatise and bring home to members of Dionysus' cult the divine aspect of the god's nature, making it directly available as a force for inner transformation. Through the well-known techniques of Dionysian ecstasy devotees could hope to become one with the god himself. Inevitably, therefore, the Dionysian Mysteries enshrined in some form (as do all Mysteries, not excluding the Christian Mass itself) the primary mythical experiences of the deity concerned – in this case Dionysus' miraculous transformations, his sacrifice and dismemberment, his divine rebirth from the thigh of Zeus, his perilous journeys, his escapades and triumphs. And the character- istic tools and symbols of Dionysus – his music and dancing, his alcohol, his *thyrsus* and ivy-plant, and eventually his overpowering and confirming ecstasy itself – must all have had their sanctified place within the rite.

In this the Orphic Mysteries can have been no different, except in matters of detail. And certainly there is some evidence that, as in the Dionysian cult, there was a ritual dismemberment and eating of the sacred body, if not also a drinking of the wine that had originally been Dionysus' own life-blood. In its ancient Dionysian aspect the former seems to have involved the eating of the raw flesh of a sacrificed child. In its later form, and certainly as practised within Orphism, the human victim would have been replaced by a young animal such as a foal. Orpheus, after all, is credited with having inveighed passionately against human sacrifice. Indeed, for the Orphics, the occasion was the sole one on which they ate meat at all – the justification presumably being that because, on this occasion, the creature's identity was fixed and known (since it was, by definition, the god in person), there was no risk of inadvertently eating anybody else, be it one's reborn grandmother or any other unfortunate.

Other aspects of the myth are also known to have surfaced in the ritual. There was, for example, a sacred marriage in which the white-robed neophyte became the snake-bitten bride of Orpheus by dint of allowing a golden serpent to pass through his clothing from top to bottom. Sacred songs and dances, chanted poetry and various presentations of esoteric lore must also have featured in the rite. And the occasion must, as in every ancient initiatory cult-ritual, have been preceded by a whole sequence of ritual purifications and ablutions.

But central to the Mysteries was undoubtedly the Orphic lyre itself. The magic of its sound must have pervaded the whole occasion. So much so that it was this aspect of the cult that went on to influence and inspire Pythagoras and his school possibly more than any other. Since the music of Orpheus' lyre of was the very key to heaven, it followed that the close study of it might eventually lead to an intimate understanding of the cosmos itself. It was this study that Pythagoras therefore embarked upon, duly discovering, in the course of experimenting on its strings, the mathematics of musical proportion, which he then went on to apply to the rest of the universe as well. The science of universal harmony was born – a science that was subsequently to find applications in spheres as diverse as Kepler's astronomical laws and the deep mysteries of modern subatomic physics.

Thanks to Orpheus and his lyre, in other words, Pythagoras contrived to lay the foundations of the mathematics that has underlain Western science ever since.

Thus it was that the Dionysian cult of ecstasy was turned by Pythagoras, via Orphism, into its opposite – a cult of Apollonian reason and science. Not for nothing was Pythagoras himself honoured specifically as a 'son of Apollo'. The results are there for all to see. Thanks largely to the efforts of those later 'sons of Apollo' who were his direct successors – namely Socrates, Plato and Aristotle – the world has been transformed. At the same time, however, the Western world in particular is today immersed, as we noted at the outset, in rampant dualism and reductionism. Apollo's science is widely assumed to be the *only* science. The head reigns supreme, while the body and emotions are officially despised. And Dionysus, having thus been traduced, deformed and, indeed, dismembered, is consequently showing every sign (as his myth would indeed require) of being reborn anew among us, and of inflicting on us a terrible revenge of alcohol-abuse, drug-addiction, self-immolation and a frenzied resurgence of the unconscious.

Yet the legacy of Orpheus is not *all* bad news. Not only our science, but also our religion owes much to the influence of Orphism. And even those of us who profess no religion at all continue to be largely conditioned by assumptions that ultimately have their roots in the ancient cult of Orpheus.

Base their idealism though both Christianity and Islam may on a typically Orphic devaluing of life as it is – and of the natural human instincts and emotions in particular – both nevertheless have a great many achievements to their credit. Insofar as the teachings of Jesus and Muhammad have managed to survive and permeate the institutionalised religions that have been erected on the basis of them, they have given rise to a great deal in modern society that we today assume to be virtually axiomatic. Our ideas – however flawed – of social justice, of concern for the poor, of human rights, of decency and morality owe their genesis at least in part to the characteristically Orphic idealism of the two religions' founding fathers. The monastic movement which assured, almost alone, the survival of the lights of ancient Greek and Roman learning through the European Dark Ages was conceived almost entirely in the spirit of purest Orphism. And even today the typically Orphic faith of both religions in a purer, ideal world beyond the grave continues to bring comfort and relief to the downtrodden, the hopeless, the outcast and oppressed throughout the world.

To this extent, of course, such religions faithfully fulfil their proverbial role as Marx's 'opiate of the people'. They represent a temporary expedient, a short-term means of assuaging our current pain and grief. But to exactly the same extent they also anticipate, in the expected Kingdom of Heaven on earth, the possibility of a final, long-term cure. Marx saw this in terms of the advent of pure communism when, the state having finally withered away, Everyman would sit unmolested (as Marx's own ancestral Jewish dispensation would have it) under his vine.

By the same token, that same Everyman's wandering days would be over. He would have achieved his goal. And that goal would have been his final homecoming, his ultimate return to earth.

But it is to the need to return to earth that Orpheus himself fails to open his eyes. His gaze remains fixed on the heavens. And so the myth goes on to spell out his inevitable demise. Our society as a whole, similarly, seems set to discover the same truth.

The knowledge of Orpheus, admittedly, is one to which we may well wish to commit ourselves at some stage in our lives. We shall be the poorer if we fail to do so. But we also need to recognise that religio-mystical experience has its own inbuilt obsolescence. It is not built to last. And so, when the time is right, we need to move on, to resume our pilgrimage, to return home with the accumulated spoils of our journey in order that we may finally integrate and make sense of all our experiences.

Orpheus as teacher

Curiously enough, even this last-mentioned necessity is nevertheless signalled by the Orphic myth. For, whether in the person of Orpheus himself or in the practice of his cult, one characteristic in particular stands out more clearly than almost any other.

Orpheus, as we have seen, is not only an idealist, *but a missionary and teacher, too*. His self-chosen task is to initiate the young.

Now, whether the fact is widely recognised or not, teachers are almost universally agreed about one thing: namely that *teaching is itself a way of learning*. As academic wisdom has it, in a class of thirty children with a teacher there are in fact thirty-one pupils.

Perhaps this is because teaching necessarily involves organising and formulating one's knowledge into a form that will convince the pupils. Perhaps it is because talking about an idea has the effect of objectivising it, of apparently placing it 'out there', where it can be looked at dispassionately and in better perspective. Perhaps it is simply because, in order to teach, one has first to find out.

Whatever the mechanics of the process, teachers almost universally report the phenomenon, and writers, too, discover that merely by writing they unearth thoughts and ideas that they never realised they had. To this the present writer is no exception: indeed, it is his fundamental *raison d'écrire*.

One of the best ways of learning something, in other words, is to teach it to others. One of the best ways of discovering what one knows is to write it down. And the prime benefits of education as normally practised thus accrue *to the educators*.

As, indeed, the history of world-wide Christian missionary-activity in particular makes abundantly clear, if often in strange, perverted ways.

This, then, is the peculiar grace of Orpheus. Distort reality though he may, temporarily stunt his own further development though he almost certainly does (teachers are not, after all, universally noted for their maturity!), he does at least start to 'get it together'. He takes his experience as Dionysian youth and as Apollonian man, together with his acquired knowledge as the wandering Hermes, and starts to make sense of it all. In Orpheus's case, that sense may not extend very far since, although he harbours within him something of the child and a good deal of the lover (however sublimated), he consigns his experience as woman to the darkness of the underworld, and limits his role as mother and father exclusively to his teaching.

Yet the lesson and example remain for us. Having *ac-knowledged* both our maleness (in **Apollo**) and our femaleness (in **Artemis**); having followed **Pan** into the wilderness and **Dionysus** into the realms of ecstasy; having loved with **Aphrodite**, duly borne fruit and taken responsibility for that fruit; having first acquired power with **Zeus** or **Athena** and then abandoned it; having then set out on the path of pilgrimage with **Hermes** and as yet reached no certain goal – we need simply to stop for a while and *take stock.*

We need to assess our experience thus far, to make sense of it, integrate it, assimilate it and *ac-knowledge it as being inseparable from ourselves.* We need, in other words, to learn to know our various knowings and to start fashioning them into a *single* knowing. For each of us is ultimately a single being, not a collection of separate beings. As even Orphism itself proclaimed in its day, our experience as a whole sequence of separate identities is but a preliminary to our final Self-realisation.

There is no future in self-dismemberment.

And so the advent of Orpheus in our lives is pre-eminently signalled by a growing urge to share our experiences with others, to formulate and express our ideals, to teach those who are prepared to listen, to write down our thoughts, our observations, our conclusions – even though, in the light of subsequent experience (and, for this very reason, there needs to *be* such experience), those thoughts may later turn out to be unthinkable, those observations frankly unobservant, those conclusions very far from being conclusive.

Teaching is the very instrument of Orpheus's salvation. By teaching he learns, and by learning he begins to know. And the upshot of that knowledge is that the assumed conclusion is not, after all, the end of the story, and that the time has therefore come to resume the search.

Such is the destiny and path of Orpheus. Descend into hell with him though we may, and lose all that we hold most dear though we almost certainly shall, the harvest of knowledge remains. We have only to take stock of it and, having taken stock, to move on.

VITAL ACTIONS

Whereas Apollo is an idealist, Orpheus is specifically a *religious and spiritual* idealist, and one with a missionary calling, at that. Getting to know him therefore involves recontacting those same aspects of ourselves not only inwardly, but also in the world 'out there'.

As usual, however, the process needs to start with careful self-assessment and diagnosis.

1. Self-enquiry

Take time out, then, to examine yourself, your attitudes and feelings from the point of view of Orpheus.

(a) Accepted aspects

Are you an idealist? Are you overflowing with love for your fellow human beings? Are you constant and faithful to them through thick and thin? Do you hate cruelty, whether to people or to animals? Are you teetotal, a non-smoker and/or a natural vegetarian? Are you courageous, even self-sacrificial in the service of your ideals? Are you committed to soothing and healing the sufferings of others? Are you a good conciliator? Are you musical? Do you have a good voice? Are you capable of using it to persuade and convert others? Are you a natural teacher? Are you particularly popular with children and young people of your own sex? Are you in favour of sexual abstinence and purity? Are you opposed to promiscuity? Are you inclined to be celibate? Are you able to sublimate your sexual urges in the interests of your calling? Are you religious? Are you drawn irresistibly to spiritual studies? Are you a monotheist, and faithful to your God? Are you quite prepared to be persecuted for your beliefs?

If the answer to most or all of these is 'Yes', Orpheus is truly alive within you.

However, Orpheus has other, less welcome aspects – and these, too, need to be considered. Do not be surprised, therefore, if you find the following list of questions increasingly disturbing. If you find yourself angry or affronted at what they seem to imply, that is actually a very healthy and promising reaction, as we shall go on to see.

(b) Rejected aspects

Are you just a little too loving to be true – to the extent that it could just be an act, whether conscious or otherwise? Are you altogether too fond of the sound of your own voice? By contrast, do you hate your own body? Do you suffer from guilts, regrets and/or depressions? Do you find it increasingly difficult sometimes merely to stay sane? Do you suffer from epilepsy?

Are you over-idealistic? Are you a bit of a Holy Joe? Are you rather straight-laced and moralistic? Are you narrow-minded? Are you a kill-joy? Are you a bit of a wet blanket where parties and mixed gatherings are concerned? Are you afraid of members of the opposite sex? Do you find it difficult to relate to them? Do you find it difficult to attract or retain a partner?

Are you sexually repressed? Are you ever so slightly maso- chistic? Do you have bisexual or homosexual tendencies, whether hidden or otherwise? Are you subject to severe sexual temptations at moments of weakness? Are you possibly a bad influence on the young people of your own sex who are attracted to you? Do you sometimes deliberately manipulate them?

Do you assume that you are always right? Do you think you and your ilk have a monopoly on the truth? Are you so obsessively immersed in religion and spirituality as to devalue the nitty-gritty of everyday life? Are you out of touch with the material concerns of ordinary people? Are you a bigot, and possibly loud-mouthed with it? Are you a hypocrite? Are you an out-and-out religious maniac?

Once again, most of these 'rejected' aspects of the Orphic archetype are potentially fraught with emotion. It would be unusual if some of them at least did not arouse strong reactions within you. At the same time, though, the very strength of those reactions has an extremely helpful function. It suggests that the characteristics to which you are reacting are in fact *rejected aspects of yourself.* They pertain, in other words, to your own darker aspect, just as they pertain to the darker aspect of Orpheus himself, and for that reason they are normally hidden from you – however obvious they may be to others. Indeed, much the same may even apply to the *positive* aspects listed under (a) above – in which case therapy is doubly urgent.

What is important now, therefore, is to learn to *re-cognise* and accept not only the first list of characteristics, but the second list too (whether or not you actually put them into practice) – for if you are rejecting them you are by definition rejecting large parts of Orpheus himself.

(c) Total non-recognition and projection

As ever, though, the most dangerous case is possibly where you have failed to identify with – or to react to – the listed characteristics at all. If this was so in your own case, go through the second list especially for a second time now and ask yourself whether you associate the qualities described mainly with *other people*. Are you suspicious of people who are always gritting their teeth and smiling? Do you wish that they would actually lose their tempers sometimes? Do you suspect those who are always mild and loving of covering up a darker, much nastier side to their characters? Do you hate Holy Joes and people who are moralistic? Do you detest all religious bigots and hypocrites? Are you intolerant of narrow-minded kill-joys? Do you despise those who cannot relate to the opposite sex? Do you find those who prefer to remain celibate incomprehensible? Are you contemptuous of masochists? Are you incensed at bisexuals, homosexuals and people with pederastic inclinations, even if they are not actively so? Are you enraged at them especially when you feel that they threaten to exercise a bad influence on children and young people in the very name of religion and spirituality? Would you like to see such people expunged from society, imprisoned, deported, castrated, sterilised or even physically eliminated?

Once again, there are many who take such attitudes – often for reasons which they regard as perfectly logical, natural and moral. But those attitudes actually say more about the people who adopt them than about the people whom they are so anxious to condemn. The very strength of feeling with which they do so reveals that the characteristics concerned *are actually part of their own Shadow*. Having rejected those qualities within themselves, they are now (naturally enough) unable to *re-cognise* them there, and so are forced to project them onto other people, where they can now safely go on rejecting and condemning them to their hearts' content.

This, as we saw earlier, is a recipe not for healing, but for continued division – whether in the inner or the outer world.

In such cases, then, therapy is especially urgent.

(d) Total acceptance

As ever, this is the ideal. We all need eventually to be able to accept Orpheus within ourselves not only in his more welcome aspects, but also in his darker manifestations. We need to be able to accept all the characteristics listed with easy-going equanimity, *re-cognising* that they are at very least potential or latent within ourselves – even if, as autonomous adults, we choose not to express all of them in practice.

If you can already manage this degree of acceptance, in all probability little in the way of extra therapy is needed beyond what you naturally undertake as part of your normal life-routine. If you cannot do so, though, some kind of deliberate therapy will be needed – and the ancient myths can as usual be relied on to suggest suitable measures to take.

2. Invocation

Start, then, in the usual way. Name the young, idealistic musician and priest of Apollo and welcome him unconditionally into your life. Seek out pictures of him. Even bearing in mind that the sites associated with him in ancient Greece are severely limited – being restricted mainly to Antissa on the isle of Lesbos, where no specifically Orphic remains survive – you could still get a good sense of his presence by visiting *Apollo's* sites as listed on page 60 above. (By the same token, you could profitably apply all of Apollo's therapies as outlined on pages 60-69.)

If you have the chance, buy a statuette of him. When you get home, consider setting it up in your bedroom and making a 'shrine' around either it or his picture. Then meditate before it each morning and evening. Affirm your willingness to accept Orpheus's basic characteristics in their entirety, both in yourself and in others, and express your refusal henceforth to feel either guilty or ashamed at what in fact are perfectly natural and normal aspects of the instinctive spiritual idealist who is hidden within us all.

Meanwhile, invoking the gods also means deliberately giving yourself the chance to encounter their characteristics within yourself and to recognise them for what they are – and, as ever, thanks to our *penchant* for projection, this means (among other things) exposing yourself to outer circumstances that reflect them. In the case of Orpheus these characteristics are primarily his sense of idealism, his longing for purity, his spiritual and/or religious obsession, his musical gift, his attraction to young people of his own sex and his natural skill as a teacher.

Clearly, then, you will need to explore the world of religion and spirituality for yourself. Investigate any one of the great monotheistic faiths such as Judaism, Christianity or Islam and study their scriptures and writings. For preference, choose a sect in which singing, dancing and ecstatic adoration play a large part. Thus, the Jewish Hasidim, the Islamic Sufis and a whole range of charismatic and evangelical Christian sects all merit your attention. Equally, the Roman or high Anglican churches, with their ancient tradition of sacred music and complex ritual, are also highly suitable. Indeed, Christianity is, of the three religions mentioned, possibly the most other-worldly orientated and thus the best suited to your needs – as might be expected in view of its obvious Apollonian antecedents. Attend its services and masses, then. Listen to regular broadcasts of choral evensong from the major cathedrals. Attend concerts of sacred music, and especially of masses and oratorios. If possible, participate in the services of your local church. Join the choir. Learn the organ. Help to run the services. Consider joining the lay ministry, if not the actual priesthood. Consider becoming a hermit, monk or nun – or at very least going on regular religious retreats.

If you are more drawn to the Eastern religions, consider involving yourself with the various Krishna sects of Hinduism, or with ritual Mahayana Buddhism, taking a particular interest in their teachings on karma and reincarnation. Read their literature. Visit their centres, attend their lectures, participate in their courses. Alternatively, make contact with various of the organisations involved in the New Age movement – especially those with a strong deistic and devotional emphasis – and participate in their activities.

Once you have become a regular member of the group or organisation concerned, become a group-leader if possible. Run workshops and seminars. Give talks and lectures. If appropriate, become a lecturer in a seminary or theological college. At very least take up some recognised form of teaching – whether merely at Sunday school, in the context of Scouts, Guides or Brownies, or as a full-time profession (preferably in a single-sex institution).

In these and similar ways you can successfully re-invoke Orpheus and learn to *re-cognise* his presence within you. Indeed, it is literally vital that you should. Otherwise you will be ignoring the spiritual idealist who is hidden deep within you, and your knowledge of yourself will for ever be only partial.

3. Meditation

Merely by 'being fully with' the activities already mentioned you are, of course, already participating in an appropriate form of meditation. But most of the cults and sects mentioned naturally have their own direct and specific forms of meditation, and you would therefore do well to try them for yourself over an extended period. Those most appropriate to Orpheus will have a strong contemplative and idealistic emphasis and a tendency to ecstatic adoration of the central divinity. They will, in a sense, amount to a kind of focused, or 'guided' meditation, rather than the more formless and anarchic kind of meditation which merely aims to put you in touch with reality as it is. They will also make full use of ritual adjuncts such as music and movement. The power of the word, whether sung or spoken, will also be very much in evidence. In the oriental context, both *mantra* and *mudra* will have an important role to play, with communal chanting high on the agenda.

Meanwhile, you should consider Orpheus's typical symbols.

Are you ready to lift your head in praise of heaven like the poppy, in the process being prepared to distinguish yourself sharply and obviously from all those around you if necessary? Are you willing, in other words, to stand out from the crowd – and to be castigated for doing so – rather like the black ewe or kid? Are you, indeed, prepared to be regarded as the proverbial 'black sheep' for the sake of your beliefs – i.e. as a positive danger to established society? Are you, like the alder, ready to raise your arms to heaven in supplication, for all the fact that your feet are firmly planted in the mire and mud of earthly life? In the eternal light of the constellation Lyra, are you prepared to set your heart on things heavenly, and then to seek to bring the celestial harmony back down to earth again?

Do not merely *think* about these things. Seek out their physical presence. Use as many as possible of your senses on them. Then allow yourself to *become* them, each in turn. Merge your identity with them. Immerse yourself in their essential reality.

Then finish your meditation by asking yourself the following questions:

Am I adequately expressing my selfless love for all – preferably in practical ways?

Am I feeling unnecessary guilty about my celibacy or ashamed of my spirituality?

Am I sincere in my religious beliefs – and sufficiently sure of them to keep asking questions and to pursue them to the very end?

Am I making full use of my musical and poetic gifts?

Am I using the adulation of the young people around me for their benefit, or rather for my own?

Am I *ac-knowledg-ing* and developing any healing and soothing powers that I have, and using them to the full?

Ponder on your answers, and consider whether this is the moment to adjust your way of life to reflect them.

4. Remedial activities

On the basis of the myths, there are a number of activities that seem designed positively to encourage you to develop your Orphic aspects. You may wish to consider taking up some of them, perhaps on a trial basis initially. Several of them pick up on themes that have been mentioned already. Add any favourite activities of your own that seem appropriate and natural to you. For convenience, the activities listed are as usual divided here into two categories:

(a) Recreational and general

Wear clean, white clothes. Pursue religious, spiritual and/or esoteric studies. Join a monotheistic sect. Get to know its religious music, poetry and sacred dance. Participate in all of them. Practise its approved forms of meditation. Seek solitude and contemplation. Go on spiritual retreats. Participate in sacred rituals. Practise vegetarianism. Avoid alcohol, drugs and tobacco. Seek sunlight. Sunbathe regularly (see under **Apollo**). Allow any prophetic gifts you may have to develop and flourish. Seek the company of children and young people of your own sex. Learn to accept any bisexual or homosexual tendencies you may have, but preferably remain celibate. Practise mild asceticism of various kinds.

(b) Professional

Particularly suitable areas for encouraging the development of Orpheus within you are: music, poetry, philosophy, reforming politics, conciliation, religion, the priesthood, life as a member of a religious community, evangelism, teaching, and work with children and young people, especially of your own sex.

SUB-PERSONALITIES OF ORPHEUS

As something of a specialist 'one-off', Orpheus seems not to have any further 'sub-personalities' associated with him – i.e. further entities expressing various of his major characteristics, at least as expressed in Greek myth. Perhaps the closest is Hippolytus, whom you will find listed under **Apollo**.

SUMMARY

By fully *ac-knowledg-ing* Orpheus you will eventually learn to *re-cognise* your own idealistic and spiritual side and to express it in your daily life. True, in time you may learn that even this approach, like any approach, has its inherent limitations, and come to realise that you need to go beyond it. For the time being, however, committing yourself to an ideal represents a vital part of your self-development, and should not be skipped merely on the grounds that it may not necessarily be forever.

We do not refuse to eat on the grounds that we shall only get hungry again, or decline to wash on the grounds that we shall only get dirty again. In his due time, Orpheus is more than food to us, and his cleanliness, purity and atoning skills are more than sufficient to wash out all our self-imposed guilts and imagined sins.

10

TIRESIAS – THE WAY OF THE SAGE

One impulse from a vernal wood
May teach you more of man,
Of moral evil and of good,
Than all the sages can.
William Wordsworth: 'The Tables Turned'

TIRESIAS is the archetypal *blind seer*. In a sense he is the final, mature version of Hermes. Having 'seen it all', he is the ultimate bearer of human wisdom, and therefore has no need to seek therapies. That is why you will not find him listed in the *Personal Diagnostic* at the beginning of this book. If you are not already animated by Tiresias, then it is of absolutely no use to seek to be. If, on the other hand, you *are*, then you have no need of this book. For enlightenment is now... or not at all.

The myth of Tiresias

Tiresias is a mere mortal, not a god. Yet he is one who has truly *taken stock*. That *stock* is his stick, or staff, and he is using it not to lean on permanently, but to help him on his way. It is a long and lonely way leading through the dark woods that clothe the slopes of Mount Cyllene, and sometimes he fears that he may lose it altogether.

As he is forcing his way through the undergrowth, however, he stumbles across two snakes in the act of mating. Immediately they both attack him. Taking his staff, Tiresias strikes and kills the female.

And lo – a miracle!

In a trice Tiresias is changed into a woman. And not just a woman. His new destiny, he discovers, is to be nothing less than a *whore* – and a celebrated one, at that.

All of a sudden, in other words, Tiresias is forced to know life – and sexual life in particular – from the angle of the subjugated female, with all its griefs and sorrows, its trials and degradations. He learns to know it thoroughly, obsessively and to the core.

For all of *seven years* this new life continues, until eventually the time comes when the now-female Tiresias feels ready to continue the original journey. Taking her staff, she once again sets out through the forest.

But then, while stumbling through the undergrowth, she again comes upon a pair of snakes mating. Once again they both attack. Taking her staff, Tiresias defends herself, this time killing the male.

And lo – a second miracle! In a trice she is transformed back into a man again.

As news of the story spreads, **Zeus** and his wife Hera, who are engaged in one of their celebrated and interminable slanging-matches, call in the newly-restored Tiresias as an arbiter on the question of whether it is men or women who gain the greatest pleasure from sex. As one who has been both, after all, he ought to know. When Tiresias pronounces nine-to-one in the woman's favour, Hera (who has been arguing the contrary) is so incensed that she strikes Tiresias blind, apparently concluding that that is what he must surely be already. But Zeus, grateful for his support, compensates him with *inward* sight – i.e. deep, visionary wisdom and the gift of prophecy – as well as extending his life to no less than *seven* generations (that number again!).

Not that this is the only account of how Tiresias ('delighter in signs') becomes the archetypal blind seer that he is. In another version he is blinded by Athena (Zeus's militant daughter and brainchild) when he inadvertently catches sight of her in the bath. (Whether this is intended as a subliminal commentary on her beauty or on the alleged effects of sexual excitement is not made clear.) In this case it is Athena herself who, at the plea of the unwitting miscreant's own mother, sympathetically orders a serpent to clean out his ears so that he may henceforward understand the language of prophetic birds.

Two stories, one outcome – and the race of the serpent is common to both. Moreover, there is a sequel, for even when Tiresias does eventually die, he is granted a special favour by Persephone, Queen of the Dead (see under **Artemis**). By virtue of his advanced wisdom he is allowed to keep his wits about him even in death, and so is alone among the spirits of the dead in retaining his understanding for all eternity.

The meaning of the myth

What can be the meaning of this extraordinary story? Clearly, it enshrines some very deep truths; but equally clearly they need decoding.

The first task would seem to be to establish Tiresias' state of consciousness *before* his traumatic encounter with the twin serpents of the first story. Initially he is on a journey through a difficult environment – possibly, then, some kind of pilgrimage. This would suggest that he is already *ac-knowledg-ing* the Dionysian element within him. Since he has evidently dropped everything and left the familiar world behind him, he is no doubt *ac-knowledge-ing* his Hermetic aspect, too. Both the staff and the twin snakes, after all, specifically suggest the presence of **Hermes**. And meanwhile his route takes him through the greenwood – so that, staff in hand, he seems to embody **Pan** the goatherd, too.

Then comes the first encounter with the snakes, and with the female snake in particular. The serpent is by definition a denizen of the underworld, an emissary from the very womb of Mother Earth, and so, as at Delphi, it bears with it Mother Earth's own gift of prophetic wisdom.

Tiresias, however, strikes it dead.

Clearly, then, he is not yet ready for the burden of its wisdom. And the nature of his unreadiness is indicated by what befalls him next. As yet, it would seem, he has failed to *ac-knowledge* the feminine side of his being. And so he must now spend a whole week of years as a woman. He must learn to know first **Artemis**, who herself haunts these woods, and then **Aphrodite**, who flaunts her charms here, there and everywhere. Only when he has experienced sex repeatedly from the woman's angle is he at last ready to re-encounter the essentially bi-polar wisdom which is that of the mature Earth Mother (**Gaia**). And this he does when for the second time he is faced with, and attacked by, a pair of mating snakes.

This time, however, it is the male serpent that he strikes dead. In other words, he finally abandons the exclusively male-orientated wisdom of Pythian **Apollo** (as represented, for example, by the Delphic oracle) and, having proved the point to the very King and Queen of Olympus, becomes a true seer. And not just any old seer, but a *blind see-er*. Blind because, in the second, alternative version of the story, he has seen the mystery that is the effulgent radiance of Athena, who is literally the brainchild of her Divine Father, the male in female form. In the true, bi-polar spirit of the Earth Mother, he has finally resolved the mystery of the opposites. In the mischievous spirit of **Hermes**, god of journeys and transitions, he has become the very incarnation of cosmic paradox.

And henceforward even the gods will defer to his wisdom.

No doubt it is in token of this fact, then, that the number seven twice surfaces in the story; for numerologically (as Pythagoras himself realised) it is the number that signifies true human perfection – or rather the ultimate union of the spiritual with the physical, of the Above with the Below.

Knowledge of the selves

But what is it that has made Tiresias eligible for this lofty status? It is the fact that he has finally gained not anything so lofty as Self-knowledge, but simply *knowledge of his selves* – not merely the head-based knowledge of **Apollo**, but also **Artemis**'s knowledge of the heart, **Pan**'s direct knowledge of the material world and of his own physical instincts, **Dionysus**' knowledge of ecstasy, **Aphrodite**'s knowledge of love, **Zeus**'s knowledge of power, Poseidon's knowledge of aggression, Hades's increasingly resigned knowledge of approaching death, **Hermes**' knowledge of insecurity and no doubt, too, **Orpheus**'s knowledge of the mystical. In the light of all these, he finally qualifies for the all-embracing and compassionate knowledge of the Earth Mother (**Gaia**), who bears within her the total knowledge of all earthly life, of things outer and inner, of things past and things to come.

His knowledge, in other words, is nothing more or less than the sheer fruit of experience.

It has been a long journey, inevitably, and not without its hitches and setbacks. Indeed, there are curious, veiled hints in the mythical canon of just how great those setbacks may have been.

For Tiresias is a native of Thebes. Moreover, he is not the only celebrated blind man who hails from that city. The accursed King Oedipus, it will be remembered, also stumbles out from its walls either blind or – more likely, perhaps – in a blind rage, after discovering (as most men eventually do and every obsessive hero surely must) that the woman he has been married to for all these years is really his mother, and that all the enemies that he has slain in conquering his kingdom of individuality are really his father in disguise.

Psychology apart (to say nothing of Freud and his celebrated, if possibly misattributed 'Oedipus complex'), there is a further symbolic oddity, too. For Thebes is repeatedly referred to in myth as '*seven-gated* Thebes', almost as though it were intended as an allegory of Oedipus's own body with its seven orifices.

Could it be, then, that the blind king who staggers out of the city into the wilderness and the blind seer who eventually stumbles back into it again are one and the same? Could it be that Oedipus is one who, having achieved the material power and success of a **Zeus**, finds himself forced by the stress of circumstance – the crisis of midlife, perhaps – to seek his truth somewhere *beyond* the mere confines of the physical body? Could it be that Tiresias is merely an older version of the same person – one who, having reaped the fruits of bitter personal experience in life's wilderness far outside the limits of conventional society, finally returns home with his new-found wisdom? And could it thus be that the ex-king's sufferings and consequent blind gropings are actually a *precondition* for the wisdom of the sage?

It could well be so. Our negative as well as our positive experiences, in other words, are essential factors in our eventual total knowledge of the world 'out there', and consequently of ourselves too. Without either one of them it would not be total. We need both the good and the bad if we are to get to know reality, for reality does not take sides. It is the *whole spectrum* of experience that alone can teach us who we really are.

Yet not instantly. That experience, acquired step by step, needs to be first digested, then excreted (i.e. rejected, or at least *re-viewed*), and finally profited from – i.e. made fully our own, with all its eventual lessons applied in practice. It is not sufficient for the pilgrim merely to set out. In order that the archetypal learning-process shall reach its triumphant conclusion – as **Orpheus**, for his part, is all too prone *not* to discover – all three of its essential aspects need to be satisfied. First we must return home again and get our feet back firmly on familiar ground. This may well mean initially rejecting what we have learnt as being merely the second-hand wisdom of others. Then we must settle down, plant our own garden and become a householder. We need, in other words, to rediscover the newly-encountered wisdom *for ourselves*. Otherwise our pretended learning will be no more than reduplication, our supposedly newly-won enlightenment mere spiritual regurgitation.

And that lesson is as applicable to the sage as it is to anyone else.

What makes Tiresias a sage rather than merely a mystic, in other words, is the fact that, after all his travels, both outer and inner – his thinkings and feelings, his sensations and spiritual ecstasies, his sexual encounters, his physical pilgrimages, his power-trips and his metaphysical flights of fancy – *he has finally come back down to Earth (or **Gaia**) again and made it his own*. Even though that Earth may now, for him, be totally transformed.

Thus, he is no mere **Orpheus**. He is not some kind of idealistic, other-worldly being. Whatever he may once have been, whatever he himself may now realise he is in the light of his new, transcendent consciousness, he is a totally *human* being. He exists totally in the here and now, push back the boundaries of both to an infinite extent though he may. He is finally *at home with him-Self*. He knows that This Is Where It Is At – all of it, warts and all. And so he does not wish that it were different or try to change it.

He simply *is*.

It follows, then, that there is nothing else 'out there' for him to know. And so, like the Buddha of a myriad statues, he can cheerfully let go of his outer sight, totally confident that his *in-sight* will henceforth be more than sufficient to guide not merely himself, but all the others who come to him for guidance, too. Not least because he now knows that between himself and those supposed 'others' there is in reality not a jot of difference. The world they know is the world he knows. The selves they know are the self-same selves that he himself experiences. They are the gods, the archetypes, the eternal guarantors of their shared humanness.

Perhaps it is for this very reason that he does not normally make the mistake of *seeking* to guide anybody. From the rare cases where he does – notably that of Oedipus himself – he soon discovers that any such attempt is liable to result in *dis-aster*. Still less does he endeavour to explain or impart the secret of his wisdom. If people come to him for advice, he will give it, but he is under no illusion that the wisdom involved is either his to dispense or theirs to receive. He has no personal axe to grind, no gospel of his own to preach. He is merely the intermediary, the interpreter of the 'prophetic birds' for those who wish to listen to what they have to say.

With the dancing Jesus of the apocryphal Acts of John, therefore, he can now sing:

To you who watch, a lamp am I,
To you who gaze, a mirror.
To you who knock, a door am I,
A way to you who wander.

In a word, he is a true *guru* – one who simply reflects back to those who seek him whatever they currently need.

As one who has discovered his destiny in *simply being*, after all, how could he possibly teach it to anybody else? All of them, did they but know it, are 'simply being' already, yet they are firmly convinced that the truth by definition lies somewhere else. How can you tell a traveller on the yellow brick road that the end of the rainbow is really in his own back yard? How can you tell a person who is asking the way to his final goal that he lives there already, and that there is therefore nowhere to go? Their inevitable reaction will be to reject the advice, to regard the sage as an idiot.

Which from their point of view, of course, he is.

Tiresias' knowledge, in any case, is no longer a collection of separate pieces of information. It is whole and indivisible. It cannot any longer be divided into parts, sections, concepts, words or things. Therefore there is *no-thing* to teach.

All that Tiresias can possibly do, then, is simply to *be*, and to hope that, eventually, other people will *real-ise what he is* and get the message that they are it, too. Or rather not to hope at all, and instead to let people get on with their lives – which is ultimately what living is for, and the sole means of actually learning anything at all.

Every teacher worth his salt is perfectly well aware of this. He knows that the best he can do is provide his pupils with suitable contexts for learning. True, he knows that he himself is part of that context. But he also knows that attempting to 'teach' what he knows is at best a way of reinforcing his own knowledge, and at worst an exercise in reinforcing his own ego. He knows that it is not actually possible to 'teach' anything at all. Any dunce can confirm the fact. Knowledge can only be *learnt*. And the desire to 'teach' it (or rather, to make the information available to others, for that is the best that can be hoped for) is merely a function of the process – for it is one of the most powerful motivations and vehicles for learning, as every examiner knows.

Tiresias, then, is not a teacher, for a teacher is by definition one who is still learning. Instead he is a *master*. And so we are faced with a paradox.

Teachers are not masters. Masters do not teach.

Or, as Lao Tzu's *Tao Te Ching* prefers to put it, 'He who knows, speaks not: he who speaks, knows not.'

The master who can be found is not the true master. The true master, on the other hand, cannot be found. And this, presumably, because the only way to discover the true master is to *become* the true master.

Whence, no doubt, the celebrated Zen maxim, 'If you see the Buddha on the road, *kill him!* '

The path of Tiresias

Such is the way of Zen. But the story of Tiresias is very different from the typical way that Zen proposes. It lays no claim to being a path of instant enlightenment. It suggests that true mastery is to be attained only through (or at least after) profound and accumulated human experience – much of it, possibly, painful. It is normally the result not a of a single flash of knowing, but of a whole series of separate knowings that eventually flow together to make a single, *comprehensive* knowing. True, that final illumination (as is often the way with illumination) may well itself occur in a flash. But it is inherently more likely to arise in maturity, or even in old age, than in youth.

However much we may prefer to resist the idea, however impatient we may be to attain our ultimate goal with the minimum of effort and delay, coping with life is something that is best learnt by living it.

This is the lesson that Tiresias himself has succeeded in learning. Having seen life from the point of view of man and woman, of child and adolescent, of lover and father, of pilgrim, of mystic and – in his case, finally – of Mother Earth herself, he is transformed, if at some physical cost to himself. For the first time he is in a position to see things whole and entire. No longer, therefore, does he need Apollo's light of day to *tell things apart* and dismantle the universe around him into disconnected, comprehensible bits. No longer does he need eyes, for he knows that male and female are one, that Yang and Yin are *Tao*, that reality is indivisible – and that he therefore does not stand outside it.

He himself *is* that reality.

Thus, there is no more knowing to be done. The basic duality on which all knowing depends is finally dissolved. Tiresias can finally *take leave of his senses* and simply *be*. True, he is also *aware* that he is, but he does not make the mistake of deducing that there is a separate Self for him to know. The knowing *is* him-Self. The being and the knowing are one. At essence, then, *he is consciousness itself.*

And from that fusion of being and knowing only total serenity can ensue.

Sat (being), *chit* (consciousness), *ananda* (bliss) – such is the ancient Hindu formula for the supreme self-knowledge that constitutes the Divine Reality itself. And implicit in it is the *realisation* that there is ultimately no Self to know, but only a consciousness to be.

The Knower *is* the Self: consciousness *is* being. And once that truth is fully *real-ised* – and not merely *taken account of*, as Apollo might approach it – all human striving comes to an end in a blissful and timeless ocean of *not*-knowing.

VITAL ACTIONS

As ancient oriental wisdom has it, *the guru is within*. The sage who is Tiresias is an ever-present inner entity who constantly guides our footsteps, informs our choices and extends our awareness. Nevertheless, he normally remains unseen and relatively unknown until a comparatively late stage in our life's pilgrimage. He does not emerge fully into the light of day until our other selves are more or less fully known. *Re-cognising* him, consequently, will depend very largely on our having already *re-cognised* our other major gods.

And by that stage no further striving will in any case be necessary.

Thus, *no* therapies are appropriate to Tiresias. However, his presence will tend to lead to one particular form of meditation...

Tiresian meditation

What form does Tiresias' typical meditation take? The myth suggests that it is essentially a kind of continual, even obsessive cogitation, pursued while sitting, standing, walking or whatever one may happen to be doing at each succeeding moment of the day. In a person of such obviously fluctuating identity as Tiresias, the focus of that cogitation has to be the simple question 'Who am I?' Am I this body, this mind, this fluctuating sense of identity? If so, who is the I who is looking at them? Who is the observer, the knower? And if I can identify that observer or knower, who is doing the identifying? Pursue the question ever further backwards, until the realisation eventually dawns that there is no knower, but only a *knowing*. At the basis of all your awareness, all your cogitation lies . . . consciousness itself.

Become that consciousness, then. Identify with it, rather than with the body, mind, thoughts, feelings or personality of which it is conscious. Become not yourself, but the watcher of yourself. Become not the world, but the watcher of the world. Become that which stands behind the whole of existence – and even behind the watching. Become the 'I' that *eyes*, the reality that *real-ises*, the ultimate *be-ing* that is. Become who you really are, rather than who you think you are. Become, in short, *your Self.*

For, once you are truly your Self, there is nothing in the universe from which you can ever again be separate.

Not even yourself.

Your meditation, consequently, is never-ending. It begins with yourself and ends with your Self. It completes the circle, encompasses the whole of reality. It is life and death, the inner and the outer, the Above and the Below. It is the Alpha and the Omega, the existent and the non-existent.

How, then, can it possibly end?

Henceforward your meditation is your life, and life your meditation. Your practice is the practice of the presence of ever-present consciousness. You have understanding of things past, things present and things to come. You have the very key to eternity. And, turning it, you have direct access to the unimaginable secrets of the infinite.

Appropriate activities

It follows, then, that *all* activities are appropriate. Once Tiresias is present, his nature accepted, his archetypal paradigm fully *re-cognised*, there is nothing to be judged, nothing to be rejected, nothing to be avoided. Your freedom is total. Your potential is unlimited.

Precisely because you are who you are, however, you will always do what is fitting. Not because it is right or moral, nor because it is approved, but because it is simply the next thing that needs to be done. Yet certain activities in particular may well recommend themselves to you in the spirit of the mythical Tiresias.

If so, you will no doubt take them up. Seek wilderness. Go rambling alone, especially in the forest and the mountains. Practise walking meditation. Seek contact with snakes, birds and other wild creatures. Learn to know their ways and to interpret their behaviour. In the full spirit of the principle of synchronicity, use them as personal omens. Stay in close contact with the Earth. Be aware of nature in all her moods. Contemplate life as experienced by members of the opposite sex. Actually adopt their typical roles and duties. Experimentally reverse all your attitudes to life. Make a point of using your left hand to perform the tasks normally assigned to your right (and vice versa), to the point where you can use either hand impartially. And all the time take care to learn the lessons of sheer time and painful experience. Pursue your current path to the end. Remain constantly aware on all levels. And, in the end, be prepared even to watch yourself die.

But then Tiresias, if he is truly present within you, will know all this already.

As to what you become, what profession you pursue or what pastimes you engage in – all these are of little or no importance any more. What matters is not what you become, nor even who you become, but who you are and have been all along.

And what you do is not going to alter that in the slightest degree – though who you are may very well alter what you do.

SUMMARY

To *re-cognise, ac-knowledge* and finally become the sage Tiresias, in short, is finally to become your Self. It is also fully to know and to be all *your selves*. And so it leaves only one question unanswered.

Can there really be any difference between the two?

And, to that, Tiresias is quite content to respond with total silence.

EPILOGUE

THE UNKNOWABLE SELF

This above all: to thine own self be true,
And it must follow, as the night the day,
Thou canst not then be false to any man.
William Shakespeare: 'Hamlet' (I. iii. 78)

To conclude, then, we can return, like the archetypal pilgrim, to the point where we started with some prospect that we may truly know for the first time and, knowing it.

In order to know your Self it is first of all necessary to know *your selves* – for it is those selves that are going to have to do the knowing. *Knowing yourself* is necessarily a two-sided affair. There has to be a knower, and there has to be a known. Only out of that duality can the knowing, and thus the healing, then arise.

Yet it is precisely the triumph of Tiresias the *blind see-er* that he has succeeded in *transcending* duality. He has literally *over-come* it. That he has done so has in turn been dependent on his *real-isation* that no way of knowing is the 'right' way of knowing – i.e. that duality is no more applicable to reality itself than it is to our way of knowing it.

All the gods embody their own ways of knowing, and our true being – i.e. our total Self – duly reflects their whole pantheon. It not only looks out through the eyes of **Apollo**, but feels through the heart of **Artemis**. It responds to **Pan**'s gut-instincts and primal sensations, is *beside it-Self* with the ecstasies of **Dionysus**. It commits it-Self to the love of **Aphrodite**, sacrifices it-Self for the posterity of **Gaia**, forcefully expresses it-Self with the mighty voice of **Zeus**. Having set out beyond the immemorial crossroads of **Hermes** and embarked on the uncertain commerce of the World Beyond, it initiates it-Self into the mysteries of **Orpheus**, only to discover, with **Tiresias**, that the pot of gold lies all the time under the hearth of home.

Even though that home has first to be abandoned before, in retrospect, it can be seen that it is where the end of the rainbow really lies.

In the absence from our personal world of any one of these major gods or archetypal entities, however, our knowing necessarily remains incomplete and, to the extent that our 'outer' knowing and 'inner' knowing are ultimately one and the same, the knower, too, remains largely unknown. The mirror that is the outer world reflects only a portion – the external, front half – of the one who is looking into it.

In the quest for self-knowledge, then, it is first of all essential to *close the circle of knowing* (see frontispiece). We need to learn to see the world not merely from one particular angle, but from *all* angles – even if not necessarily from all of them at once, or in any particular order. All of the archetypes demand our *re-cognition* – particularly the fundamental ones that we have been considering, who are the very guardians of our developing *self-consciousness*.

But this is where, as Apollonian adults, our weak point generally lies. We tend obsessively to see the world from a particular, fixed point of view. We are not merely single-minded, but largely one-eyed, too. That is why the world is so full of division and conflict. We cannot see that there are other points of view, all of them just as valid as our own – indeed, *identical* to our own at some other time or place (for whatever we reject is by definition some 'dark', disowned aspect of our own Self). We too easily assume, consequently, that 'we' are always right, that 'they' are always wrong. We too easily imagine that 'there is no alternative'.

As Robert Burns was to put it:

O wad some Pow'r the giftie gie us
To see oursels as others see us!

He, clearly, was well aware of the problem. And his well-known words hint specifically at the solution. We need deliberately to invoke those 'Pow'rs' – i.e. those gods, those modes of consciousness – that are best capable of helping us to know ourselves again as it were from 'out there'. We need especially to seek out those aspects of ourselves that we perceive as being on the opposite side of the circle from our current selves. For they are nothing less than our own familiar shadows, for all our present refusal to *re-cognise* them.

It is in the act of perceiving those antithetical modes of consciousness, in other words, that we are most likely to *come across our Selves*.

But in order to do any such thing, we need first of all to learn to *re-cognise* which gods in particular are missing from our lives. Fortunately this is not a difficult matter to resolve. When a god or goddess is suppressed or *un-ac-knowledg-ed*, he or she does not merely leave a vacuum. He or she fights back, relentlessly and even savagely. The more violent the suppression, the more negative and traumatic the resistance.

On the world stage, consequently, the neglected **Artemis** comes back at us through our militant feminism, our aggressive Amazonian lesbianism, our marriage-breakdowns, our one-parent families, even our Hecatean occult obsessions; **Pan** through our loveless sex, our extreme sexual practices and our headlong flight from the cities; **Dionysus** through our world drugs-problem, our alcoholism, our vandalism, hooliganism and crude adolescent indiscipline – to say nothing of our suicide-bombers; **Aphrodite** through our sex-mania and promiscuity, and ultimately through diseases such as AIDS; **Gaia** through our global environmental crisis, as well as through the collapse of the inner ecology that is our psychological balance; **Zeus** through our political confrontations, our international disputes and industrial power-struggles; **Hermes** through our restlessness and addiction to travel, as well as through the self-contradiction with which our general attitudes are riddled; **Orpheus** through our far-out cults and crass religious fundamentalisms; even the younger and as-yet ill-formed **Tiresias**, possibly, through our now almost commonplace transvestism (especially among women), our general sex-role confusion and our determination to attack and destroy whatever we do not understand.

And **Apollo**, who is not so much neglected as habitually abused, comes back at us all the time in almost everything we do.

On the personal level, similarly, we have only to take a look at the most difficult and troublesome areas within our lives – our psychological hang-ups, our problems of relationship, even our physical illnesses and accidents – to identify the particular gods whom we personally have neglected or offended. Indeed, thanks to the mechanism of psychological projection, we need (as we have seen) only to identify those characteristics that most irk us *in other people* to discover which of the rulers of our inner Olympus are facing us from the far side of the eternal circle of awareness – for it is always *through other people* that the gods most love to wreak their vengeance upon us. Once having identified those gods, we can then make appropriate adjustments to our lives in order to bring the archetypes that we have neglected and/or rejected more fully into play and so *ac-knowledge* and honour their presence not merely 'out there', but deep within us, too.

It was in my earlier book *The Healing of the Gods* that I first outlined a comprehensive system for achieving this, and suggested for it the name *theotherapy*. This involves using one's problems and symptoms as detectors to identify which of some seventy-odd gods and mythical entities one is neglecting or dishonouring, and then applying a range of possible therapies based on the associated myths to rectify the situation. The purpose of such archetypal therapy, however (and this needs to be stressed) is not to *suppress* the symptoms, nor to drive from our lives the gods that are currently 'troubling' us, but the reverse – to welcome them in, to encourage them to function, and thus to allow their more 'negative' symptoms to subside of their own accord.

The system, in other words, is essentially homoeopathic – and it is the one that consequently informs the current volume.

Closing the circle of knowing

Thus it is that, once our primary archetypes have been duly *ac-knowledg-ed* and their lessons fully absorbed, the circle of knowing can finally be closed. True, it is a task that may take a lifetime – and indeed, there must be more than a suspicion that that is precisely what a lifetime is for.

Self-knowledge, in other words, is the most natural and

spontaneous thing in the world, and not something to be achieved by act of conscious will. Our primary task as human beings is not, after all, to seek the highly Apollonian ideal of personal enlightenment, but simply to live out our successive selves to the full. And then we are likely to discover – no doubt when we least expect it – that the light has unaccountably dawned (as it does every day in nature) of its own accord.

True, living life to the full is not something that necessarily comes easily to sophisticated Westerners, with their highly specialised outlook on life. To the inhabitants of the 'developed world', who owe their very development to the supremacy of Apollo, it tends to be no less demanding a task than that which traditionally faces the Egyptian goddess Isis, as she collects and re-assembles the dismembered body of her murdered husband, the Lord Osiris. It involves not only our finding, but our eating and fully digesting – and thus *re-membering*, in the basic spirit of the ancient Mysteries – all the parts of the scattered divinity that is our ultimate Self, so that we, too, may at last be made whole.

The process is one that life in more 'natural', 'primitive' societies than ours seems designed positively to promote. There, ritual or social opportunities are constantly provided for men to act as women and women to 'play the man', for adults to become children again or to act as animals, for older people to re-experience through music, drugs and dancing the *ec-stasies* of youth. Sexual love is familiar to all, parenthood an experience that is common to the tribe as a whole. The Hermetic journey (in the form, for example, of the Aboriginal walkabout) and initiation into the ancient mysteries are built into the very fabric of the rites of adolescence, as into a whole host of other rituals as well – with the shaman, or medicine man, the virtual incarnation of Hermes himself, if not also of the priestly Orpheus. And the elders, as bearers of the tribal wisdom, are traditionally expected to fulfil the role of sage.

In our own society, by contrast, the multicoloured rainbow of selfhood tends to be far more elusive. Positive obstacles are constantly placed in the way of our *developing our selves*. We are all – even the women among us – expected to be 'sensible, rational men'. It is taboo (if perhaps somewhat less so than once it was) for men to be womanly, for adults to be childish, for the sane to 'go mad', for the unmarried to love, for fathers to be motherly, for the settled to up-sticks and go walkabout, for the religiously minded to join exotic cults, for teachers to promote strange beliefs, for the aged to be enlightened.

But that it not the half of it. It is even taboo for *women* to be womanly, for *children* to be childish, for *the mad* to go mad, for *lovers* to be caught loving, for *mothers* to be seen mothering (especially where giving birth or breast-feeding are concerned), for *vagrants* to go walkabout, for *drop-outs* to join exotic cults, for *strange believers* to peddle strange beliefs, for *the enlightened* to be enlightened – let alone for the aged to be seen to do what the aged have to do, namely grow old and die.

Such is the devastating legacy, it seems, of Apollo's exclusively head-orientated outlook.

And so, with our natural drive towards closing the circle of knowing largely thwarted, it may well be necessary for us deliberately to invoke the ancient archetypes anew by act of will, using a series of carefully-chosen conscious measures to rekindle the embers of our long-neglected developmental instincts. The vital actions already outlined are designed specifically to assist in this task.

For Westerners especially, then, the process of self-discovery is no longer half as natural as it may once have seemed. The difficulties are legion, and much hard work may be necessary before the circle of knowing can finally be closed and healing achieved. Yet eventually, for those who persist long enough, the time must inevitably come when the task is complete, and the outer world is known from *all* angles and seen through *all* eyes. Consequently it is the moment, too, when all conflict ceases, all warfare stops, all division comes to an end. Mythologically, that moment is the self-same instant when the wandering Tiresias, like Osiris, *becomes himself once more* – and, in his case, is simultaneously relieved of his sight.

Now wisdom reigns, and *in-sight* becomes total. In the light of it, the outer knowledge is seen to be merely the reflection of the inner knowledge. The universe is myself. As the Hindu scriptures prefer to put it, *Thou art That.*

Thus it is that the knower is finally known. The magician is bearded in his cave. The watcher is revealed.

Now at last, then, the great search can commence, the great question be answered. With the knower fully known and the watcher, in consequence, whole and complete, the immemorial quest for the Self can finally begin.

But at this point there is a curious and humbling technical hiccup. As we try to set out on our search, the door resolutely refuses to open. And this for a ridiculously simple reason.

There is nowhere else to go.

Since all is now 'here', there can be no more 'there'. Since all is now 'I', there can be no more 'you'. Space has been swallowed up in infinity, time in eternity. And in the light of the new wholeness, the entire world of duality is seen to be an illusion.

There is *no-thing* more to be known, and *no-body* left to know it.

And so the great quest founders in a simple paradox. Until the knower is fully known, Self-knowledge is not possible. But once the knower *is* fully known, Self-knowledge is not necessary – for now there cannot possibly be any separate Self for the knower to know.

The conclusion is therefore inescapable – as, ultimately, Truth always is. And, in the event, it turns out to be *truly* the conclusion.

The knower *is* the Self. The knocker at the door is already within the house. The beholder, in his limitless totality, also turns out to be the totality of the psyche, of the soul, of consciousness and all that it is aware of. There is no division, no difference. Thus, he himself is the cosmos incarnate, Reality immanent, heaven on earth, God in human form. In him microcosm and macrocosm are eternally one.

With the pilgrim finally back home again, the human journey – and with it, the human being undertaking it – is at last complete.

SELECT BIBLIOGRAPHY

Berve, H., Gruben, G., & Hirmer, M.: *Greek Temples, Theatres and Sanctuaries* (Thames & Hudson, 1963)

Campbell, J.: *The Masks of God* (Penguin, 1976)

Encyclopaedia of World Mythology (Peerage, 1975)

Facaros, D.: *Greek Islands* (Cadogan, 1986)

Facaros, D. & Pauls, M.: *Turkey* (Cadogan, 1986)

Graves, R.: *The Greek Myths* (Pelican, 1960)

Grimal, P. (ed.): *Larousse World Mythology* (Larousse, 1973)

Hillman, J.: *Archetypal Psychology* (Spring, 1985)

Hillman, J. *et al*: *Facing the Gods* (Spring, 1980)

Jung, C.G.: *Man and His Symbols* (Aldus/Jupiter, 1964)

Jung, C.G. & Kerényi, C.: *Science of Mythology* (Ark, 1985)

Kerényi, C.: *The Gods of the Greeks* (Thames & Hudson, 1951)

Kerényi, K.: *Apollo* (Spring, 1983)

Kerényi, K.: *Goddesses of Sun and Moon* (Spring, 1979)

Kerényi, K.: *Hermes, Guide of Souls* (Spring, 1986)

Kirk, G.S.: *The Nature of Greek Myths* (Pelican, 1974)

Lemesurier, P.: *The Healing of the Gods* (Element, 1988)

Levi, P.: *Atlas of the Greek World* (Phaidon, 1980)

Miller, D.L.: *The New Polytheism* (Spring, 1981)

Paris, G.: *Pagan Meditations* (Spring, 1986)

Robertson, D.S.: *Greek and Roman Architecture* (Cambridge University, 1945)

Roscher, W.H. & Hillman, J.: *Pan and the Nightmare* (Spring, 1972)

Rossiter, S. (ed): *Blue Guide to Greece* (Benn, 1973)

Stein, M.: *In Midlife* (Spring, 1983)

Stillwell, R. (ed.): *The Princeton Encyclopaedia of Classical Sites* (Princeton University, 1976)

Tomlinson, R.A.: *Greek Sanctuaries* (Elek, 1976)

Ziegler, A.J.: *Archetypal Medicine* (Spring, 1983)

O

is a symbol of the world,
of oneness and unity. O Books
explores the many paths of wholeness
and spiritual understanding which
different traditions have developed down
the ages. It aims to bring this knowledge
in accessible form, to a general readership,
providing practical spirituality to today's seekers.

For the full list of over 200 titles covering:

- CHILDREN'S PRAYER, NOVELTY AND GIFT BOOKS
- CHILDREN'S CHRISTIAN AND SPIRITUALITY
- CHRISTMAS AND EASTER
- RELIGION/PHILOSOPHY
- SCHOOL TITLES
- ANGELS/CHANNELLING
- HEALING/MEDITATION
- SELF-HELP/RELATIONSHIPS
- ASTROLOGY/NUMEROLOGY
- SPIRITUAL ENQUIRY
- CHRISTIANITY, EVANGELICAL
AND LIBERAL/RADICAL
- CURRENT AFFAIRS
- HISTORY/BIOGRAPHY
- INSPIRATIONAL/DEVOTIONAL
- WORLD RELIGIONS/INTERFAITH
- BIOGRAPHY AND FICTION
- BIBLE AND REFERENCE
- SCIENCE/PSYCHOLOGY

Please visit our website,
www.O-books.net

SOME RECENT O BOOKS

Daughters of the Earth

Cheryl Straffon

Combines legend, landscape and women's ceremonies to create a wonderful mixture of Goddess experience in the present day. A feast of information, ideas, facts and visions. **Kathy Jones**, co-founder of the Glastonbury Goddess Conference

1846940168 240pp £11.99 $21.95

Maiden, Mother, Crone

Voices of the Goddess

Claire Hamilton

This is a vividly written and evocative series of stories in which Celtic goddesses speak in the first person about their lives and experiences. The sources of the narratives are explained in the book and there is a glossary of names and pronunciation. The book enables the reader to reconnect with a neglected but resurgent tradition that is a part of the advent of the feminine in our time. **Scientific and Medical Network Review**

1905047398 240pp £12.99 $24.95

The Sacred Wheel of the Year

Tess Ward

A book of prayers intended for individual use. Divided into monthly sections, with a week or prayers for each, it incorporates Celtic Christian and Celtic Pagan traditions in a single pattern of prayer.

A spiritual handbook full of wisdom, grace and creativity. It dips into the deep wells of Celtic tradition and beyond to gather the clear water of

life. This is a book of prayer to be treasured. **Mike Riddell**, author of *The Sacred Journey*

1905047959 260pp £11.99 $21.95

Savage Breast
One man's search for the goddess
Tim Ward

An epic, elegant, scholarly search for the goddess, weaving together travel, Greek mythology, and personal autobiographic relationships into a remarkable exploration of the Western World's culture and sexual history. It is also entertainingly human, as we listen and learn from this accomplished person and the challenging mate he wooed. If you ever travel to Greece, take Savage Breast *along with you.* **Harold Schulman**, Professor of Gynaecology at Winthrop University Hospital, and author of *An Intimate History of the Vagina.*

1905047584 400pp colour section +100 b/w photos £12.99 $19.95

Tales of the Celtic Bards
With CD

Claire Hamilton

An original and compelling retelling of some wonderful stories by an accomplished mistress of the bardic art. Unusual and refreshing, the book provides within its covers the variety and colour of a complete bardic festival. **Ronald Hutton**, Professor of History

Harp music perfectly complements the book in a most haunting way. A perfect way in to the tales of "the Strange Ones". **Wave**

1903816548 320pp with CD 230/152mm £16.99 $24.95 cl.

The Virgin and the Pentacle

The Freemasonic plot to destroy the Church

Alan Butler

The author unfolds the history of the tensions between Freemasonry and the Catholic Church, which he sees as reflecting that between patriarchal and matriarchal views of the godhead. It is essentially a power struggle that continues to this day. He makes a valuable contribution to the relationship between inner and outer history. **Scientific and Medical Network Review**

1905047320 208pp 230/153mm £12.99 $17.95 pb

Way of the Druid

The renaissance of a Celtic religion and its relevance for today

Graeme K. Talboys

Enjoyable and revelatory...goes into closely argued debate on the nature of belief, religion and the Celtic metaphysic. Should be on library shelves-public and academic-and on the personal shelves of all those who already call themselves Druid. **Liz Murray**, Liaison officer, Council of British Druid Orders

1905047231 304pp 230/153mm £17.99 $29.95

The 7 Ahas! of Highly Enlightened Souls

How to free yourself from ALL forms of stress

Mike George

7th printing

A very profound, self empowering book. Each page bursting with wisdom and insight. One you will need to read and reread over and over again! Paradigm Shift. I totally love this book, a wonderful nugget of inspiration.

PlanetStarz

1903816319 128pp 190/135mm £5.99 $11.95